AMAZING AUSSIE BASTARDS

LAWRENCE MONEY

ALLEN&UNWIN

AUSTRALIAN GLOSSARY
OF BASTARDS

You old bastard, *n*: traditional term of endearment between Australian males of any age, usually reflecting a lengthy period of mateship

Lucky bastard, *n*: appellation for a bloke who has had good fortune. Carries undercurrents of both grudging envy and fraternal good cheer

Poor bastard, *n*: an unlucky bloke whose life, or part thereof, has gone arse over turkey

Mongrel bastard, *n*: less friendly term, mostly hurled at footy umps and other forms of low-life

Not a bad bastard, *n*: understated expression of admiration which places the bastard on something of a pedestal

Cheeky bastard, *n*: an Aussie bloke who has demonstrated above-average chutzpah

Amazing bastard, *n*: an Australian male who does stuff that other bastards wouldn't try in a month of Sundays

Allen & Unwin
83 Alexander Street
Crows Nest NSW 2065
Australia
Phone: (61 2) 8425 0100
Email: info@allenandunwin.com
Web: www.allenandunwin.com

Cataloguing-in-Publication details are available
from the National Library of Australia
www.trove.nla.gov.au

ISBN 978 1 74331 499 9

Set in 12/16 pt Goudy Oldstyle by Midland Typesetters, Australia
Printed and bound in Australia by Griffin Press

10 9 8 7 6 5 4 3 2 1

For Helen, my bonny Scottish bride, with love

The lives of most men are like street-cars running contentedly along their rails ... I am fascinated by the men who take life in their own hands and seem to mould it to their own liking.
—W. Somerset Maugham

ABOUT THE AUTHOR

Lawrence Money survived a hanging at the Victorian County Court in the 1980s (Judge Fricke bought one of his paintings) to launch a career of 34 years (and counting) as a newspaper columnist on the *Melbourne Herald*, *Sunday Age* and daily *Age*. He has twice won the Melbourne Press Club's Quill Award for columnist of the year.

Lawrence has done many years of commercial and ABC radio, has written four previous books and is the inventor of the Murfett board game Holiday. He follows the struggling Melbourne Demons footy team, strives vainly to recapture his 13 golf handicap, speaks for the Saxton agency, blogs and tweets as @lozzacash ('because some cheeky bastard had already grabbed @lawrencemoney').

Lawrence is the elder son of actor-director Alan Money and journalist Doris van der Hagen, the longest-serving Miranda columnist on the *Weekly Times*. They divorced when he was seven. 'There was never a dull moment,' says Lawrence.

All suggestions, congratulations and abuse to the author at amazingbastards@gmail.com

CONTENTS

INTRODUCTION

There have ever been such men. Blokes whose goals seem hopelessly beyond their outstretched fingertips yet they reach them anyhow. Blokes who seem undaunted by failure, refashioning setbacks into stepping stones to later success. Blokes who—to misquote Robert F. Kennedy—see wrongs and try to right them, see opportunities and make sure they grab them, see mountains unclimbable and scale them anyhow. And bugger those who say they can't.

Writing for Australian magazines and newspapers over the years, I have met many for whom there is only one apt description: Amazing Bastard. They seem to have an extra gear, a booster switch and usually a healthy contempt for petty Down Under officialdom. As per Bruce Woodley's classic anthem 'I Am Australian', their bloodlines come from all the lands on earth, including the great southern continent itself, and they run the gamut of human dynamics—from the buccaneering Ian Kiernan, Derryn Hinch and Bob Katter, who never seem to have had a self-doubt, to Hard Knocks choirmaster Jonathon Welch, whose journey to inspiring a nation with song was accompanied by many bruises. With some, like pianist (and, yes, horse whisperer) David Helfgott and comedian Carl Barron, their natural-born talent makes their craft appear effortless; for lesser-known names like Tasmania's Bob McMahon, who led Australia's longest protest movement and felled a giant timber company's pulp mill, success has been achieved through gritted teeth.

There are Amazing Bastards famed nationally for what they do—globe-trotting World Vision chief Tim Costello, fiery Sydney broadcaster Alan Jones, Melbourne courtroom warrior Colin Lovitt—and amazingly gutsy bastards like Victoria's solar pioneer John Hoerner, who, after losing his sight during a series of devastating strokes, became the nation's first blind photographer. There are eccentric bastards, like the mesmeric Peter Janson and the multiskilled cook and cartoonist Peter Russell-Clarke, to whom rules and regulations seem to be merely excess baggage. There are blokes like Kevin Russell, who works at healing Indigenous Australian families fractured by the government-endorsed separations of years ago and who carries a torch lit during the nineteenth century by his great-grandfather, the acclaimed humanitarian William Cooper.

There are marvellously cunning bastards, like Western Australian farmer Len Casley, who, in the time-honoured Aussie tradition, gave the federal government the one-digit salute in 1970 after being dudded on wheat prices and, outsmarting the best legal brains the government had to offer, cut his property off from Australia and declared himself Prince Leonard of Hutt, head of a new micronation. Len's Hutt River Province still thrives today, and his rebel yell rang around the world, inspiring the creation of many other microstates.

Amazing Bastards are many and varied. They include fearless South Australian polar explorer Tim Jarvis, Sydney retail wizard Gerry Harvey, national real estate crusader Neil Jenman, globe-trotting foreign correspondent turned IT geek Garry Barker, veteran Melbourne actor and playwright Alan Hopgood, South Australian wine pioneer Wolf Blass, wunderkind chef and restaurateur Shannon Bennett, trailblazing internet publisher Stephen Mayne and former pop star Ronnie Burns, who turned a wild idea into a Tasmanian utopia for needy kids.

You've got to love these blokes. The road has not always been easy. Variously, they have bounced back from cancer, blindness, injury, sexual abuse, financial disasters, law suits, depression, divorce, the sack and road blocks erected by unamazing bureaucrats. Sassy, inspiring, often obstinate, always determined, they march to their own drum, showing lesser bastards what can be done if you reach out hard enough, often enough, far enough. And they're bloody handy to have around when the going gets tough.

Cometh the hour, cometh the Amazing Bastard.

PETER JANSON

Sultan of the tower

If it featured anyone other than Peter Janson, the Tale of the Two Swedish Tourists, the Naked Penis and Lord Rathcavan would probably seem rather far-fetched. But if you do feel that way, you obviously have not had dealings with Percival Pierre Gustaf Janson, the cigar-smoking, whisky-drinking, car-racing Amazing Bastard who appeared in Melbourne in the early 1960s and turned the empty tower of a city hotel into a high-rise apartment that swiftly became a cross between a London private club and a Hugh Hefner bunny hutch.

Of course, to those who have had dealings with Peter—and tens of thousands of their names are carefully recorded in his dog-eared contact book—very little about this ageless mystery man comes as a surprise. The unexpected is entirely expected, the eye-poppingly outrageous is mere commonplace. Besides, the story of the Swedish tourists and the naked penis is a first-hand account for which I can vouch, having played a cameo role in a sojourn that began in the early 1990s when Peter, with whom I had previously travelled through India, suggested that I write a travel piece on Vienna for *The Sunday Age*, the newspaper employing me at the time. He said he was heading through Austria and had contacts there, so I checked with the travel editor and, yes, her section would be most interested in an article. While Peter's Austrian connection got to work on accommodation and flights, I began collating the necessary research material. But less than a week later this was rendered unnecessary by a call from Peter's domestic lieutenant at the time, Sean O'Brien.

'Crow,' he said, using the nickname Peter had bestowed upon me, a process he applies to most of his pals. 'Janson wants a word.'

Peter came to the phone. 'Crow, the buggers in Vienna are mucking us around. Your accommodation is okay, but they refuse to cover your meals. They can't treat you like that!'

I scoffed that it was no problem and that I would be happy to cover those myself, but Peter remained incensed.

'No, Crow, fuck 'em, we'll go to London instead.'

London? But the Pommy capital had been covered in travel journalism a zillion times, and unless there was something topical it was doubtful that my newspaper would be interested. I hesitated. 'I'm not sure about that, mate.'

However, my concerns proved immaterial, for within days Sean rang again. 'Crow, Peter wants a word.'

He was outraged once more—while complimentary five-star London digs had already been arranged there was a growing dispute over extras. 'They refuse to provide a butler,' Peter roared.

A what?

'A butler for your room, Crow, so bugger 'em. We'll go to Northern Ireland.'

Butler? Northern Ireland?

The mind boggled, the travel plans swirled before me like a London pea souper, and God only knew what the travel editor would make of it all. But there was no time to deliberate: within the week Peter and I had kangaroo-hopped for 36 hours through Austrian and British and Irish airports (somehow seated in first-class Lauda

Air with economy tickets) and were sipping tea in the kitchen of a country villa owned by Lord Rathcavan and his family, a three-storey mansion on 400 hectares outside Belfast.

Splendid fellow is Rathcavan, a journalist and hereditary peer by the name of Hugh O'Neill, a pal of Peter whose children greeted him like a beloved uncle. Rathcavan suggested a boat ride the next day, and thus it came to pass, but the Irish Sea was wild and icy cold, the howling wind whipping spray across Rathcavan's open-topped boat, and we were all chilled to the marrow. We returned to the villa as Rathcavan's charming missus was preparing a picnic lunch to be enjoyed in their gardens. The spring sun had finally begun casting about its warming fingers, the grass glowed green, birds twittered on the branches—a bucolic scene indeed, but one that was destined to be upended by the Great Doodle Disaster.

I galloped up to my second-floor room, thawed out under a hot shower, changed into dry clothes and rejoined the assembly below to find Peter dozing in the sun on a banana lounge. He had removed his red cravat, white undies, black socks and black shirt, which were arrayed along a hedge to dry out in the sun. He was wearing only his black pants with the red braces, which he had slipped off his shoulders to encourage an even tan.

Various people began to arrive, including Sven, a Swedish tourist, who, with his wife, had rented one of the small cottages on the massive estate. Rathcavan was keen to introduce them to his colourful pal from Australia and approached the slumbering figure, barking his name. Peter awoke abruptly—indeed, too abruptly—and leapt to his feet, extending a hand to Sven and his missus and expressing his great pleasure in making their acquaintance. He has remarked in the years since that, for a fleeting instant, he thought he was a bit of a chance with Mrs Sven, given the way her eyes had travelled so swiftly from his face to his mid-groin, where they remained transfixed. But it was for only an instant.

Mrs Sven's horrified expression—and a startled 'I say, old chap!' from Rathcavan—alerted Peter to the sorry fact that, in springing to his feet, his unbraced trousers had fallen to his ankles and, with undies still drying on the hedge, there was naught to screen the naked Percy doodle-dandy. There it hung, still somewhat reduced in dimension by the chill Irish Sea but sufficiently stout to wiggle slightly in the gentle Celtic zephyr that wafted across the lawn.

Alas, Peter's attempts to remedy the situation served only to compound it. As he sat down again on the banana lounge, reaching desperately for his strides, the immutable laws of physics came into play and the impact of his derrière on the seat's central section triggered an equal and opposite reaction in the hinged lounge terminations. Each flap rose up to smack him on either side of the head, sending him tumbling backwards onto the lawn, a fleeting glimpse of Antipodean buttock being his final salute. As witnesses observed later, the great Charlie Chaplin himself could not have performed better.

Those who know Peter Janson well will not be surprised by this report. Certainly not John Haddad, the Federal Hotels chief who found Peter at his Melbourne office door one day in 1967, wanting to know what plans there were for the empty five-storey tower atop the company's historic Federal Hotel on the corner of Collins and King streets. 'I told him it was just gathering pigeon droppings,' says Haddad, 'and he asked what we would charge if he built an apartment there. I said if he paid for the work he could have it for very little.'

There were builders and cranes and delivery trucks there before you could say 'Amazing Bastard', and the city's first high-rise bachelor pad was up and away. Once it was completed, *The Australian Women's Weekly* was there in a flash, reporting in October 1967 that the new resident was 'young man-about-town Peter Janson', who had a 'reputation for extravagant parties and for being addicted to luxury'.

Peter told the *Weekly*, 'I think one should either live in the heart of the city or way out in the country. I hate suburbia.' The *Weekly* said he had spent $20 000 converting his tower into an apartment, describing a 'magnificently restored rosewood staircase spiralling from the bottom floor to the top of the tower and carpeted in a rich dark gold'.

However, behind the scenes there were a few teething problems. Within months the hotel building manager noticed that the telephone bill for the property had soared, and an inspection revealed that, through some silly error by workmen unknown, Peter's phone lines (which have always been in the plural) had somehow been spliced into the hotel's network. The bearded sultan of the turret did his best to look surprised at this discovery and even more so a month later when an escalating hotel power bill prompted management to check the wiring, only to find some foolish workman had spliced the wrong cable into the wrong socket, leaving Peter feeding off the juice for the Federal.

He uttered his favourite apologia when things go awry: 'I haven't been so embarrassed since my helicopter was repossessed.' It is a line he has employed many times since, because, well, Peter's Projects—and there have been many—do tend to push the envelope. He came to Melbourne as a racing-car driver and was the first to overcome the ban on advertising on the windscreen of racing cars at the famous Bathurst 1000. Back then, only the driver's name was permitted on the windscreen, so Peter temporarily changed his name by deed poll to N.G.K. Janson, greatly pleasing the NGK spark plug company, which remunerated him handsomely.

Peter then laid the foundation for the small city of luxury entertainment marquees that now springs up at the Melbourne Cup, importing a red London double-decker bus as a mobile hospitality unit, which he would park near the Flemington Birdcage sporting an adjacent annexe. In the evolving tradition of so many Jansonian projects, his Melbourne Cup hospitality centre grew annually in size and luxury, eventually incorporating fountains, waiters and entertainers, and even allowed for an outside-broadcast booth for radio. As with his parties, the guests ranged across a broad spectrum and, sometimes unexpectedly, cross-pollinated.

Such a pairing on one occasion was that of sexual disciplinarian Madam Lash and a knight of the realm, who were seen entering a mobile loo together. Michael Muschamp, an old Janson chum, observed at the time, 'There was all sorts of shaking and rattling in there, and the knight emerged wearing her Biggles helmet. Madam Lash came out wearing his top hat and a large grin.'

The London bus had its erotic moments too. The late judge Sir Richard Kirby is said to have recoiled at a report of one such carnal episode inside, exclaiming, 'Good heavens, what time was this?'

Replied the informant, 'About three-thirty, Sir Richard.'

The beak was much relieved. 'Well, at least they had the decency to wait until after the running of the Cup.'

Kerry Gillespie, a former executive at Moonee Valley Racing Club, says there was soon a second London bus, which Peter used to transport his guests to the great race. Again the doting *Weekly* magazine rushed in, reporting that this latest bus was the 'last thing in comfort—carpeted, curtained, set with tables and seats (which convert into beds): it also has a stereo, television, refrigerator—and telephones'. Peter eventually had eight buses which he also used to transport sons of the British aristocracy, who during their holidays were sent to Australia by their parents, to live and work at his abode in what was termed the Janson Finishing School. 'He was fantastic with them,' says Kerry, 'very strict but fair. He would sometimes drive them down to Portsea in the bus—the locals' eyes were like organ stops at the sight—and they would rock up our driveway with an Esky full of chickens and grog, have a chat, have a swim, eat the chickens, get back in the bus and drive back to town.'

By the 1970s Peter's high-rise pleasure domes had become notorious. He had been forced to move out of the Federal when it was marked for demolition, although his mate Jack Joel, now in his eighties, says the hotel had to turn off the water supply to force him out. Jack, who eventually built up the nation's largest car-leasing firm, was looking for an office, so Peter knocked down one of the hotel walls to make space.

'Poor Johnny Haddad,' says Jack. 'We gave him buggery. I wanted an en suite so we knocked down another wall, brought in a dunny then filled the roof spouting with tea, floated a couple of plastic turds in it and called the maintenance bloke. Just about killed him. We never did get the toilet connected. We'd have regular lunch in the tower, made our own champagne we called Chateau le Tour, as in "tower". If you drank enough it made you blind, but we enjoyed it. We'd compete with each other for guests. I brought Arthur Calwell as a guest. You know, the bloke behind the White Australia policy. He really loved it. I remember he stroked my hand one time and said, "Never forget the colour of your skin." There are a million stories. Peter's knowledge of the Bible is incredible. There was one night after he first arrived when a Salvation Army bloke was spruiking on the corner of Collins and Russell streets and Janson began screaming out, "It wasn't like that, my good man!" He finished up on the box and delivered the Sermon on the Mount.'

The briefly homeless Peter, who by then was using the title Captain from a two-year stint with the Indian military, soon bobbed up on the rooftop of the historic Windsor Hotel in Spring Street, where he swiftly built another exotic bachelor pad. According to the man himself, this move was almost an act of charity. 'Their occupancy rates were way down,' he says sympathetically, 'so I said I would help them out.' Again, *The Australian Women's Weekly* was fascinated, and in October 1975 reported on the new penthouse, which had been created out of a 'maze of rooms once used for staff quarters but uninhabited for 80 years'. Peter told the *Weekly*, 'We had to cart out 400 boxes of rubbish.'

The Janson rooftop bachelor pad certainly added some glitz to the establishment. Celebrity guests were a frequent sight, trotting through the foyer en route to the penthouse—Omar Sharif, Jimmy Edwards, Quentin Crisp, Edward de Bono, Spike Milligan, Stirling Moss. The *Weekly*'s social diarist Di 'Bubbles' Fisher was invited up to a 'super champagne party' in 1980 and reported, 'Peter sent a car to collect me and in no time at all I was sitting by a roaring log fire on a velvet sofa with his alpine dingo licking my left ear and Olivia Newton-John talking in the other!'

British prime minister Margaret Thatcher's daughter, Carol, lived there for a year and, says one long-time pal, fell in love with Peter. 'Oh yes, Carol would do anything for him. At one stage she wanted to go hiking so he bought her a pair of army boots and made her march in them, knees up high, down Collins Street, to test them out while he followed in amusement, twenty paces behind and smoking a cigar.'

One visitor recalls taking his leggy first wife to the Windsor penthouse, which was bedecked with the Janson trademark stuffed animal heads, Persian carpets and bookcases, and incorporated the hotel's two towers. 'I had a suburban property with a tower which I wanted to sell and thought he may be interested,' the visitor recalls. 'It quickly became apparent that Peter was more interested in my wife and we left. I had this feeling I was being set up as a cuckold.'

These were Peter's wild days, when stunts such as the Tram Hijack were entrenched in Melbourne folklore. 'The conductor wouldn't change a £10 note,' he recalls indignantly. 'So when the driver got out for a minute to do something I grabbed the lever and took off and gave everyone a free ride. I was banned for life.'

Court appearances were not entirely unknown to the dapper Captain Janson, who was up before Melbourne's Magistrate Proposch in November 1972 on a charge that surprised even the most seasoned Janson-watcher: bringing a live monkey into Australia in the passenger compartment of an aircraft. As *The Age* reported earnestly at the time, the female gibbon was 'seized by customs officials at Perth airport' after Peter took it aboard in a wicker basket. 'The monkey travelled in first class,' he told the bug-eyed beak. 'She pinched someone's transistor radio and camera during the trip and I had to return them. That was rather embarrassing. She would wake me up and I'd take her to the toilet, where she would sit and go, as long as no one watched.' But as for the preposterous suggestion that he had 'smuggled' the creature aboard, this was utter tosh. 'Heavens,' Peter said to the court, 'you can't hide them. Their singing can be heard for a range of three and a half miles.' Sadly, it was not long before the singing simian was heard no more. It died of hepatitis some weeks later, which, the court was told, it caught from an animal keeper who had been caring for it at Perth Zoo. 'They are very susceptible to colds and hepatitis,' Peter told the beak, presumably referring to the monkey, not the keeper. While finding the charge proved, Proposch declared that Peter had not meant to disobey the law and gave him a $20 fine.

Playboy magazine latched on to the Janson shenanigans in 1979 and, under a headline reading 'Living It Up with a High-Revving Hell-Raiser', ran a six-page report by Phil Jarratt.

> He doesn't drive around town often but when he does there is usually trouble. 'I have two speeds,' Janson says, 'flat-out and stopped.' He was flat-out near Dandenong one night last year when a police car beckoned to him to pull over. Janson offered a friendly wave and kept going. The police slapped their removable siren on to the roof and indicated that they were quite serious. Janson retaliated by producing his own magnet-based ID—a flashing light with 'JANSON' written on it in large letters—and the chase was on. A road block at Phillip Island was his undoing.

Due largely to the efforts of John Phillips QC, Peter was eventually disqualified from driving for only six months and given a small fine. Phillips rose to his defence on many an occasion, once after one of the rooftop parties went pear-shaped. Police were called, but Peter threw Sergeant Geoff Woods' cap into the air then fell on top of him. Phillips told the court, rather quaintly, that 'Mr Janson does not scorn the common consolations of mankind in company and the product of the grape.' He explained (but failed to note that this was hardly unusual) that Peter had had 'successive visitors' that day and had acted in a manner out of character with his normal behaviour. 'He had somewhat more than the norm in the way of drink,' said

Phillips, presenting three glowing testimonials to his client's pristine character: from Aussie Rules giant Ron Barassi, Olympic champion John Konrads and John Carrodus, manager of the hotel where the cap-tossing and cop-squashing had taken place. All swore to the 'impeccable' character of the man in question, who escaped with a twelve-month bond.

Happily, Peter managed to keep his nose clean in one of the most infamous episodes of his monkey era: the Case of the Exploding Egg. Without disclosing too much incriminating detail, it can be recorded that, many years ago, the good captain's esoteric collection of knick-knacks had come to include a box of 'eggs'—live military hand grenades—one of which was mishandled by a guest in a certain non-Australian hotel on a particularly booze-fuelled evening. 'He pulled the safety pin,' recalls Peter. 'I had only one option: I reached down the toilet, placed it past the S-bend and flushed the cistern. It blew the wall out two floors down.' No casualties, apart from the sewer pipe. Baffled hotel management blamed it on an airlock.

Kerry Gillespie met Peter soon after he arrived in Australia. 'I grew up in Sydney and met him at a cocktail party there when I was in my twenties,' she recalls. 'All I can remember are those naughty eyes that danced all over the place and looked right through you. He was extremely compelling and debonair, and I was very pure and naive, although I had lots of fun. Anyhow, next day he appeared at my flat, I don't know how he got my address, just appeared at the back door while I was in the kitchen cutting up a salad. He had come to ask me out. He was so electric and I was so nervous I almost chopped off a finger.'

Back then, as now, the origins of the dashing Captain Janson were shrouded in self-generated mystique. Had he come from New Zealand, where long-time pal Michael Muschamp, a former quiz champ, says he was born and raised? Was he from India, where Peter was reported to have gained his rank in the Indian army? (Fleet Street gossip columnist Nigel Dempster once quipped in the *Daily*

Mail that that his captaincy was for 'courageous partridge shooting on the Bhutan border'.) It was in India that he and I were once greeted like royalty at Delhi airport, a delegation of three government suits decking us out with some sort of glittering garland at 2 a.m. and ushering us to a waiting limousine untroubled by customs. Certainly, I found that Peter seemed to have known various Indian powerbrokers, like Dr S.K. Misra, a former private secretary to the Indian prime minister, since childhood.

Or did Peter hail from the Emerald Isle, where Lord Rathcavan's kids greeted him like one of the family? Or what about England, to where he disappears every Christmas for Yuletide festivities with the Duke of Beaufort?

Peter is a master at avoiding answers to such questions. 'Britain,' he says, if you ask where he came from, but he brushes off any attempt to acquire further detail. In 1979, *Playboy* magazine stated that he had been born 'somewhere in New Zealand either 35 or 40 years ago but details are sketchy'. Peter has kept them sketchy ever since, replying to those rude enough to ask his age, '45 to near death.' And the method by which he earns the income that keeps him living in such style? 'Professional gentleman' is his standard response.

Fact is, the captain rarely leaves Rutherglen House, his five-storey city home since 1982, other than to visit a single-storey near-replica he built in the country some years ago, filled with the same sorts of bookshelves, taxidermy, Persian carpets and exotic bric-a-brac. But he does not need to get about town: as in all his various city abodes, there is a never-ending stream of people who come to see him.

For decades, Tuesday has been party night, and the breadth of the guest list over the years has been unrivalled. Everyone from the late John Phillips, who went on to become chief justice of Victoria, and Ted Baillieu, the man who became the Victorian premier, to millionaire pollster Gary Morgan, British tycoon Lord Vestey and News Limited executive Ian 'Cookie' Moore, whose glass eyeball somehow found its way into the fireplace one ribald evening and exploded in a shower of fragments.

Tuesday is still party night, but, rather than informal weekly gatherings, Peter holds what he calls 'big ones' every month or so, with hundreds of guests. He has always issued the invitations personally by phone, although in recent years some of that task has fallen to former girlfriend Nicola Paull, an actress now married to ex-Seeker Keith Potger, who sends an SMS. As ever, new guests are awe-struck at the theatrical flair and exotic decor of Peter's domain and take off on guided tours as if at a museum.

Rutherglen House rose from the shell of a bluestone warehouse, one of the first five buildings constructed in the Melbourne CBD. The stylish conversion so impressed *Victorian Homes* magazine that it devoted twelve pages to a spread in 1988. 'Implementing the Janson "grand design" was no easy task, even for one so well-known and respected in the field of renovation as Oliver Sperway ... But the transition from mammoth empty mansion to splendid, quite extra-ordinary and exceptional home has been the achievement of the owner himself.' The female writer, who one suspects was irradiated by the Janson charm offensive, goes on gushingly, 'The acquisitions of an astute and avid collector and the mementoes of an incredible life have been blended in to a sequence of sumptuous settings that intrigue, entice, dazzle the senses and arouse the curiosity'.

The author no doubt encountered Peter's Coffin Room in her tour: a low-ceilinged alcove behind a fireplace containing a polished casket, professed to be the way a friend settled a debt. The satin-lined timber coffin bears an engraved plate reading, 'Peter Janson: wine, women and contra, not necessarily in that order', and for many years a mannequin's hand in a shirt sleeve has dangled out from under the lid. Peter claims to have slept there on occasion as a 'test run', although, as Kerry Gillespie says, 'he'll outlive us all.'

But, for all his pranks and derring-do, Melbourne's eternal playboy is not to be underestimated as a trailblazer. He galloped to the defence of his old digs the Windsor Hotel when demolition was a real possibility in the 1980s and championed a plan for development at the rear. 'We saved it by about six weeks,' says Peter.

'I was offered big money to get out, but I went to the government instead. The development was needed. I said it was like a lady with or without a hat; it didn't matter. Even at 110 per cent occupancy the hotel couldn't make a profit as it was.'

Peter also pushed Victorian premier Dick Hamer to clean up the shabby industrial areas on the banks of the Yarra River. 'I told him we were the only city in the world that turned its back on the river,' says Peter, who was among the first of what became a flood of people going back to live in the CBD.

He claims the city's first rooftop garden and had a hand in founding the Melbourne Cup's 'Fashions on the Field'. His business connections and networking skills are formidable, and his racing career was no mere hobby either. At Bathurst, regarded as one of the toughest races in the world, he chalked up two seconds and a third over twenty years.

In 2005 *Australian Muscle Car* magazine dubbed him the 'prince of the Bathurst privateers' and devoted ten pages to mark the 25th anniversary of Peter's best result at Bathurst, a second placing with co-driver Larry Perkins behind Peter Brock in 1980. 'If Brock was the most successful Group C Bathurst driver,' said the magazine, 'then Peter Janson was undoubtedly the era's biggest character. Channel Seven's massive Bathurst audience lapped up his pit lane antics when he exited his car after a stint, quickly swapping race helmet for deer-stalker cap. The captain would inevitably end mid-race interviews with a statement like "better freshen up with a Cherry Ripe and a Schweppes lemonade." He was a race sponsor's dream'.

AutoAction magazine also saluted the anniversary with a big spread, quoting Peter's team manager, Ian Tate, as saying, 'With Janson you never knew what was going to happen next. There was a disaster every day and you dreaded the phone ringing.'

Peter says that he and Larry got on famously, apart from the time he 'went a bit over the gravel to throw Cherry Ripes to the marshals.' Then Larry rewrote two of the Ten Commandments just for Janson:

thou shalt not throw Cherry Ripes out the window; thou shalt not smoke cigars in the car.

Peter finally hung up his helmet in 1996, but not without war wounds. 'I had a prang years earlier driving a Ferrari in Europe,' he says. 'Front axle snapped. A pole went through the window and straight down my throat. The surgeons used part of my ribs to patch up my jaw—that's why I wear a beard—and they took some skin off my bottom for my mouth. I'm the only one who can say "Kiss my arse" and get away with it.'

And so, Captain Peter Janson's extraordinary life rolls on, his phone rarely quiet, his farewell call of 'Rev-rev' as boisterous as ever. Even for an Amazing Bastard he is a hard bloke to categorise, but the best effort perhaps came in the 1990s in—of all places—Mauritius. Enjoying pre-dinner drinks on the beach behind Le Paradis Hotel, I was chatting to the hotel manager, a suave Frenchman named Jean Marc Lagesse, and mentioned my recent sojourn in the Far East. 'I went with a mate,' said I. 'You wouldn't know him. Name's Peter Janson.'

Jean Marc's eyes lit up. 'Ah, Peter Janson, yes, I know heem.' What? A Frenchman in Mauritius knows Janson? How on earth does that happen? 'I was managing another 'otel years ago,' explained Jean Marc, 'and there was, 'ow you say, zee power blackout. Next thing I know, zees naked man wearing only zee towel, he is at my door, shouting, "What zee fuck is going on?" He 'ad been in zee shower and zee water stopped. Turned out to be Peter Janson from Australie and I got to know eem well. He drank all my whisky, smoked all my cigars, but hey, what a guy!'

RONNIE BURNS

Lord of the flies

Ronnie Burns can still reel off some of his spiel from the Leviathan department store in Melbourne, where he started working life as a lift driver. 'Ladies and gentlemen, this is men's work wear, industrial wear, women's clothing ...' Shoppers could never have imagined the bloke at the controls would become one of Australia's biggest pop stars; nor would they have guessed he was scared witless. Ronnie hated lifts—had always hated lifts.

A few years later when he performed at the opening of the Sydney Opera House he squeezed into a lift with another performer, actor Reg Varney, and a mob of musicians, and his nightmare came true. 'It was supposed to hold six passengers but there were eleven of us,' he says. 'The door slid shut but we didn't move and then smoke started coming through the cracks. I was panicking because I was at the back and I started farting because I couldn't control myself. I saw newspaper headlines: "Reg Varney and Ronnie Burns die in fire".' Well, of course they didn't die—not of fire, and not even of the fragrant aromas with which Ronnie had filled the car.

Ronnie's bus to work in those days often carried another passenger destined to carve a career in showbiz—Ian 'Molly' Meldrum. 'He was travelling to university—so he said—to study law and economics,' Ronnie says. 'He was living across the road from us, above a shop with his aunties. We would compete for a bit of attention on the bus although we didn't know each other. One day he got on board with all these law books and when the bus started to go—he planned it all—he pretended to trip and tossed all the books down the bus and they landed in everybody's lap. That night he appeared at our back door asking if I had seen one of the books because he had lost it. Then after half an hour he asked whether my mother and father would let him come to stay for a couple of weeks. I told him that was unlikely but he could ask them himself. To my amazement my dad said yes. Two weeks turned into nine and a half years! So much music came out of there; in a way, all these records—Colleen Hewett's "Day by Day", Russell Morris' "The Real Thing", my biggest song, "Smiley"—they all were produced from the lounge room of that house. Molly would come home and play the records and we'd talk about things … He's had extremely wide interests over the years. Surfing, music, theatre, collecting.'

Ronnie had been hooked on music since the age of seven. He had worked odd jobs to save enough to buy a guitar, and then older brother Frank bought a drum kit and started a folk band. 'He asked me if I could learn a couple of songs for a gig in Collingwood Town Hall. So I learnt the songs and brought the music along, but when he said, "Here's my brother Ron Burns," I just got frightened and wouldn't move.'

He conquered the yips at a later gig and became part of the band, but it was not long before he was approached by a couple of young musos wanting to start a new group. 'The Beatles were around then—and Buddy Holly and The Crickets—so we called ourselves The Flies. Not something you'd choose today.'

In contrast to the room-trashing ways of wilder bands The Flies were almost too nice to be true. 'It's about being courteous and respectful of other people,' says Ronnie, 'and not acting like a son of a bitch, because that puts people offside.' As if to emphasise the point, Flies bass player Themi Adams (who had been heroically christened Themistocles Adamopoulo) went on to become a Greek Orthodox priest in South America! 'I really loved those guys,' says Ronnie. 'There was never any drama, although I did get drunk once and jump into a swimming pool. John Farnham saw me go in, and when I didn't come up he jumped in fully clothed. But I was very happy sitting on the bottom—I had been drinking champagne. I can't remember being drunk since.'

That's not to say the boys hung back from the plentiful supply of groupies who are an integral part of the standard pop group package. 'We were young bucks of about eighteen, and the girls were always there,' he says. 'It was just part of it. There was a fair bit of promiscuity but one day I said to the boys, "I'm not going to do this any more; I want to find someone I can be with for more than a one-night stand." Of course they thought I was crazy, but I'd bought a magazine called *Honey* which had The Beatles on the front and inside there was a shampoo advertisement with a picture of a really beautiful girl. I cut it out and framed it and put it next to my bed. That was the sort of girl I wanted to meet, and three months later I did.'

His dream girl was named Maggie Stewart, a classical dancer, who had never heard of pop star Ronnie Burns. 'She was doing a show called *Dig We Must* for the ABC. She was dancing and I was singing, and when I walked into the studio for rehearsal I saw her up on the stage and all my lights went on, I was besotted, but I can't say the same for her. However, I met her again at a party a couple of nights later and I asked her to go with me to Geelong, where I was doing a few songs in a show. She came along but I didn't even dare hold her hand—I thought it was a bit early for that! I suggested she come back into the dressing room after my numbers, but two security blokes saw her and threw her out. When I came back I didn't know where she was. Eventually she found her way back in, but she couldn't believe it: because she came from a classical background, she didn't understand that girls would be screaming and carrying on. She couldn't believe you could be thrown out.'

The budding romance survived this early setback, and in 1970 Maggie became Mrs Burns. The union made the front cover of *TV Week* magazine as the 'Pop Wedding of the Year', with a follow-up feature four months later when they got around to a delayed honeymoon. They set off for two months' travelling around the world, with Ronnie cutting an LP in London with Barry Gibb of the Bee Gees, who wrote all the songs and produced the album. 'I'll always be indebted to Barry for his guidance and influence,' says Ronnie, who first met the group in 1965 when he was sent several of their songs to consider for a single. When he flew to Sydney to record two of them the future millionaire superstars picked him up from the airport in a beaten-up kombi van. 'I paid for some petrol to get us home,' Ronnie recalls. 'At their house they told me they had only limited means and had to share one guitar. It had only two strings—an E and an A.' It was the same two-string guitar the group used to compose 'Spicks and Specks', which catapulted them onto the world stage.

In the *TV Week* feature Ronnie and Maggie gushed enthusiastically about a 'fortune-teller' they had been consulting. 'The woman we go to is uncanny,' said Ronnie. 'She told me lots of things that were on the way, plans that were only half-formed in my mind so she couldn't have known about them.' It was a subject which Ronnie pursued years later when he produced and hosted a TV show called *Prophecy & Prediction: Threat or Warning?*, which took him around the world.

Drummer Danny Finley, who was married to Colleen Hewett, recalls that Ronnie was always a steady hand. 'If there's one word I'd use for Ronnie it is "focused",' says Danny. 'He always knew where he was going.' They first met in the 1970s when heading to Sydney to perform in the same show. 'We flew up together from Melbourne,' says Danny, who was in a band with Mike Brady called MPD. 'I was quite traumatised because Colleen and I were splitting up. We had agreed that she would be leaving the next day and I wasn't feeling good at all. When we got to the hotel in Sydney they didn't have a room for Ronnie so he shared with Colleen and me. I told him about the split and I said I didn't know how I would get through. He told me I'd be right and, you know what? He came back to Melbourne with me on the flight and for the next two years I virtually saw him every day. He helped me. He and his wife, Maggie, never said a negative word about Colleen, never criticised me, just helped me and I've never forgotten that.'

Yes, Ronnie Burns was not your usual pop star. For many years he was a vegetarian, despite the fact that his father, Bob, was a butcher. Bob would ride a bike 16 kilometres to work, from Footscray to Elwood, six days a week. 'Little bicycle clips on his trousers,' recalls Ronnie. 'He must have been very fit.' Wife Maggie and children, Lauren and Michael, also became vegetarian. The lack of a meat diet did not seem to hamper Lauren, by the way: she won the gold medal in taekwondo at the Sydney Olympics, in 2000.

Despite the name, The Flies hit the big time. In 1964 they had won a competition during Melbourne's annual Moomba festival, as 'the band most like The Beatles' and were among the first to sport the soon-to-be-obligatory shoulder-length hair. When The Beatles toured Australia that year Ronnie and his pal Molly Meldrum went to the Melbourne concert and Molly earnt one of his many newspaper headlines by being ejected from the stadium—he was accused of 'yelling too loudly'. Promoter Garry Spry hired The Flies as the resident band at his new club, Pinocchio's, then booked them in to Sydney, where the long hair irked the local gendarmes—the boys were all charged with vagrancy. It was a publicist's dream.

Upon its return to Melbourne the group posed for photos at a women's hair salon. Ronnie had taken along a guitar and sang a couple of numbers, and one of the salon apprentices joined in. She was so good Garry signed her on the spot and, bingo, another Aussie pop star was born—Lynne Randell.

By 1965, members of The Flies were wanting their music to move in different directions, and Ronnie decided to go solo. He was an instant star and was named Australia's King of Pop the following year, but the status had its drawbacks. At the Trocadero in Sydney one night the surging crowd of adoring females grabbed him by an arm, an irresistible force that dragged him off the stage. The crowd parted as he fell, and Ronnie hit the concrete floor. He was taken to hospital with concussion and still cannot understand the hysteria that grips young female fans. 'It's the same for the Justin Biebers today,' he says. 'I don't know what becomes so emotive for the females but their ages can stretch from 12 years old to 25. I think there's a momentum effect where they see other girls doing it.'

While Justin Bieber's career blossomed through YouTube, the music industry in Ronnie's era was in its infancy. 'Back then we were pioneering the business. There were people who are still around today—Normie Rowe, Russell Morris, Johnny Young, Dinah Lee. We were looking towards America and the United Kingdom and we started to formulate our own style and write our own songs.'

By the early 1980s, after a long stint on the Sydney club scene, Ronnie had tired of the weekends away from home and made a career change of startling proportions: he launched his own house-building business. No formal training at all. 'But I learnt the basics renovating my own home,' he explains. 'I was on the tools myself a bit but got other contractors. The regulations were not as tight as they are today. One of the first jobs I did was a huge renovation for Johnny Young and his wife, Cathy, in Kew. He threw me in at the deep end, wanted the whole thing: pool, tennis court, garden. They were very happy with it and it went from there. I became a registered builder—still am—and started work as an interior decorator. I did a lot for people in the industry—a bit for Molly Meldrum,

Sue McIntosh, Johnny—and then the work started to roll because I could showcase my work.'

However, the Ronnie Burns bandwagon eventually hit a speed bump. 'We got into property development and took on a really big project in Hawthorn by the Yarra, a two-storey Victorian home with a pool and views all over the city. It was 1987 and two weeks before the auction the property market crashed. Instead of getting $1.5 million we had a fire sale and had to flog it for $900 000. I was devastated. Two things came out of that. I learnt there are rises and falls in markets and you have to be careful you don't come in near the end of the wave, and the other thing, if I had kept doing it I probably would have had a heart attack and be dead. It just consumed my life.'

TV producer Gavan Disney had taken note of Ronnie's housing ventures, however, and sought him out. Would he be interested in co-hosting a new show for Ten called *Healthy, Wealthy and Wise*, acting as the resident expert on architecture and design? 'He gave me a lifeline and it was fantastic,' says Ronnie. 'I had four years in that and it was the forerunner to a lot of lifestyle shows.' Oddly, the producers had to pay $4000 to the Hare Krishnas for the rights to the name. Ronnie, showing his business flair, produced a coffee table book to cash in on the success, *The Australian House Book*.

But after four years, after a dispute over contracts, in 1995 Ronnie switched to Nine to host a 5 p.m. quiz show called *Strike It Lucky* and, after that wound up, he found backers for a production of his own, *Prophecy & Prediction*. 'Because I was reading books about the notion of prophecy,' he says, 'I set out to find out if it really exists. Can you really predict the future? Could Nostradamus, John the Apostle? I wasn't going out as a messenger or prophet but asked people how that worked. I talked to a clergyman, astrophysicist.' The network decided it would start on 8 September, which happened to be Ronnie's birthday (who could have foreseen that?), and it rated so well that it was re-run a year later.

The show also answered a few personal questions for Ronnie. Despite a blessed run with family and career, he had long felt there was a piece missing from the personal jigsaw. 'It's always been like that for me,' he says. 'Who am I? What's the reason I'm here? How can I help other people? There were four messages from some very eminent people on that show. First, we have to stop desecrating the forests. Second, we have to protect our water supplies. Third, we must stop this destructive thing called war. And fourth, we must protect our children and leave them a future.'

Ronnie and Maggie had long had a plan to retire in Tasmania. Ronnie had been impressed by the state's natural beauty during his touring days, but now the retirement plans were put aside. They would go to Tasmania to tackle that fourth challenge—to protect the children. 'We've always loved children,' says Ronnie. 'Maggie was the choreographer of *Young Talent Time* for twelve years, and I'd always loved our children and all their friends. So we had a powwow with our two kids, told them the plan and they said yes, we had to do it.'

So the couple went to the Apple Isle, bought some land with a large house near Cradle Mountain and launched the dream: a respite centre called Appin Hall for children who were traumatised through illness or grief. Maggie recalls, 'There was nothing there when we started. We spent the first three years picking up barbed wire and cleaning the property. It was a huge project. You would go to bed at night and there was not one muscle in your body that wasn't aching. But you got up and did it again.'

Says Ronnie, 'We were novices, of course, and at first we were thinking, *Oh my God, have we done the right thing?* How could we accommodate the children? How would they get there? We had no money left.' However, using his background as a builder, and with $2.5 million in funds provided by corporate and community groups like Tattersall's and Rotary, Ronnie erected 8 of the 46 proposed structures for the project. Once the doors opened it was easier to sell. The couple went to hospitals, oncologists, doctors, social workers, shelter groups, the Salvos, groups dealing with children with the same message: here is a children's retreat; give us the children.

The couple gathered a board of savvy people who could help, such as a lawyer and a professor of nursing. Initially, accommodation was short-term, up to a week, and the kids were those with serious illnesses like cancer, leukaemia, HIV and cystic fibrosis. It was not long before there were 200 volunteers working there with around 30 children resident at a time.

But Ronnie was thinking big—up to 130 kids at a time and about $45 million in funds to build it all. 'We need a huge dining hall, accommodation for 130 kids, plus the staff to manage them,' he says. 'Thirty-eight more projects. But I'm not daunted by those figures—this project actually exists already for me. Maggie and I can envisage it all built. However, I'm going to the state and federal governments because we will burn out if we continue like this for the next ten years. The Tasmanian government already knows that Appin Hall will eventually be of state significance to the children of this country.

'One of our aims is to share the old-fashioned values that we grew up with and were shown by our grandparents. We have already shown the kids how to propagate seeds and grow vegetables, make plum pudding, churn butter, bottle fruit, make sauerkraut, that sort of thing. My grandkids come here and the first thing I do is take them for a walk by the creek, give them a ride on the tractor. When children first arrive here we find they are texting on their mobile phones. By the next day the phones have disappeared.'

Maggie is not surprised by the former pop star's ultimate life path. 'When we were young, Ronnie would often do hospital visits. He would be asked to see kids in the children's ward and he would genuinely love to do that. He has always had that warm heart. He was a wonderful father with our children, he just adored them, and we were very fortunate that he would be home all week and would book work only at weekends. He is just a big kid himself, really. He's always had that humour in his life.'

Maggie and Ronnie are now in their sixties and, while their spirit burns bright, the flesh grows weaker. 'You have to be realistic about age,' says Maggie. 'I'm looking forward to sitting on a swing seat with Ronnie one day and watching all the young people hard at work in the garden. We want to see a committee of young people on our board, because this is about children and their needs.'

PRINCE LEONARD OF HUTT

The mouse that roared

Leonard George Casley, son of a Western Australian railway worker, was born in August 1925 with a weak muscle in his right eyelid that kept it half-closed until his 86th year. That was when he had surgery to give him the 180-degree vision that most other people enjoy. 'Why are you bothering after all this time?' asked wife Shirley, but Len had made the decision and, as history has proved, that is usually the end of the matter.

A shrewd operator is Len. He had proved years earlier that, lazy eyelid notwithstanding, he had a rare ability to read the fine print. You may know Len Casley more readily as His Royal Highness Prince Leonard of Hutt, the self-appointed monarch of Australia's only secessionist micronation, Hutt River Province Principality, founded in 1970 amid a media and bureaucratic firestorm. Prince Leonard, raised in remote Kalgoorlie, left school at fourteen yet ended up outsmarting the state and federal governments' best legal advisers, befuddling at least two prime ministers and a state governor. More than four decades later, with the prince approaching 90 years of age, his principality seems to stand apart from the Australian taxation system and has its own currency, stamps and visas. It is regarded by some, says the Lonely Planet book *Micronations*, as 'the world's most established (and lucrative)' homemade nation and something of a template for others to follow. More than 13 000 people throughout the world have become official Hutt River citizens, some of whom (Sir Paul Hasluck included) were accorded this great honour post-humously. The late artist Pro Hart, some of whose works hangs in the principality's gallery, was made a Hutt River knight, and Norfolk Island–based author Colleen McCullough has been made a dame. Even the local Nanda Aboriginals have saluted the Hutt River monarch, making him 'protector of the legends'. So, all hail Prince Leonard, the outback Aussie farmer and bush lawyer who pioneered a micro-secessionist movement that inspired dozens of other micro-nations across the world.

One finds the sun-baked Principality of Hutt River some 520 kilo-metres north of Perth, a dusty 75-square-kilometre sovereign state that takes its name from a spasmodic trickle that might have been more accurately named Hutt Creek. It was to Sir Steven Baikie, aide-de-camp to HRH, that one first made entreaties for an audience with the prince for the purposes of this book. The thrust of one's initial communication was that should HRH graciously consent to an interview it would need to be via telephone due to the remote location of his unique domain. Sir Steven, whose stationery also denotes him as 'Acting Minister of Electronic Communications and the Inspector General, Diplomatic Security Force', responded with welcome alacrity:

> *Your email was forwarded to me for my attention. I have taken a look at your links and some other sources and then presented your request and supporting information before Prince Leonard for his consideration. I am pleased to advise*

that HRH Prince Leonard would be happy to speak with you by phone. It is difficult to catch him but the best time to try would be between 4.30 p.m. & 6.30 p.m. WST when he usually sits down near the phone as time set aside for that purpose.

And so it came to pass one spring evening that HRH answered one's call. It is a trifle unnerving, speaking to royalty, even though one has done the most thorough research in preparation. And, of course, that research had quickly shown that an astute and agile brain had been at play here, a brain that was able to deploy such forgotten corners of the law as the English *Treason Act* of 1495, by which Prince Leonard stymied Sir William McMahon, and the law of torts, which he used to fight a federal government wheat quota. But first things first. To the firm and feisty voice on the other end of the line, a voice belying its owner's 87 years, one had to ask the question 'How on earth did all this begin?'

'In the late 1960s,' HRH replied, 'the Australian government was giving the farmers a guaranteed price for wheat and that guarantee was up for renewal. But the government was worried that if they gave an open guarantee and the farmers overproduced they might be up for a lot of money. So they said to the states they would not renew the guarantee unless the states restricted the farmers by quota. The states agreed.'

Back then, of course, Prince Leonard was just an Aussie wheat farmer named Len Casley, who had put much money and effort into the property he had bought in 1966 and who, with the 1970 season promising to yield 600 hectares of lucrative crop, was finally looking forward to seeing all that hard yakka pay off. Then came the shock. On 20 October 1969, wheat quota certificates were issued by the Western Australian government and Len's, number 018366, was for just 40 hectares.

'During the previous twenty years,' recalls the prince, 'we had cropped around 5200 hectares of wheat each year at my previous property in Westonia. I raced to Perth to have a look at the act of parliament for the quota, but I was amazed to find they didn't have one—they had jumped the gun: all they had was a wheat quota bill. I had a look at it and two clauses concerned me. The first said that no appeal would be allowed and the second that there would be no compensation. In my opinion that cut across all sense of justice, because, if an injustice were done, there would be no right of remedy. So I lodged three protests: one to the Wheat Quota Board, one to the Western Australian premier, Sir David Brand, and a third to the Western Australian governor, Sir Douglas Kendrew. The first two didn't reply, but the governor, in a letter dated 10 December 1969, said it was out of his hands. No alteration to the quota would be considered. He was acting in the name of the queen.'

Len, with an uncommonly savvy grasp of legal process, then sought help from the law of torts, which empowered any subject of Her Majesty the Queen to claim compensation 'in all cases in which there is a claim against the Crown for injurious affliction'. Len lodged a claim for 600 000 extra hectares of land, worth $52 million, at that time the largest claim ever received in the state. 'That's what we would have needed, based on the government's quota formula, to crop the acreage we had cropped before,' he says. 'After that claim was lodged, I had a meeting with a minister of the Western Australian government, and a proposal from that meeting went from the state government to the Commonwealth government to England. England then flew a British lord out to have a three-hour luncheon with me that was arranged by a member of ASIO, I found out later, and at the meeting that lord was pushing for us not to pursue getting land with a coastal strip because if we got it we would have to spend money protecting the coast.'

Meanwhile, accentuating the pain, two wild storms wiped out Len's entire crop, even the 40 hectares the quota allowed him to sell. But even as his claim sat festering in bureaucracy's too-hard basket (where it remains today), the Western Australian government began drawing up another bill to acquire compulsorily any lands it needed—and you scarcely needed to be Einstein to work out that Len's storm-battered farmland would be first cab off the rank if he caused them any more grief. Len wrote to the governor, telling him this 'intent to resume the land' was unlawful. 'The title for the land is a legal document,' said Len, 'and on the title it is stated no more than one-twentieth of any of the land could be resumed for any purpose whatsoever'.

There was silence from the governor, but Len's beady left eye had spotted another legal lifeline: under international law, Hutt River had the democratic entitlement to secede and form a 'self-preservation government', a move warranted by two circumstances: that his economy was being taken and that he was threatened with loss of land. 'And both of those matters were being dealt with directly between myself and the sovereign through the governor,' recalls the prince. 'I couldn't just sit there and let them walk away with it.'

An ancient English law decreed that a government was not permitted to threaten a citizen's livelihood. Also, the Montevideo Convention on the Rights and Duties of States, under international law, dictated four requirements for statehood: permanent population, defined territory, government and capacity to enter into relations with other states. Hutt River qualified entirely, and thus it was that on 21 April 1970 a startled Premier Brand received a notice of secession.

Len then notified the tax department of the new arrangement. At this stage he was the administrator of a republic and advised that he would pay taxes on what he owned in Western Australia—but would not pay taxes on Hutt River. 'They sent an inspector who spent a week with me in my office in Perth,' he says. 'Back then I had a block of 60 flats, a few shops and a couple more blocks of flats. We came to an agreement, but there was a change of prime minister and the new one, Billy McMahon, decided he would change the rules and started to get heavy. He wrote to the Western Australian premier to say he'd put the full powers of the Commonwealth at his disposal to deal with us. So I sold up everything—our two-storey house in Perth, shops, flats—so we had nothing there. And then they couldn't use that for tax because if you have a home in Australia they claim you have to pay tax wherever you get your money from.'

Len then scoured the law books and came up with a master stroke. The 1495 *Treason Act* from England, which also applied to Australia via the Commonwealth of Nations, protected the citizens of a sovereign state from nasty bully-boy neighbours, such as those foreigners across the Hutt River border in Australia.

Administrator Len gathered his people together and explained that they would have to declare themselves a principality. He recalls, 'I told them that under the imperial *Treason Act* any person helping a prince (sovereign) attain his office cannot be charged with treason and a person who hinders a prince (sovereign) attain his office may be charged with treason. That thrust the responsibility back on Billy McMahon—we told the media that he had to be very careful; otherwise, he could be charged.'

Meanwhile, the world awoke to a new royal family: Prince Leonard, his wife, Princess Shirley, and their seven royal offspring: crown princes Ian, Graeme, Richard and Wayne, and princesses Kay, Sherryl and Diane. The new royals quickly formed a government (Prince Ian was prime minister, Prince Wayne minister for Foreign Affairs) and drew up a constitution to comply with international law. It left the federal and Western Australian governments agape— Prince Leonard had done 'em all like a dinner. 'We had no further trouble with McMahon,' recalls HRH with much satisfaction.

By now you are asking yourself, *How did this bloke, son of an outback railway worker, get to be so sharp?* It is a question HRH is happy to answer. 'When I was sixteen years old I worked in the office of a shipping and forwarding agency and, if I had a quiet day, I would get hold of an act of parliament just for the fun of reading it. And part of my job was lodging claims and it is a lot easier when you know the law, so I taught myself.' One day he advised the manager of the agency, James Kiernan Pty Ltd, that he had checked the *Stamp Act* and had found the firm was paying stamp duty unnecessarily on their cargo documentation—it should have been paid by the issuer of the bills. He proved to be right.

At age eighteen and still working with James Kiernan, Len had staff of his own and a storehouse on lease, which he used to hold feldspar ore. Approaching nineteen, he left to serve three years with the Royal Australia Air Force, and then launched his own exporting firm with a three-storey warehouse and a truck fleet. His legal smarts came into play again, this time with Len waving a copy of the *Restrictive Trade Practices Act*, as he forced the Grape Growers Association to back down from an attempt to thwart his exports.

Says Prince Leonard, 'Actually, three years after secession the universities in Australia began inviting me to address their law faculties. I met all the law professors and they agreed that everything we had done at Hutt River was perfectly correct. I also studied to become a qualified accountant, although I have always been too busy to work as one. Before we got involved in the secession I was also involved in writing articles on gravity and physics for NASA and universities. I was a bit of an academic and you develop a bit of knack of knowing where to reach for information. So when we got into the secession I dropped NASA and the universities. I wasn't working for them—I would just write articles and they would circulate them among their scientists. But I'm still doing research into that now. I was using solar astronomy to calculate the velocity of gravity and I did get a close estimate of it, and lately I have got up some formulas which I think verify what I calculated before. When NASA lost three satellites over the poles I took out the calculations and told them what the problem was. They sent me a thank-you—but not a cheque.'

Evidence of the prince's canny grasp of matters scientific is to be found in a letter from the department of astronomy at Indiana University dated 4 January 1963: 'We would like to offer congratulations to you on the recent publication of your papers on relativity and the solar system', wrote Messrs Fernandez, Arata, Ki and Karthas. 'We believe you have made the first fundamental contribution in this field since Copernicus.'

All pretty impressive, especially considering Prince Leonard's beginnings. He was three years old when his parents, Myrtle and George, moved 400 kilometres east from Kalgoorlie to Rawlinna, where George's employer, the Commonwealth Transcontinental Railway, operated a major siding. It was a desolate place surrounded by the vast Nullarbor Plain, but it tended to engender a spirit of enterprise and independence among those who lived there.

Several years later the family moved again, this time to an outback railway town in South Australia named Quorn, where Len went to school until the age of eight. The final six years of his education were regularly disrupted, as they moved back and forth to Kalgoorlie with breaks in Fremantle and in the tiny town of Boulder.

It was in Fremantle that the young Len showed early signs of commercial nous, picking wildflowers and making bouquets that he took down to the wharf to sell to passengers on the liners anchored there. It also led to one of his first clashes with bureaucracy, as the port authorities eventually banned his fledgling trade.

Years later, as Prince Leonard of Hutt, he felt the bureaucratic backlash in his childhood hometown once again, when, at the invitation of a local businessman, he travelled to Kalgoorlie on a 'royal tour'. A grand cavalcade was scheduled to terminate at the local school, where excited youngsters, furnished with small Hutt River flags, were ready to wave and cheer. But when word reached the ear of the state's Minister for Education he forbade such a carry-on. On this occasion it was bureaucracy that lost out, Prince Leonard graciously declaring a school holiday and inviting the students to go home. Soon afterwards, there was nobody at the school but the teachers.

By this time it was nothing new for Prince Leonard, who had been cocking a snook at foreign governments for decades. But that is not to say he has not extended the olive branch occasionally. At one stage, while organising a Prince Leonard shipping register, the gracious sovereign offered the Western Australian government a share of the revenue. 'Sir Charles Court took offence,' says the prince, 'and asked the Australian government to stop the register.' But the Australian government, apparently powerless in the matter, wrote to the American Government for assistance. While there is record of the request, stony silence (and possibly disbelief) seems to have been the only response.

Malcolm Fraser, fresh from his 1975 triumph over Gough Whitlam, was another who tried to take on the prince. 'I was told Fraser had instructed the tax office to go after us and break us,' he says, 'and three court cases in a row came up. So one day I said to my cabinet: we have to do something about Malcolm Fraser. He is waging a state of cold war so let's make it a real war—that set the cabinet members back until I explained the strategy and they agreed. First, I sent a telegram to the governor-general saying that a state of war now officially existed between Hutt River and Australia. Three days later I sent another telegram saying the war had officially ceased and that I hoped the Australian government would respect the rules of war, under which some things are automatic for an undefeated country. I also gave notice that we, as an undefeated country, did accept and apply the Geneva Conventions of 12 August 1949, which is *Act 103* of 1957 of the Commonwealth of Australia, and conveys the duties of the government to the occupying power, which was my government. So by Australian law mine was the only government authorised to govern this territory. By the way, it's interesting to note that the transcripts of those three court cases, kept by the Crown prosecutor, have all since got accidentally lost.'

Ah yes, life in the Hutt River principality has had its dramas and, like many a royal court, it may even have endured an attempted coup. In the 1980s a chap named Kevin Gale was appointed Hutt River's prince regent and worked assiduously to bring in a buck, boosting production of stamps and coins and selling Hutt River titles to those around the world who craved them.

Back in September 1994 Prince Kevin mailed me a pile of literature at my request, letters of thanks from clubs and charities, photocopies of press articles, but—one was puzzled to note at the time—they seemed to feature Prince Kevin rather more prominently than the founding prince himself. Several letters even addressed him as Lord Kevin Gale, and the *Royal Herald*—the 'official newsletter of the Hutt River Province Principality'—of July 1994 carried no fewer than six photos of him, one showing him in a friendly wrestle with ex-pugilist Joe Bugner. There was none of Prince Leonard.

One also noted that the *Royal Herald* had a mailing address in Burleigh Heads, Queensland, a long way indeed from the blessed royal patch on the Western Australian coast. Lonely Planet's *Micronations* claims Gale was an

> *enigmatic and, by all accounts, charismatic figure who operated as a maverick from his base in Queensland … capitalising on the fame of the Province but reportedly operating without the authority of Prince Leonard. Kevin Gale died unexpectedly in 1995, amid rumours that he and his associates were planning a coup. Some say there was even a plan to relocate the province to an island in the Pacific. He was posthumously declared a traitor. These events are not included in any official history of the Hutt River Province. To this day Prince Leonard declines to comment.*

However, good Prince Leonard does not hold back in his remarks about the province's epic battle with the Australian postal service. After the birth of the new micronation the postie happily continued his deliveries in and out, complete with the new Hutt River stamps, until an unwelcome order came through from head office. 'They put a blockade on us,' says HRH, 'said there was no such place as Hutt River. I got that lifted, then they put another mail embargo on us so if you posted a letter to Geraldton, for example, which is not far, it went from here to Canada before it got delivered. After six months of that they took us to court to try to knock us out, but the court ruled that our Hutt River stamps were legal and valid, so the post office said they would handle our mail if we put our Hutt River stamps on the back. The main concern was that the mail had to keep moving.' Prince Leonard says the mail has flowed freely ever since—all without Australian stamps. 'You can't use foreign stamps on mail from here,' he explains patiently.

In fact, a Hutt River post office was part of a new administrative building erected in 1973, a complex that also contained a cafe, souvenir shop and chapel. There was much joy among the Hutt Riverians over their new headquarters, but on the eve of its official opening the local council, Northampton Shire, was foolhardy enough to challenge the legitimacy of the work. There had been no permits, said the council, so the building would have to be demolished.

Prince Leonard fired off another of his letters to the Western Australian attorney-general, but the A-G backed the council. However, this time the principality had no need of the law—after three years of media coverage the public in that foreign land over the border had taken the Down Under royals to their heart. 'Leave that Amazing Bastard alone' was the general sentiment from the Australian citizenry, and Northampton council eventually backed off.

After all, by then the tourists were trekking from all over to check out this phenomenon, bringing lovely tourism dollars to the region. 'We still greet about 30 000 tourists a year,' says Prince Leonard, who was swamped by around 60 000 a year in Hutt River's heyday. 'Could even be a bit down on 30 000 now. I notice that there are not so many young ones from Europe these days, but those from Hong Kong, China and Taiwan have increased vastly in numbers.'

The farm he worked as commoner Len Casley still operates under three of the princes, but HRH has not dug a hand into the soil for 25 years. In the 1979 official history of Hutt River, *The Man*, author R.C. Hyslop sums up the saga thus:

> *Prince Leonard has calmly taken over the sovereignty of a part of a nation. He has done it within the very laws of that nation. Then when there appears to be a conflict he will turn*

up on the steps of parliament in Canberra for discussions and
tell the government that he is there to deal with any problems
the government may believe exists between them. Although
he stands there, apparently quite alone, no government
has ever shown desire to discuss opposition with him. He has
instead been taken to friendly luncheons and dinners.

Sir Steve Baikie—elevated to Lord Steven, Earl of Tankerness, by Prince Leonard in 2012—has known the royal rebel since 1974. 'He is certainly one of a kind,' says his lordship. 'In the early days I attended court cases with him where he always represented himself and I watched him run rings around Crown prosecutors and even magistrates at times. At age 87 HRH's mind has still not slowed down one bit and I find that alone amazing. Not bad for a bloke who virtually never went to school and, what schooling he had, he walked away from at age fourteen.'

Like any self-respecting sovereign nation, the Principality of Hutt River has envoys and representatives around the world and has applied—unsuccessfully so far—for membership of the United Nations and the Commonwealth of Nations. On the principality's glorious 30th anniversary, in the year 2000, Prince Leonard's man in London had a surprise. 'He presented me with a certificate from the Universal Star Listing,' HRH says, 'showing that a star in the Virgo constellation had been named after me. I have a certificate giving its coordinates.' And the Prince Leonard star has been shimmering over this blessed Antipodean patch ever since. God save the prince!

ALAN JONES

Wirelessaurus Rex

At the height of the great 'dying of shame' uproar of 2012, Sydney broadcaster Alan Jones was in full flight. 'You absolutely gutless wonder,' he declared on his top-rating 2GB breakfast show, referring to Mercedes-Benz executive David McCarthy, who had demanded the return of Alan's complimentary limo. 'You big hero, Mr McCarthy,' said Jones, cranking up the attack. 'They can have the damn thing back straightaway.'

Yes sir, the brickbats were flying. Many jumpy advertisers had suspended commercials on the Jones show, wary of the backlash over his ill-advised remark to a university dinner that Prime Minister Julia Gillard's father had 'died of shame' because of her 'lies' to parliament.

The broadcaster quickly realised he had made a major blue. 'There are days that you have to man up and say you got it wrong,' he said, and apologised, but the Prime Minister, who had been caned before by Jones, said she would never darken the door of his studio again. A social media tsunami enveloped him, and for a week, in an unthinkable move, the station suspended all ads on his program. Liberal silvertail Malcolm Turnbull declared that Alan had copped a 'dose of his own medicine.' Melbourne's *Herald Sun* ran an editorial declaring he should 'get off air', and every Labor MP in sight somehow managed to blame the whole thing on their nemesis, Tony Abbott. Melbourne radio producer and broadcaster Justin Smith penned an article for the Fairfax papers saying Jones would never regain his previous power—quipping that he was a 'Samson with a buzz cut'.

Conversely, Jones' loyalists were incensed and swore to shun Mercedes and the other deserting sponsors, while, in the dark world of the internet, venomous exchanges raged for days. Perhaps the weirdest turn of events was the cameo appearance of Sydney's other radio icon, John Laws, who fronted the ABC's *7.30 Report* in sunglasses and scarf, sipping on a glass of Wild Turkey with ice (or, as journalist Tracey Spicer tweeted, it could have been Valvoline), the drink held in a hand that sported a giant silver ring. In his familiar booming baritone, the Golden Tonsils declared that 'we all make mistakes' and that his one-time airwave rival was a 'very very competent broadcaster,' even though Laws was then reminded that he once said Jones would win a gold medal in an Olympic Games for hypocrisy. Everyone was talking about the Jones boy, and not for the first time in his extraordinary career.

But let us leave this urban war zone briefly to visit the domestic patch of broadcaster Jones, a gentler, less combative world that few outsiders ever see. Tonia Taylor is the daughter of Alan's sister, Colleen, and, in her words, has 'pretty much seen him every day for sixteen years.' At age fifteen, she travelled from her family home in Toowoomba to stay with Alan in Sydney, pursuing a career in professional tennis. 'Alan has been the rock of the family,' she says. 'We'd be lost without him. He provides a security blanket and he has done that pretty much since I was born. I'm told I was a pretty ugly baby myself, but Alan was the only one who thought I was beautiful. I was the apple of his eye.'

Like Alan, Tonia was a natural at tennis and made the top 500 on the world tour before retiring, aged 20. She had been working for eighteen months on the Gold Coast, where she had met her future husband, tennis coach Justin Taylor, when Alan gave her a call. 'He said he had a job for me, so we moved down and I was still working with him when I had my three children. Hunter was first. He was due on Tuesday 17 September but I worked until Friday the 20th. I went into labour that night and had Hunter the next evening. Alan was speaking at a testimonial for New South Wales cricketer Gavin Robertson but was getting updates. He came in to see us at midnight after the function.'

Alan had decreed that Tonia 'would not have a job' unless she brought her new son to work, so Hunter was part of the radio station from the age of four weeks. 'I had my portable crib in there,' says Tonia, 'and if Hunter cried, Alan would pick him up. Didn't matter who he was with. People soon learnt that the best way to butter up Alan was to play with Hunter. I remember Max Markson, the publicist, in there one day crawling under the table and playing hide-and-seek on the floor. Hunter came to work until he was two—he'd sit on Alan's desk pretending to read the paper.'

The next two children, Hamilton and Elizabeth, also went to work with Tonia, Alan being godfather to all three. 'He's amazing,' says Tonia.

But cuddly old Uncle Alan can be a hard man on the airwaves. A year before the 'dying of shame' uproar, he had told his 2GB audience that Julia Gillard and the paradoxically named Greens chief Senator Brown should be 'shoved in a chaff bag and taken as far out to sea as they can,' where they should be left to paddle home. There was no explanation as to how one goes about paddling inside a chaff bag, but Jones later suggested the same treatment for Sydney's lord mayor Clover Moore—she and Julia to be squeezed into a chaff bag and tossed into the briny.

While this did much to raise the profile of Australian chaff manufacturers, it also triggered shrill howls from the feminists, the human-rights push, the political correctness pundits and maybe even the coastguards, who have a thing about political leaders bobbing around in the shipping channels. The Australian Communication and Media Authority swooped in—a sort of slow-motion swoop that took eleven months—but let the air out of the protesters' tyres by decreeing that calls to bag and toss prime ministers 'did not incite violence or hatred based on age, gender, race or other characteristics'. In fact, the ACMA remarked that 'it was clear that the comments were not genuine invitations to violent behaviour but were figures of speech'.

However, the 'dying of shame' furore seemed to reactivate the ACMA, which took another unprecedented step: it directed that Jones and the rest of the 2GB crew should attend 'fact-checking' school, citing an arithmetic error Jones had made months earlier when he had told his audience that human-produced carbon dioxide made up 0.001 per cent of carbon dioxide in the air, although curiously no mention was made by the ACMA of what the figure *should* have been. (That's probably because it seemed to range from 3 per cent, as reported in some sections of the press, to as much as 30 per cent, as declared by *Media Watch*'s Jonathan Holmes.)

Some years earlier, journalist David Salter had hissed in *The Monthly* magazine that Jones had achieved a 'mastery of populist nonsense', but, while seemingly disliking Jones' 'prissy … semi-sour' voice, Salter simultaneously acknowledged that 'it's a voice that speaks to a dominant share of the Sydney talk-radio market every weekday morning'. Salter was right there: the first ratings survey after the 'dying of shame' furore saw Jones' figures rise 0.5 per cent to 17.3 per cent, while nearest rivals 2Day and 702 ABC fell away. In *The Sydney Morning Herald*, columnist Paul Sheehan wrote, 'The Alan Jones show has surged back to the top of the market. It is again bristling with ads. His number of listeners—all voters and consumers—is showing a healthy glow'.

It had been a similar story after the ACMA's earlier 'chaff bag' rebuke—the Jones show rose 1.8 per cent to 18.5 per cent, a Black

Caviar–type lead on nearest rival 702 ABC, which rated a lowly 12 per cent. And in the same set of numbers, commercial rival 2UE, where Jones once top-rated as breakfast king, scored an embarrassing 5.1 per cent. By November 2012 Macquarie Radio Network boss Russell Tate was able to report to the network's annual meeting that Alan's ads were 'almost back to normal.' Of 647 individual advertisers, only 15 had said they would not return. While conceding that around $1.5 million advertising revenue had been lost during the exercise, Tate said happily, 'All the nonsense was from people who don't even listen to the program and never will. They are not 2GB listeners. Alan Jones' audience doesn't care about the advertiser departure.'

But the politicians do care about that big juicy Jones audience, even though it is not always a pleasant experience fronting up for a grilling. Here's Julia Gillard phoning in from Canberra in happier times, in February 2011.

ALAN. Prime Minister, can I just make a minor point? I've got
    my job to do; you've got your job to do. Your people rang here
    yesterday and it was agreed that this interview would take place
    at ten past seven, and we accommodated that and cancelled
    someone who was to be here. Ten past seven is ten past seven,
    isn't it?
JULIA, *voice fast losing its initial chirpiness*. Well, I'm sorry about that,
    Alan, but I've been delayed on another interview.
ALAN. I can understand you may not want to come on or you
    can't come on, but surely courtesy has to be part of the way the
    public are treated?
JULIA. Alan, I believe I am a very courteous person and (if I can
    finish my sentence, Alan) I am also a very busy person.

When the interview finally got underway Jones quoted his listeners: some were calling the Prime Minister 'Jul-liar', he said, because of her broken promise on carbon tax. Another listener had pointed out—rather oddly—that, because Gillard was living at the Lodge, taxpayers were shelling out for her toilet paper. It was not a happy experience for the Prime Minister, but she had ventured onto the Jones show for the same reason previous leaders of all hues had done before her: that 'dominant share' of the morning audience. The clout of this Wirelessaurus Rex is such that an unauthorised biography about him by Chris Masters was entitled *Jonestown*.

How did the biggest city in Australia become stamped with the name of a kid who grew up in the tiny Queensland town of Acland, son of poor miner Charlie Jones and his wife, Elizabeth? 'Mum was tough,' says Alan, quoting the lesson she drummed into him: 'The only thing you get without hard work is failure.' Father Charlie was a hard worker too—he went down the coalmines when the great drought shrivelled up their dairy farm—and he was the bloke who pioneered the chaff bag concept. 'It's farmer's lingo,' says Alan, who scoffs at the fuss. 'On the farm if anything was useless he'd say, "Chuck it in a chaff bag."' Of course, Charlie would have had no idea that this would be extended one day to Australia's first female prime minister. The gag got a second run, by the way: a bloke from Woolworths got a laugh with a novel gift for the charity auction at that fateful university dinner—a shirt made from a chaff bag.

Alan, who bought the novel garment, says he works 21 hours a day, though 'I sometimes have a nap for twenty minutes in the car when I'm being driven somewhere.' When he ventured into musical theatre in 2012, playing the role of wheelchair-bound President Roosevelt in John Frost's production of *Annie*, he broadcast his 2GB breakfast show without missing a beat, rising at 3.30 a.m. to start work, just a few hours after returning home from the theatre. Some days he did his 3-hour radio show plus an *Annie* matinee and evening performance.

Tonia, who now works as his personal assistant, says her uncle did not miss any of the eight shows a week in Sydney, Brisbane or Melbourne. Hyper-driven Jones—who then shot off to London for the Olympics, handing over the theatre role to Bert Newton—even managed to squeeze in a protest rally in Melbourne one chilly Sunday afternoon during the show's run, telling the modest gathering that climate change science was 'propaganda and witchcraft.' Said Alan, 'Common sense will tell you it's rubbish: 97 per cent of all carbon dioxide occurs naturally; 3 per cent around the world is created by human beings.' There was no mention of *Media Watch*'s 30 per cent figure, but Jones has been none too keen on that program since it roped him and his latter-day supporter John Laws into the infamous 'cash for comment' radio-sponsorship controversy in 1999.

Again, it irritated the tripe out of his critics that Jones not only survived that scandal—and another flare-up in 2004—but also actually grew more influential than before. And much wealthier. In 2002 Alan clinched one of radio's great deals, accepting an offer from rough-diamond ad man John Singleton to switch to his station, 2GB. Jones' pay packet was gargantuan and included a huge wad of shares in the station itself. Singleton believed that Jones was perhaps the only radio performer in Australia able to take his audience with him, and he was right. The move transposed the fortunes of the two stations, with Jones' former employer 2UE flopping after he left and new station 2GB climbing rapidly to the top.

Alan says his decision to leave 2UE was prompted by the failure of the station to look after his staff. 'I've never told the story before,' he says. 'The station wanted to renegotiate my contract in 2002, but I said, "Before you do that, renegotiate the contracts of my staff, because they get up at two-thirty or three-thirty every morning." It's a massive sacrifice, family and all the rest of it. I told them, "We are making all the money; this is what I want my people to be paid." They said it couldn't be done, that it would set a precedent. I said, "We are creating the precedent: we keep on winning. If you can't sign them, you can't sign me." That's the reason I left and all five of them came with me.'

Amazingly, Australia's highest paid radio opinionator owes his start on the airwaves to rugby—and his start in rugby to teaching. Alan's first job in 1960 after leaving school was as a teacher at

Ironside State School in Brisbane; then he moved to Brisbane Grammar, and then The King's School in Sydney. A talented tennis player who had reached national junior level, Alan began coaching tennis and also rugby. Within four years of joining King's he had taken the school rugby team to a premiership. His coaching prowess was noticed, and in 1982 he was appointed manager of the New South Wales rugby union team, taking over as coach of Manly a year later. It was unprecedented—he was the first Manly coach who had not previously been a Manly player—but the team went on to win its first premiership in 32 years. Another leap, another bound by the caped crusader, and Jones was coach of the Australian side, the Wallabies. 'We then won the grand slam,' he says. 'England, Ireland, Wales and Scotland on the one tour—no one had done that—and then we beat the Barbarians, which is a combination of all of them plus France. Then we came back and went to New Zealand and beat them in New Zealand. Never been done before.'

The natural assumption is that it was the Jones hot-gospelling persona that lifted those teams to glory, but the man himself says not. 'I'm not into all this motivational stuff,' he says. 'Look, if you don't know what you are talking about, you are not going to be motivating anybody. The biggest motivation is knowledge and people knowing what you are about. Okay, I can stir people up a little but that wasn't the issue. If you are talking rubbish Monday, Tuesday, Wednesday, Thursday and Friday, you are not going to motivate them on Saturday.'

But there was no doubt that, where John Laws had the booming baritone, Alan Jones seemed to have kissed the Blarney Stone, and his winning way with words during the tour of the United Kingdom came to the attention of 2UE program and sports director John Brennan. Says Alan, 'I had agreed to take calls from 2UE during the tour. At that stage everyone thought the Wallabies were hopeless, so I thought if I could get just five minutes of publicity anywhere I'd do it. I told Brennan, "Don't mind when you ring," and of course they were ringing Australian time when I was in bed, at two in the morning. I didn't mind and he got the inside oil on a few occasions, so he was able to break news. After we got back Brennan rang me one Sunday morning—he said he wanted to talk to me about going on radio. I'd never been inside a radio station but I went over and did some dummy stuff.'

It is now radio legend that Jones was offered the services of a typist to take down some notes to prepare a couple of sample editorials, but he said he did not need it and delivered a couple of word-perfect opinion pieces off the top of his head. Brennan was agape and soon afterwards offered Alan a job on mornings, co-hosting with a woman, a shift John Laws had just vacated. Says one station staffer, 'Alan wasn't interested. He said he'd do it alone or not at all. Not sure if the woman ever knew—she's still quite high profile in Sydney. Anyhow, he was signed as a solo performer for ·$130 000. He admitted later he was only expecting about $25 000.'

Three decades later, Matthew Knott of The Power Index, rates Alan among the top ten communicators:

> Alan Jones is not a man; he's a force of nature. Cyclone Alan has been written off as a spent force many times, but he keeps spinning, wreaking havoc and destroying anyone who stands in his way.
>
> He's got energy, persistence, hide and an ego as big as the Sydney Harbour Bridge. No other broadcaster can match his track record of elevating stories into scandals, amplifying his listeners' anxieties and nagging decision makers until he gets his way. Jones is not just a radio host: he's a self-appointed ombudsman on a mission to right society's wrongs.

And on this great crusade ol' Al doesn't mind handing out a few bruises. The year 1993 was a beauty. He said the choice of Aboriginal musician Mandawuy Yunupingu as Australian of the Year was a 'disgrace' and clashed with Aboriginal activist Charlie Perkins in a TV debate, asserting it was 'Australia's nation', not the Aboriginals'.

Charlie called him a redneck, saying Alan had 'sat on your white bum at 2UE in Sydney all your life so you wouldn't know what goes on out there.' Alan rounded off the year with a prosecution for contempt of court after he caused a trial to be aborted.

However, like his niece, friends insist there is an old-softie side of Jones that most people rarely hear about. 'Eighteen months before the 2008 Beijing Olympics,' says one pal, 'Alan was speaking to Sarina Bratton, the former diver who founded Orion Cruises. She showed Alan a video clip of a young Queensland diver named Matthew Mitcham. She said he'd been turned away by the Queensland Institute of Sport for some minor infringement—missed training a few times or whatever—but he had a lot of talent. Alan agreed, got in touch with the young bloke, started to sponsor him, arranged coaching by a top bloke in New South Wales and talked to Matthew pretty much every day to get his confidence up. Alan has always done this sort of mentoring. Anyhow, Matthew won the gold medal at Beijing off the 10-metre board. It was unheard of. The Chinese had pretty well dominated it for years.'

In 2011 Alan's multifaceted career took another turn when he had a call from producer John Frost: would he consider filling the role of President Roosevelt in the musical *Annie*? For once, the radio titan, who featured in costume on huge posters in the various theatre foyers, had to play second fiddle. He was sharing the spotlight with Australian stage heavyweights Nancye Hayes and Anthony Warlow.

'On the first day I had never felt so humiliated,' he says. 'They had one of those scenes where you all sit around and meet each other. Usual stuff. John Frost said a few words then suggested perhaps we go around the room and say what we do. I thought, *What the hell am I going to say? That's Nancye Hayes, Anthony Warlow! How quickly can we move on?* My turn could not come too slowly. When it did, I think I said something like, "Well, apparently I'm the president, and I know he's very left wing." Thought it might get a laugh.'

Alan soon found he had cause to be awe-struck: he says Warlow turned out to be an entertainment freak. 'He has an incredible store of jokes about any subject you can name,' says Alan. 'He's an illusionist. He can reach over and produce a 50-cent piece from your coat pocket. On the night of the launch in Brisbane he was surrounded by people, so I went up and said, "Can you give me 50 cents?" and he said, "Excuse me, I'm the great Oliver Warbucks and I'm a millionaire; I only deal in paper money," and he produced a $5 note out of the air. Everyone was stunned but he just said, "Don't be surprised, there's a lot of money in the room," and put his hand in the air and produced another one. Unbelievable!'

There was more. 'He can impersonate anyone,' says Alan. 'Tony Blair, me, a Yorkshire pig farmer. He sometimes does it on stage when he has his back to the audience to liven things up. Once we had a fire drill at the theatre—Warlow was standing with us in the corridor when he said he was sick of waiting and did the sirens, all the sounds, fire trucks; there were people running everywhere. Truly amazing! Sharing the stage with Warlow and Nancye Hayes is like sharing a tennis court with Novak Djokovic.'

By the same token, Alan is apparently a fair entertainer himself, with phantom calls of the Melbourne Cup being his favourite party trick. 'Which year do you want?' he says when you ask him what Cups he can replay from memory. 'Yes, all useless stuff.'

He prides himself on public speaking without notes, much as he did years ago in his trial run for 2UE, so you would assume that memorising his *Annie* lines would not pose a problem. Surprisingly, however, the veteran broadcaster admits to nerves on this one. 'Nancye and all the rest say the same thing: you always get a bit nervous that you won't remember the lines, which is good. I'm not at all worried about giving a speech or going out to coach, but this is placing yourself in a space where you've never been. It's funny like that.'

However, *Annie* was not Alan's first venture onto the stage: he produced and acted in plays at various schools during his years as a student and teacher. And in 2007 he rubbed shoulders with opera star Teddy Tahu Rhodes, filling a small guest role in the Sydney opera *Dead Man Walking*. It was billed as 'the story of a nun who befriends a death-row inmate, prompting her to campaign against capital punishment'. Again he felt awe-struck by the experience. He has a passable singing voice but he says that 'shouting at footballers buggers it up'. Still, it was a little harsh of the theatre critic who wrote in the Melbourne *Age* after the opening night of *Annie* that Alan was 'so utterly lacking in acting talent, the decision to keep him looks like the result of some drunken dare'.

Warlow and Hayes hit back later, saying that their new radio buddy was an 'absolute team player who took notes and direction like the true professional he is,' that he had 'always endeavoured to give his best' and that it had been a 'great pleasure to get to know and work with him.' We may see more of stage performer Jones as the years roll by—the sort of late-life career embraced by his successor in *Annie*, former radio star Bert Newton. 'As they say,' smiles Alan, 'my management is open to offers.'

Alan's reverence for achievers probably comes from his late mother, Beth. 'It is important to be appropriately deferential when people have a measure of accomplishment that merits recognition,' he says, unable to resist taking the line of thought further. 'That's sometimes the weakness in the political system: you have to respect the office—prime minister, treasurer, for example—but you may not respect the people. There was that big kerfuffle when politicians' salaries were raised. I said I think the Australian prime minister should be paid more. But should Gillard and Wayne Swan, the treasurer, be paid anything at all? No!'

Alan, born in 1941, has had a clean bill of health since a double-whammy health scare in 2008, when he was diagnosed with prostate cancer and a benign brain tumour. 'I've had the lot,' he says, 'but I don't think about it. I just have good doctors and keep going. Too many people philosophise and hypothesise about all this, but you have to get on with it!' He is rattled by the diseases that strike down compatriots so suddenly. A Sydney acquaintance had been recently diagnosed with a lethal blood clot and had only weeks to live. 'Just astounding,' he says. 'It just comes at people.'

Wolter Peeters, Fairfax Syndication

DAVID HELFGOTT

The man with the runaway mind

I t had been badly treated, that horse. You could tell by the way the poor creature stood way up in the far corner of the paddock, shunning human contact, too skittish for a bridle. Probably only good for the knackery, to be honest, but this was an animal that got lucky three times. First, it was given to a sympathetic woman who put it out to graze in the faint hope it might recover. Second, that paddock happened to be next door to the home of pianist David Helfgott at Bellingen, on the coast of New South Wales. And third, most unusually, David and wife Gillian were at home for five weeks between his relentless concert tours, and every morning the man with the runaway mind would stand quietly by the fence, soothing the troubled beast.

'You would hear him out there,' says Gillian, 'calling it "darling," saying hello, and slowly, day by day, the horse came further down the paddock. At the end of the month David was patting it and giving it carrots. The woman came to see me and said, "Gillian,

David is a horse whisperer; he has healed that animal." It's not in the paddock any more; the new owners can ride it now.'

Gillian Helfgott is married to one of Australia's most unusual men. They met in 1984 when, as a 52-year-old divorcee visiting friends in Perth, a bare-chested David—dripping wet from a swimming pool—rushed up to wrap this stranger in one of his famous hugs. Three decades later he is still doing it. 'He comes straight out of the bath and hugs me,' says Gillian, who was once asked by a make-up girl before a TV interview, 'Does it ever worry you, him hugging all those women?' Gillian laughed. Of course not, that's just the way he is: a man who loves animals, loves people, loves the world.

You never forget a meeting with David Helfgott, who, even for an Amazing Bastard, is fair-dinkum astonishing. It was early afternoon when I arrived at his son-in-law Scott's Melbourne house and was greeted by a human whirlwind on the stairs to the front door.

'Lawrence, Lawrence, what's your last name, your last name?' David's body—or half of it—was above me on the landing, but his head suddenly craned back to quiz Gillian about this new visitor. Then he was all over me like an excited puppy, head nuzzled into my neck, arms hugging me, and next thing I knew we were in the lounge room reading verse in unison from an antiquarian book.

'Look, look, look, Lawrence, the word "sword" also means—does that say "means"?—means, means cleanness and death. This book would cost a fortune; can you read that to me, Lawrence?'

Soon, the reason for his choice of book, which Gillian said later cost $1500 through Amazon, became clear.

'Look, look, T.E. Lawrence, not D.H. Lawrence, different Lawrence, different Lawrence, Lawrence of Arabia.' Gillian stood alongside in quiet amusement, but David was utterly engrossed in the text. 'What's that word? "Battered." Not "mattered". Must have the right word, the right word.'

David was carrying a small radio tuned to a music station and was talking over it in a cascade of words that Geoffrey Rush, his alter ego in the 1996 movie *Shine*, calls 'fluent David Helfgott.'

'Would you like some tea?' asked Gillian amid the audio firestorm, while David beckoned me to sit next to him at the piano and started to play. 'Now, David,' said Gillian, 'I think we can do without the radio!'

During the next few minutes, while Gillian boiled the kettle, the runaway train slowed down long enough to field a few questions. Born in Melbourne? 'Yes, yes, a long time ago, yes.' And moved to Perth when he was six? 'Something like that, yes, roughly about six, about six.' And is it true that he could walk on his hands for half an hour as a kid? 'Well, I used to walk down the street to meet Dad, walk the whole street; sometimes I'd hobble but you don't wobble, you hobble, don't wobble whoah-heh-heh-heh-heh.' And he had just played at Melbourne's concert hall? 'Yes, yes, I would have never believed, never imagined in a million years that I would be in this unique position. I think everyone knows me. By repute, they just know me somehow or other. It's nice to be a virtue, virtuous, virtuoso; it's a wonderful story, more of a love story, really, wonderful story.'

From anyone else this might have sounded somewhat immodest, but here is an individual who lives in his own unique bubble. 'He really is the most endearing human being,' says Gillian. 'No meanness whatsoever. David doesn't argue. He nags, but he doesn't argue. The noise is the hardest thing. He will have the radio and the TV going while he plays, and he turns them up so high that the house reverberates.'

Despite Gillian's earlier request the radio continued, and I suggested that maybe, now he was playing snatches of music, it could be turned off.

'Do you think we should? I like it, whoah-heh-heh-heh-heh, the more the merrier, I like the technology!'

No one has managed to pinpoint the precise cause of David's extreme personality. Author Beverley Eley, who tried to nail the true man in her biography *The Book of David*, eventually concluded, 'David is simply an enigma, the true mystery within a mystery … in tune with the unknown'.

Mercifully, the whirlwind occasionally subsides. At Bellingen, where the Helfgotts live on 2 hectares of beautiful garden, David says goodnight to the sunset every evening. 'Just quietly stands there watching the sun go down,' says Gillian. 'Before that horse in the next-door paddock there was a donkey. He would go out there and stand with the donkey very peacefully.' There are other quiet times too: David's daily two-hour swim and two-hour piano practice. 'He sleeps seven hours a night,' Gillian tells me. 'Sometimes he goes to sleep in the bath.'

Peace eventually descended on that suburban lounge room too. David spotted my research papers and galloped off to the kitchen to read them, his voice and semi-manic chortle echoing occasionally from the back of the house.

It was Gillian's friend Chris Reynolds, owner of a Perth bar called Riccardo's, who introduced the pair, in 1984. Reynolds told Gillian that David was 'the most unusual person I have ever met,' and she soon saw what he meant. That night, when Gillian went to the bar to hear David play, she was stunned. 'He played Rachmaninov without the orchestra. It took 44 minutes.'

The next day David, who also had a past marriage (to Claire Papp, a Hungarian-born cooking teacher), visited Gillian. 'He asked me to marry him—and you know, I almost said yes.' They saw each other for barely eight hours over the next four days, then she flew home to Sydney. Gillian, an astrologer by trade, says she and her astrologer friends had known a new man was coming into her life, but 'he was not in the package I expected!' She had been home only a few hours when she sensed that David was heading for trouble. 'I phoned to ask Chris. He said David needed help due to emotional stress and I flew back to Perth.' David's turmoil subsided with Gillian's return and, within weeks, the two were wed.

Gillian has been called David's wife, publicist, manager and protector. But she has also been a significant figure in the astrological world, publishing a book on numerology called *The Insightful Turtle*. 'You put numbers around the shape of the turtle,' she says.

'It's the first book of its type to discusses the power of the zero.' She says she foresaw both the share market crash of 1987 and the global financial crisis of 2008, and sold their shares beforehand. She has been called 'formidable' and 'rambunctious' by some sections of the media, with occasional claims that she has exploited her husband. 'When they first said it,' Gillian told *The Canberra Times* in 2005, 'it was hurtful but now I just burst out laughing. He's known all over the world, he has a beautiful house and he says the best decision he ever made in life is to marry me. Well, if that's exploitation let's exploit people.'

Half an hour with this couple makes you wonder how Gillian copes with those waves of nervous energy—a favourite Helfgott stunt is to pull out all the books from the bookshelves and all the CDs from the cupboard, and then take all the leaflets out of the CDs, leaving the lot strewn across the floor. Gillian built a library 80 metres from their house a few years ago, overlooking their Japanese garden and lagoon. Rule number one: no radio or TV. 'It is my quiet place,' she says hopefully. 'I have a pile of wonderful books I want to read. Christopher Plummer's autobiography, Adele and Fred Astaire's biography, many more. Yes, there have been times when I have almost booked David a one-way ticket to Tierra del Fuego, but no, we really do get on amazingly well. And there's never a dull day.' Gillian is fifteen years older, but David, heavily reliant on his wife's stability, is convinced they will both die on the same day. 'That has caused some of our friends to joke that they won't travel with us on the same plane. But I have to stay around a long time yet.'

Gillian marvels at the audiences that attend David's concerts. 'In Melbourne it was quite extraordinary that there were so many young people there, beautifully dressed. Most of the concert entrepreneurs are saying the audiences are getting older, but about five people commented to us about the young people. They would have been in their very young teens when *Shine* came out, so there's a new audience. And he got the most spontaneous standing ovation;

they were enthralled by his personality, the joy that's on the stage. The second half particularly was beautiful playing, and the response was just gorgeous. A very close friend of ours who has studied music all his life said no music had ever touched his heart to the degree that David's did. And there were emails: "He warms your heart; the music just flows through him". When Melbourne's Hamer Hall reopened in 2012 David was one of the stars asked to perform. He practised every night until two in the morning. Then he would rush in and wake me up to tell me how well it went. If you want to see a grumpy woman, just wake me at 2 a.m.!'

However, it has not all been roses for the pop star pianist. When David made a world tour in 1997, propelled by the success of the movie, the public flocked to see him, but he got walloped by many of the critics. In *The Sydney Morning Herald* Peter McCallum said the concerts had the 'appeal of the freak show', claiming that 'without the frenzied media and public acclaim which has greeted *Shine*, Helfgott's disjointed performances would barely merit attention'. But the Sydney public came anyhow. Kiwi reviewer Denis Dutton wrote in the journal *Philosophy and Literature* that David Helfgott was like 'Beethoven on Prozac' but the New Zealand public came anyhow. In Britain, wrote David's sister Margaret in her book *Out of Tune: David Helfgott and the Myth of* Shine, one newspaper said it was 'like watching a Muppet give a recital' while another described his performance as 'exaggerated clatter'. But the British public came anyhow. Margaret wrote:

> *In the entire history of classical music performance there can hardly have been a wider gap between critical reaction on the one hand and public reaction on the other ... Almost all his concerts were sold out well in advance and he received rapturous applause wherever he played. At the first concert in Auckland, New Zealand, the audience of 2200 rose to their feet ... In Boston a 3000-strong audience gave him four standing ovations.*

David's CD of his concert performances, *Brilliantissimo*, shot to Number 1 in the British classic music charts in 1997. Like Glenn Gould, the eccentric Canadian virtuoso pianist who would hum during concert performances, David often sings along to his music while on stage. That was another irritation for Peter McCallum: 'The reality is that his trademark chatter and wild gesturing during performances drained the music of both its balance and its artistry'. Says Gillian, 'Because they surrender to the music, they don't realise. I might say to David after a performance, "You sang a bit too loudly, darling," and he'll say, "Oh, did I sing?"' But while Gould would play only when sitting in an old wooden chair his father had made for him, avoided social functions and hated being touched, David seems the ultimate extrovert who loves everybody, takes to the keyboard at the slightest opportunity and is surely one of the most people-friendly performers in history.

Away from the concert hall David is quite a homebody. 'He makes the beds every morning, sweeps the kitchen floor and front steps,' says Gillian. 'Doesn't like vacuuming. He'll un-peg the washing but he's not much good at folding it. But David's getting better year by year so he is more of a companion, a lot more sharing of sorts. He's far more aware of everything. For example, he'll ask me if I realise I've left the oven on.' That is not to say domestic life at the Helfgotts' is becoming dull—far from it. 'He has just learnt how to operate the heating,' says Gillian. 'I have it on 22, but when I go out he turns it right up to 28. When I open the door coming home I'm just about knocked out. It's like walking into a sauna.'

David loves tea and hides tea bags around the house to foil Gillian's attempts to monitor his consumption. When they met he smoked 125 cigarettes and drank 25 cups of coffee a day, but not any longer; according to his doctors, he is in top medical condition. 'His hands are very strong,' says Gillian. 'Just try to take a teabag off him.'

The mental illness that afflicts him has never been precisely diagnosed. Medical experts settled on 'manic eccentric', but, whatever it is, the problem surfaced early in childhood. He did not begin talking until he was three years old, and at five, after starting at Melbourne's Elwood State School, David was so filled with anxiety about being away from his parents that he would frequently dirty his pants and then hide after class, smelly and ashamed, in the grassland nearby. His sister Margaret would take him home, where their mother would put him in the bath and scrub the little bloke clean. 'David messing himself was just a fact of life,' wrote Margaret, 'something we got used to. My father never whipped David for this with a wet towel as happens in *Shine*. He never hit David, nor would it have been in his nature to do so'. David's oddities continued into the teenage years. He still could not tie his own shoelaces, and his eyesight was so poor he needed thick Coke-bottle-style spectacles, a magnet for schoolyard bullies.

According to the biography on The Official Website of David Helfgott, David, born in Melbourne in 1947, was such a prodigy as a child that he won 'the state finals of the ABC's Instrumental & Vocal Competition six times'. But his family says that for the first two years of playing he seemed unable to cotton on. Until he was eight, he could not remember which note was which, despite instruction each night from his father. Then, magically, it all fell into place one evening, when he stunned everyone at home by playing Chopin's Polonaise in A-flat major, a challenging piece for any pianist.

At seventeen he studied with Alice Carrard, a former student of the Hungarian virtuoso Istvan Thoman. David went to London two years later to study at the Royal College of Music with Cyril Smith, who described him as the most brilliant student he had seen in 25 years of teaching. Smith compared David's technical skill with that of American classical pianist and composer Vladimir Horowitz, reputed to be one of the finest pianists of the twentieth century. Says the Helfgott website,

> David won a number of awards at the College, including the Dannreuther Prize for Best Concerto Performance for his triumphant performance of Rachmaninov's Third Piano Concerto. However, towards the end of his time in London,

David faced increased emotional instability and mental excitability, compounded by the death in Perth of his mentor, writer Katherine Susannah Pritchard [sic].

A period of frequent hospitalization followed during the 1970s, but by 1976 David had moved to a halfway house where he stayed for six years. The greatest crisis for David had been the loss of his inner music, but he remembers the day the music came back: 'The fog lifted, I could hear again … I survived.'

Gillian tells me that David, who is now booked two years in advance, had resumed playing ten years before the movie *Shine* propelled him to stardom. 'Yes, he had been playing in Europe,' she says, adding that they were staggered at the movie's success. 'We thought it would just be a small art house film.' In 1997 Geoffrey Rush won an Academy Award for best actor for his portrayal of the adult David, and the film was given many other nominations, for Oscars, Golden Globes and Australian Film Institute awards.

David is still called Geoffrey occasionally by overeager fans. 'I suppose Geoff gets called David occasionally too,' says Gillian. 'Geoffrey did such a good job on David's character that for a while there I felt like I had two husbands!'

The movie's producer, Scott Hicks, first saw David perform eleven years before making the movie. He was not to know that this recital, in front of a small audience, was the catalyst for three men—David Helfgott, Geoffrey Rush and Scott himself—achieving international fame. Scott told Patrick McDonald of the *Herald Sun* that it had been obvious David was struggling, but he had still managed to generate enthusiasm and excitement.

The real moment that caught my attention was after the concert finished and the audience was leaving. As they were filing out of the hall, David came back on to the stage and started to play the piano again.

So a few people drifted back and gathered around the piano. Within moments, David not only knew all their names and who they were, but they were laughing—it was an event unlike anything I'd ever seen …

He captivated people—you could just sense the love, they just adored him … That was the real trigger that led me to talk to him and … Gillian after the concert and say 'I'm a filmmaker—what's the story?' That was the beginning of a long road.

However, the movie also triggered enormous upheaval in the family, with sister Margaret's book slamming the harsh portrayal of their father, Peter. In 2001 she and sister Leslie wrote to the publication *Research Studies in Music Education* rebutting psychologist Jane Davidson's observations about David and accusing both the movie and Gillian's own book *Love You to Bits and Pieces* of presenting an inaccurate portrait of their family life. The sisters wrote that, far from being forced to play piano by their father,

David had a natural love and passion for the piano from a very early age, and was always impatient to play piano and have lessons with his father. In fact, his three other pianist siblings vied with one another for access to the piano and their father's enthusiastic tuition. Rather than our father causing David to practise for 'lengthy practice sessions' he guided him and taught him patiently in daily lessons … It should be understood that David's motivation was his own incredible love of music—he was enamoured of the piano from around age three and his virtuosity and extraordinary talent were encouraged and nurtured by our father. When Peter had taught him all he could he searched for a more advanced piano teacher for both David and Margaret. He found Frank Arndt, an accomplished teacher who refused all payment. Frank, who died in 1999, was shocked at the false, violent and cruel portrayal of Peter in the film and publicly denounced it in the Western Australian Gazette *newspaper on September 22 1996.*

Love You to Bits and Pieces was sold along with the programs and souvenirs at David's concerts. In *Out of Tune* Margaret criticised Gillian's book and quipped that the 1997 world tour was a case of 'exploit you to bits and pieces'. She suggested that perhaps David's medication had been reduced 'in order to maintain his freak appeal'. His medical team denied this, saying his medication had to be carefully balanced, calming his manic symptoms but leaving his performing powers intact.

However, Gillian says peace was eventually restored in the family. 'I worked very conscientiously to bring harmony back there. We were in Perth recently and Margaret and David were playing duets on the piano together. But David has three sisters and a brother, and his sister Susie never agreed with Margaret's view. She supported me all the way through. If you have five kids, they are all going to have different experiences with parents. Everything in the movie, as David said, had a point to it, and David did not think his father was treated harshly in the film at all. He went through terrible torment with his father—when he came back from England Peter would not speak to him. The film was about David's life, not Margaret's.'

By coincidence, that deafening day that I visited the Helfgott household was the eve of my birthday, and the discovery of that fact spurred David to even greater activity. His sensitive hands danced over the keyboard of the Steinway, playing increasingly intricate variations of 'Happy Birthday to You' in between trips to the kitchen to fetch 'gifts': three pieces of well-fingered chocolate from a family block, a 375-gram pack of Sunbeam sultanas, a can of Scottish sardines. I gave him my ballpoint pen to add to his huge collection ('He is always taking them,' says Gillian) and departed. David led me to the car by the hand, gushing 'happy birthdays' and kissing my forehead before loping with Mr Bean–like gait back up the driveway.

On the journey home I found myself smiling broadly—and laughing. Some time later my daughter Samantha, a flight attendant with Qantas, reported that David was on board her flight and had been just the same, excitedly hugging and kissing the other passengers. As Gillian Helfgott says, 'He's the friendliest person in the world.'

WILLIAM COOPER'S MOB

Warriors for justice

All these years later Kevin William Russell (pictured) can still hear the voice of his Aboriginal grandmother, Sally. 'Never forget who you are, Kevin,' she would tell him. 'My father, your great-grandfather, was a hero. Don't ever forget that.'

Kevin was an Olympic year, Australia Day baby, born on 26 January 1956, but for a long time he did not celebrate his birthday. For many Australians like Kevin, with Aboriginal blood in their veins, it is a date that tolls a death knell for an Indigenous culture that stretched back thousands of years. Long before Kevin was born, his famous great-grandfather, William Cooper, had declared Australia Day of 1938—the 150th anniversary of the arrival of the First Fleet in Sydney Cove—a national Day of Mourning.

William, son of a white labourer and an Aboriginal woman, had spent years campaigning in vain for Australia's Indigenous people, who in the 1930s still had no vote and were not even counted as human beings in any census of the population. On 13 November 1937, two months before the 150th celebrations, William's two-year-old Australian Aborigines' League, together with the newly formed Aborigines Progressive Association, held a peaceful protest march on Sydney Town Hall followed by a rally for 1000 people. However, as before, their calls for recognition fell on deaf ears. Their ten-point petition to the prime minister, Joseph Lyons, was ignored, and many years passed before Australia's original inhabitants won some justice. And it was many years too before William's quiet heroics—including a remarkable humanitarian act on behalf of Germany's Jews—were recognised.

Kevin Russell, raised in Benalla, son of the son of the daughter of William Cooper, knew all this thanks to his grandmother Sally, but the fractures of dispossessed people keep spreading down through the generations, and Kevin's youth was too troubled to allow much contemplation of his family legacy.

'With one Aboriginal and one non-Aboriginal parent there is a feeling of being displaced,' says Kevin. 'Almost like being part of the Stolen Generation, not being able to belong to one group or the other. My parents separated when I was fifteen, and as a younger boy I had copped some sexual abuse from a male neighbour. It played on my mind through my early years, so I was a little bit chaotic in my own life without the Aboriginal identity thing. Joining the army and drinking and travelling were pretty good options at the time. As part of the healing of that, I reconnected with my Aboriginality when I was going through some treatment, trying to understand what was going on. Through that process I was able to reconnect with other Aboriginal men who were in recovery. I became stronger and grew to understand my own journey. My head came out of the clouds and I decided that my job was to help others who had been along a similar path.'

And so Kevin's life finally took off along a trail first blazed by his great-grandfather. Today, he is a team manager at Link Up in Adelaide, an Indigenous support group, helping heal in others those same fractures he suffered himself.

However, to fully understand Kevin's mission and his family

legacy you need first to wind the clock back to 1861, the year William Cooper was born, near Echuca, to labourer James Cooper and Yorta Yorta woman Kitty Lewis. It was a time when disease, alcohol and violence were eating away at the Indigenous population, and when farming and land development were wiping out traditional food sources, so, at age thirteen, William moved with his mother and grandmother Maria to the Maloga Mission in New South Wales. Theirs was one of the first families there, accepting food and shelter in return for converting to Christianity.

The mission was run by clergyman Daniel Matthews and his wife, and, says Kevin, 'it was a pretty good option at the time because life along the river had become treacherous as the inland settlement continued to take its toll on our people. Towns like Bendigo, Ballarat and Echuca were thriving business centres, yet our people were on the fringes. In the period between 1851 and 1894 the sheep population of New South Wales, where Maloga and Cummeragunja missions were, had increased from 5 million to 67 million, and access to the river country was restricted by wire fences and cruel station managers. New stations that were taking our land—such as Moira and Medowie—were owned by prominent businessmen and politicians from Melbourne. They were in constant dispute with Daniel Matthews, who they looked on as a "black-lover" who lured their workers away to Maloga.'

Kevin says Daniel was often threatened and victimised, but he confronted the men about using Aboriginal women. Some females were as young as twelve, says Kevin, and were 'kept in black camps on these stations for the shearers' and labourers' pleasure.' As the word spread about Maloga, many other Aboriginals came to settle there, seeking protection. William Cooper's potential was quickly apparent to the Maloga missionaries. In a diary entry dated 6 August 1874, Daniel noted, 'The boy Billy Cooper showed great aptitude for learning, he has acquired the alphabet, both capitals and small, in three days and has been able to teach his brother Bobby capitals in one day'.

Says Kevin, 'We know in later life William was to become a prolific letter-writer, and it was here he developed those skills. As a twenty-year-old in 1881, William would have witnessed firsthand the effects of government policies in what was known as the "protection era". Unfortunately, it was those who were supposed to protect us that we needed protection from the most. Life in this period saw an explosion in the number of children born to white fathers, William included, who had their way with the women and then of course disappeared. This set the way for future policies such as the "half-caste policy", designed to deal with the increasing numbers of "not so dark children". William went on to work as a shearer, horse-breaker and labourer before he was taken to the Melbourne home of Sir John O'Shannesy, a former Victorian premier, to work as a coachman.

'In 1884, 23-year-old William returned to his people at Maloga Mission,' Kevin continues. 'He married Annie Clarendon Murri, who bore him two children. Three years later William was a signatory to the so-called Maloga Petition to the Victorian governor, urging that local Aboriginals be granted their own land: "not less than 100 acres [40 hectares] per family in fee simple or else at a small nominal rental annually with the option of purchase at such prices as shall be deemed reasonable for them under the circumstances, always bearing in mind that the Aborigines were the former occupiers of the land". Such a provision would enable them to earn their own livelihood.' As William saw time and again during his life, the requests were ignored.

William's personal circumstances grew harder. One of his children died, then in 1889 he lost his wife, Annie, too. He remarried four years later to Agnes Hamilton, and they moved to Cummeragunja, the 730-hectare reserve nearby whose name, translated from the Yorta Yorta language, meant 'our home'. It had been set aside by the government for Aboriginals to farm and clear and soon became quite successful with quality wool, grain and timber products. Agnes gave birth to six children before dying in 1910, leaving 50-year-old

William widowed for a second time, and with seven dependants. One of his daughters, Amy, became matron of the first Aboriginal girls hostel in Melbourne, in 1959, and son Lynch became a top athlete, winning the Stawell Gift in 1928 and the world professional sprint title in 1929.

Another son, Daniel, was killed in action in World War I, on 21 September 1917, aged 21. 'Killed,' notes Kevin, 'along with many of his people, fighting for a country that did not recognise him or his father or any of our people as citizens of this country. My grandmother Sally could never rest knowing her brother Dan lay buried on the other side of the world. Maybe one day I will fulfil her dream and have Dan brought home to be buried next to his father on Cummeragunja.'

At age 65, William married for a third time, to Sarah Nelson, née McCrae, of Wahgunyah and Coranderrk Mission, but had no more children. The postwar depression saw conditions deteriorate badly at Cummeragunja under the management of a man named McQuiggan, a harsh taskmaster who patrolled the reserve armed with a rifle. Residents were confined to the property and many of their relatives were forced away. There was a lack of rations and supplies, and residents had to share blankets and live in rag huts. Tuberculosis and whooping cough flared up among the elderly and the young.

In 1933 William decided to move to Melbourne, eventually setting up home in Footscray, but back at Cummeragunja, life grew ever more bleak. An Aboriginal activist and journalist, Jack Patten, one of William's fellow organisers in the 1938 Day of Mourning, was arrested and removed from the mission after trying to address the local people. In what became known as the Cummeragunja Walk-off, more than 150 residents deserted the mission and moved across the Murray River into Victoria, setting up home in the areas of Barmah, Echuca and Shepparton. The walk-off, defying the rules of the New South Wales Aboriginal Protection Board, was the first mass strike by Aboriginal Australians. The episode eventually became the subject of an opera called *Pecan Summer*, written by and starring Aboriginal opera singer Deborah Cheetham.

William was aged 77, ailing and only three years from death when he did a remarkable thing. It was November 1938, and half a world away in Germany the Nazis had begun to attack Jews. More than 90 were killed and thousands of Jewish properties damaged or destroyed in an event that became known as *Kristallnacht*, or Night of Broken Glass, because of the thousands of smashed windows. It was the beginning of one of the world's most horrific episodes, the Holocaust, and William expected people everywhere to voice their fury but was astonished to find that the world's citizenry remained largely silent. Several weeks later he wrote a letter of protest to the local German consul. Then, on 6 December 1938, walking with supporters from his home in suburban Footscray to the consulate in the city, he tried to deliver it. The letter voiced a protest on behalf of Australia's Aboriginals at the 'cruel persecution of the Jewish people by the Nazi Government in Germany' and demanded that it be brought to a halt. However William's party was turned away at the door.

Says Kevin Russell, 'William's message was that if we sit in silence when evil's happening around us, we're no better than those who are doing it. That was a powerful thing—for people, who had no status, to walk into a capital city and demand at the German embassy, "You stop this." Can you imagine what people were thinking of him? Now, we see him as a hero. Then, he was just a troublemaker. Just a stirrer. "Gotta watch him, he's a stirrer, that fella."'

It was the only such private protest on record anywhere in the world, but it took many decades before history truly recognised its significance or William Cooper's lifelong fight for his people. That fight began as early as 1887, when he was signatory to a petition to the Victorian governor pushing for Aboriginals to be recognised in their own land. In 1935 he led a delegation of Aboriginals to Canberra, urging for federal control of Aboriginal affairs. A year later he founded the Australian Aborigines' League, the first

Indigenous Australian political organisation. And in 1937 he helped to organise the Day of Mourning to mark the nation's 150th anniversary of white settlement.

As things turned out, the anniversary celebrations were a fiasco, with the New South Wales government deciding to hold a re-enactment of Captain Arthur Phillip's arrival but being stymied in their efforts to find Aboriginal people who would participate. All Indigenous groups in Sydney refused to take part, and the government was forced to bring in 26 Aboriginal men from a reserve in western New South Wales. The men—not exactly volunteers, as they were threatened with loss of rations if they did not cooperate— were locked up in the Redfern Police Barracks the night before, to ensure they would not run away.

William and his Day of Mourning were ignored by the media at the time, but true recognition can often take time. When the nation's bicentenary of white settlement arrived, in 1988, William was named among the 100 greatest Australians. Kevin says William's compassionate heart was apparent in the way his prolific correspondence invariably ended with such terms as 'I am forever yours' or 'Your faithful subject'. Says Kevin, 'Words like that just show who William was and that he knew that the way forward was not through bitterness. He started doing things the white way because he feared the extermination of our people.'

In the early 2000s the story of William's protest against the Nazis became better known in the Jewish community. In 2009, 70 Australian trees were planted in Israel in William's honour, and the Israeli ambassador to Australia presented William's grandson Alf 'Uncle Boydie' Turner with an associated certificate at Victoria's Parliament House. Five more trees were planted in William's honour, in the Forest of Martyrs, near Jerusalem, and in 2010 a memorial to William was established at Jerusalem's Yad Vashem Holocaust museum. Meanwhile, in Footscray, where William lived in the latter part of his life, the well-travelled footbridge to the railway station was named the William Cooper Bridge, and, after

Melbourne's former County Court building was renovated in 2010, it was renamed the William Cooper Justice Centre.

In 2012, on the 74th anniversary of William's thwarted Nazi protest, Kevin Russell and Uncle Boydie led a group of Aboriginals and Jews in a re-enactment, carrying a replica letter from the former Cooper house in Southampton Street, Footscray, to 419 Collins Street, the address of the former German consulate, where honorary German consul Michael Pearce SC was happy to accept it.

Uncle Boydie, son of William's daughter Amy, is now in his eighties and lives in Mooroopna, in country Victoria. He says he attained his lifelong nickname when his mother brought him home from hospital as a baby.

'Look what I've got for you,' said his mother, 'a boy!'

One of his two elder sisters said, 'A boydie!' and the name stuck.

Uncle Boydie stayed with William for many years. 'Just after I was born, in 1928, Mum took me back to a little place called Barmah, where he lived, opposite the Cummeragunja Aboriginal settlement. I lived with him there until he moved to Melbourne, in 1933. He had been fighting for Aboriginal rights for years and wasn't getting anywhere with it, so he decided it might be better in Melbourne. My grandmother came and took me down there to live with him again. He was a big man, around 1.8 metres tall and heavily built, a Christian man who didn't drink or smoke. He was very quiet but he could wind up a bit when the Aboriginal question came up. Back then, Aboriginals could not even vote.'

William walked into the city from Footscray to deliver his protest because he was on an aged pension and could not afford transport. 'He had four grandchildren in his house,' says Uncle Boydie. 'Myself and three of the children from a daughter who had died. I was the youngest.'

Uncle Boydie left school at thirteen to cut wood in the Barmah Forest. After various labouring jobs he became a plasterer. 'I was on different committees with the local Aboriginal communities,' he says. 'There has certainly been progress, because I can remember things weren't real good when I was a boy. They were taking the children away from Cummeragunja.'

According to Uncle Boydie, William organised a petition to King George V in 1933 calling for Aboriginal rights and delivered it to the Australian prime minister. 'There were 1814 signatures on the petition,' he says, 'but it was never sent to England. We're planning to fix that too. Travel to England soon with a substitute letter for the queen. That's in the pipeline.'

In Barbara Miller's 2012 book *William Cooper, Gentle Warrior*, Uncle Boydie recalled William holding many meetings at his house. He would open the door to such Aboriginal leaders as pastor Sir Doug Nicholls, who became a South Australian governor; William's son Lynch, the champion athlete; and brothers Eric and Bill Onus (credited with suggesting the name for Melbourne's annual festival, Moomba). 'A couple of white people used to come too,' he told Miller. 'My grandfather was always writing letters. Some days he was so sick he could not get out of bed but he would put a red blanket around his shoulders and keep writing. He had been writing for years before moving to Melbourne but it went into the waste paper basket because no one would listen.'

Uncle Boydie was thirteen when William was taken to hospital at Mooroopna, where some of his family were living. He died there, at age 80. 'When I asked the doctor what he died from they said he was "just worn out,"' says Uncle Boydie. 'Working as a team manager at Link Up South Australia, an organisation assisting Stolen Generation people connect with family and culture. It was a big funeral: many knew him.'

Now Kevin Russell is carrying both his great-grandfather's name and his great-grandfather's mission into the 21st century. 'It has become more clear to me over the past few years,' says Kevin, 'as I do this work and understand the enormity of what my grandmother's messages were. I had to pull my head out of the sand and see things as they really are. Most of the community who come to us for assistance are normally very disconnected people, often in fear of being rejected again should they find community or family people who don't want to connect, the pain that it might cause at the other end of the line. There are also other Aboriginal children, separated from their families at young age, who have had very successful lives in loving homes, had every opportunity, very black in colour and with very Aboriginal features, but totally disconnected from their Aboriginality in any way, shape or form. When they are reconnected to a traditional setting it can be quite overpowering. It is very complex.'

It has been a hard road, too, for Kevin, who spent more than ten years drifting about Australia seeking his life's purpose. As with his parents, his own marriage broke up as he trod an uncertain path between two cultures. 'We were a bit disconnected after Dad split up with my non-Aboriginal mother, but having that knowledge embedded in us from a young age, it was always there, and it was only a matter of time before we would explore it further.' Kevin is now 57 and more relaxed about his Australia Day birthday. 'I celebrate it openly for what it is,' he says. 'But I always take time on the day to reflect and remember those who have gone before us.'

CARL BARRON

The kid from Wompoo Street

So this cocky little bald bloke in a T-shirt and jeans saunters onto the stage at the Montreal comedy festival in 2006 looking like the love child of Mahatma Ghandi and Chris Judd, and starts telling the Canadians about thongs.

> *People don't know what I'm talking about over here. You call 'em 'flip-flops'. We don't call 'em that in Australia; we call 'em 'thongs'. You know what you call 'thongs' over here? Women's G-strings. Nobody told me that the first time I got here. Shoulda heard this conversation I was havin' with this bloke I met in the street.*
>
> *He's goin', 'Man, once she bent over you could see her thong.'*
>
> *'What are ya lookin' at her thong for?'*
>
> *'It was popping out the top of her jeans.'*
>
> *'What was poppin' out the top of her jeans?'*

'Her thong.'

'Her thong was poppin' out the top of her jeans? What's a friggin' thong doin' poppin' out the top of her jeans?'

'So, when you looked down her jeans you could see her thong.'

'She must have had loose jeans on. By the way, where was the other one?'

'The other what?'

'Thong. They always come in twos.'

'Wadda you know about thongs?'

'I wear them.'

'Do you? When?'

'When I'm feelin' hot. And when I'm cold I put a sock on first and put the thong over that. What's the big deal? Me dad wears 'em, me mum wears 'em ...'

'Are we talking about the same thing?'

'I don't think so ...'

Fair dinkum, the folks in the audience are cacking themselves at this bloke. And cop a load of his haunted eyes—like Uncle Fester in *The Addams Family*. You piss yourself just looking at him. Is this an Amazing Bastard or what? And, get this: his routine goes on YouTube, and last time I looked it was heading for 3 million views. That's more than Billy Connolly got talking about colonoscopies, and this little bloke didn't even have to stick a tube up his clacker.

Carl Barron was born in Longreach, Queensland. His old man, Rick, reckoned two women fainted at his christening because his pecker was as long as a horse's. Reckoned some sheila in the family made a jockstrap to hold this monstrous weapon, and Rick wouldn't exaggerate: he was a shearer, and those blokes never stretch the truth. Carl's not convinced, though; hey, it's his pecker, and if that was the case, what the hell has happened to those dimensions in the 49 years since?

Rick was a funny bugger, country humour as dry as a chip, all bent over like a half-open pocketknife after years of wrestling those sheep, buzzing away with the electric shears. He was often away on the shearing circuit—so often, in fact, that young Carl didn't recognise him one night. 'Who's that in bed with ya?' he asked Mum.

'That's your dad,' said Carmel.

Rick died in 2009, but not before Carl took him on a sentimental car trip from the Gold Coast back to the old house at 8 Wompoo Street, Longreach, where Carl spent his first six years. Bloody hot, bloody flat, bloody boring, but Carl and Rick visited the local hospital to find Carl's birth registered in a dusty records book: 6 October 1964, to Carmel Edith Barron, a boy, birth 'satisfactory'. It didn't take long for that to appear in his stage show. '"Satisfactory"? The doctors obviously had a quick look and said, "Yeah, that'll do."' Now that same kid from Longreach is out-YouTubing Billy Connolly. How does that happen?

It's a sunny winter day in Sydney, and Carl Barron comes to his front door in the same casual gear he wears on stage—T-shirt, jeans, sneakers. In contrast, his home in the inner west has an impeccably formal front garden, a fastidiously tidy interior and a spacious backyard with swimming pool. Delightful place. But Carl won't stay here long. Too bloody quiet. He gets bored. He was in Kings Cross before this and thinks he made a mistake coming to the suburbs. He's always moving on and, yeah, now he's got the dough, he can afford to.

'People say I can't settle down, I can't commit. But it's just that I like contrast; that's the positive way of looking at it.' He was shocked when his dad passed on. 'He had a heart problem, but he was all right, he was managing it. But Mum rang one morning— he'd gone. Dad was 80. Look, he wasn't a health fanatic—used to drink custard to quench his thirst. Smoked, didn't exercise. A very funny bloke, had natural timing. A lot of blokes from back home are like that, really good timing. That's what it's about. You see lots of people with funny things to say but their timing's off. They just don't wait for that right moment to say it; a second later and it's not as funny. It's that point—you feel your way into it. It's a feeling you have or you don't have.'

Carl seems to have had that timing from the year dot. 'One of my earliest memories is standing in front of the kids at school, just loved having a group of people in front of me, looking at me. There was something really exciting and exhilarating when I walked up the front. I felt like all I had to do was the smallest thing and I had their attention. Funny faces, y'know.'

Weird kid all right. In Grade 3 he used to walk around with one of those blue Collins mini-dictionaries jammed in his shirt pocket. 'I would sit there reading words,' he says. 'I felt the power that can give you. I read something about extending your vocabulary—you can enter a new world. I was obsessed with pens, had them in my pocket too. And I'd copy out algebra, those long formulas, and take them to the teacher and tell her I'd just done them. She'd say, "Where did you copy that from, Carl?" I loved the look of all the numbers and letters and brackets. I find that attractive. Like Egyptian hieroglyphics.'

His attraction to words constantly seeps into his stage shows. Words are just noises, after all. Who chose them? Why can't the noise for 'hello' be something else? 'Brarp'? Or maybe 'kachoo'? '"Word" is just the noise for "word",' he observed shrewdly in one show, then glanced at his watch, waiting for the audience to catch up. Carl says he has always been pedantic about language. 'I love words and reading,' he says. 'One of the first times I remember doing that sort of thing was in Grade 4, when the teacher handed me a bit of paper and said, "Write your name on the back of this."

'And I said, "You want me to write 'your name' on the back of this?" I knew I was being a smart-arse, but in some ways I knew I was right.'

He discombobulated Bert Newton on TV one night after Bert congratulated him for selling more DVDs than any other Australian comedian ever. 'You must be happy with that,' said Bert.

Carl couldn't help himself. 'Why must I?'

Bert looked a bit thunderous, but Carl is not an ill-mannered bloke—it is just this fascination he has with what humans say and do. Why *must* selling DVDs make you happy?

'It doesn't,' says Carl. 'When Artie, my manager, rings me up and tells me we've sold hundreds of thousands, I'm very grateful for that and the money you get from it, but it doesn't make me happy. It's just a really good thing I've got in my life. What makes me happy is making people laugh—live, in the moment.'

Like Bert, fans may find him a tad brusque when they offer him material, something that happens to most comedians. 'They'll say, "I've got a joke for your show, Carl," and I'll ask, "Is it long?" and they're, like, "Sort of," and I tell them, "Then I don't want to hear it."' Well, he will just have been on stage for maybe 90 minutes being funny. Would he really want to stand there listening to a long and possibly badly told joke afterwards? It's like asking Michael Phelps to watch *you* do a lap of the pool after *his* 400-metre final.

Even Carmel has been known to stray into this territory. She came back from the butcher's one time suggesting a joke about minced meat. Ah, no thanks, Mum.

Rick and Carmel never really talked much about their eldest son's climb to the top of the comedy tree, but Carl reckons they've been proud.

'Carl's a famous comedian,' said father Rick to the laconic bloke at their old Longreach house when they knocked on the door during that sentimental car trip. You gotta love those country Aussies.

'Yeah, come in,' the bloke said, not knowing them from a bar of Palmolive.

That's despite the fact that Rick had banged on the door when they arrived, calling out, 'Get your hand off it!'

Carl had brought a film crew along to make a documentary. They all trooped inside too. Carl is still gobsmacked: 'We just turn up and he asks us in. They do that in the country. Who would do that in the city? You'd be locking up and calling the cops. And what's that bloke doing sleeping on a mattress in his own lounge room?'

The doco went into his DVD box set, but they couldn't flog it to the TV stations. 'None of them wanted it, which I took as a compliment. But we had some funny feedback. One lady said, "It's a bit personal." A father and son going to their old home town. Of course it's personal!'

Carl's manager, Artie Laing, went along on that trip. 'I really enjoyed that,' he says. 'Very good for Carl, and Rick was a good bloke and good fun.'

Artie's father, Arthur Laing, managed Slim Dusty for many years, and Artie entered the same business. He first encountered Carl when organising a TV gala with disabled comic Steady Eddy. 'One of the acts pulled out,' says Artie, 'and Carl was recommended. The moment he told his first gag, that was me gone. He instantly went well, like he does everywhere. I always had a passion for comedy—used to love the comics on *Hey Hey It's Saturday*. So I have worked with some big names—Jason Alexander from *Seinfeld*, Wayne Brady, Ross Noble—but none of them can pull the number of people Carl does. He had 6500 at the Entertainment Centre in Brisbane. Despite that, Carl is very modest—I think that is part of the reason for his success.'

Carl was aged six when Rick and Carmel moved to Burleigh Heads, on the Gold Coast, where Carmel's family had a timber yard. The Barrons were Aussie battlers who went where they could find work. Carmel still says they never had any money problems. 'If you don't have any money, you never have money problems' is her philosophy. Rick would go off shearing or work at the timber yard or as a postman. For a while, he and Carmel ran a hamburger shop.

But Rick made up for life in Struggle Street with his colourful imagination. For years Carl and his three siblings—elder sister, Julie, and younger brothers, Troy and Rick junior—would hear about a wonderful place, a veritable utopia, called Morven in outback Queensland. 'Dad would always talk about Morven when we were young. It was

"Morven this" and "Morven that," how great Morven was, how his first girlfriend came from Morven. The way he used to speak about it, we thought it was like Las Vegas. When I finally went there years later it was this shitty little town in the middle of nowhere—one shop and ten houses.' Like his eldest son, Rick was big on words. Did the crossword every day. Sharp as a tack till the day he died.

The family's house on the Gold Coast was a two-bedroom duplex: parents in one bedroom, kids sharing the other. 'I was always in charge of the boys,' says Julie, 'because Mum and Dad were always working. They didn't have time to do much together. So I had to have the boys clean and tidy, but a lot of the time all we did was fight. Had wrestling matches in the lounge room, broke a few things and had to hide them.'

Rick had been adopted: Julie tells me his mother was Italian, and Carl's resultant dark olive skin caused him a bit of grief at school. 'He'd often get upset because kids would pick on him, call him names,' she says. 'But Carl was always funny at home. One time he appeared at the doorway with a string tied around him with a lettuce leaf covering his willy—nothing covering his bottom—thought it would cheer me up after school! My baby brother, Rick, used to do things like that to me too.

'Carl tried everything as a kid. He was an altar boy at the church. Used to eat big handfuls of holy bread when the priest wasn't there, and it'd get stuck up on the roof of his mouth. Then he was a paper boy: got $1.10 a week, banked a dollar and spent the 10 cents on lollies. Then when he got sick of that he tried being a magician: bought a set from the magic shop and did tricks for us every night. Then he got a doll and tried being a ventriloquist; he'd get into trouble at school for talking but not opening his mouth. Then he took up karate and then boxing: hung a big boxing bag in the car port. Then he wanted to be a professional tennis player. But he hated being a roof tiler.'

Never did Julie imagine that her cheeky young brother would end up on stage entertaining thousands of people at a time, one of the nation's most successful comedians. 'I go to all his shows,' she says, 'but I get nervous for him. Get excited and nervous. I don't know how he remembers it all. But Carl's very quiet in real life. He doesn't go out a lot and I don't push him because I know he has to be in the mood. People recognise him all the time. Some are good but some can be annoying. I came down to Sydney recently and we went out—once he had a few beers he was hilarious. Didn't care who was looking.'

Carl left school on the Gold Coast after Year 10. 'I didn't like it, struggled with a lot of subjects, had trouble applying myself. I never thought I was stupid, though. Maths I used to fail because you had to follow a system, whereas English and performance you can jump around. I think that suits my mind—I think that's the nature of minds, anyhow. So I worked for a couple years in the timber yard, then one day I was down at the pub and someone said his brother, a bloke named Spud, had broken his collarbone and did I want to fill in with some roof-tiling for a couple of weeks? Ended up doing roof-tiling for seventeen and a half years.'

Carl amused his workmates with his antics and eventually began working short weeks so he could do comedy gigs in the local pubs. In 1993 he fronted up at the Harold Park Hotel in Glebe, where hopeful comics went on Monday nights. 'You'd have maybe fifteen blokes there and you'd get three minutes. If you were bad you wouldn't get on the next week. I did well the first night, but I knew I was going to because I just knew what this was. I'd done it a million times; it didn't feel foreign to me. Felt very comfortable. I had a girlfriend once who said, "You look happier up there than you are with me."

'I said, "I am," but I didn't mean it as an insult. She went on and married and had kids.'

So work is no problem, money's now no problem: Carl Barron the comedian can pick and choose. The real challenge comes when he is *not* working. Rather than relax, the off-duty Carl tends to get cabin fever. 'The worst thing you can do is sit around not doing anything. You start going outside then think, *No, I'll have a cup of tea first*. I gotta get out. It's like being addicted to some drug. I do all these gigs in front of 1000, 2000, maybe 4000 people, then I come home and I've got a vacuum. I don't know what to do, so I go back on the road.'

Like sister Julie and brother Troy, Carl has never married. Rick junior's married, but Carl says he has never even come close, and Carmel says it would be an 'unusual girl' who could snare the remaining Barron boys. With no serious relationship to occupy him away from the stage, Carl sometimes misses a 'proper' job. 'I said that the other night to a friend—she's a psychotherapist.

'She asked me, "What's a proper job, Carl?"

'I said that for me it will always be making stuff. Sawing, hammering, mixing concrete, fixing a gutter—sometimes I wish I could go somewhere one day and do it. Comedy's not work; writing's not work.'

Artie Laing got Carl his first TV spot in 1997, on the New South Wales *Footy Show*. It lit the fuse on Carl's career. He was so popular he was asked back sixteen times. After that success, Artie offered to manage him. Carl may now be filling whole theatres, but you won't find him mixing with the red-carpet set. 'I like meeting up with one person at a time, so a mate will go, "Want to go to the beach?"

'And I go, "Nup."

'"Like to go to this party?"

'"Nup."

'I want to go somewhere quiet, glass of wine and a bit of a chat.'

The mobile phone has been a boon. He uses the voice recorder when he gets an idea. And he has a book where he writes notes. And he writes on bits of paper. He writes down all sorts of things and puts a circle around the stuff that are comedy ideas. 'Sometimes, when I feel like doing new material I get all the bits of paper together and the idea just grows.' And although his acts seem to meander all over the place, to Carl it is all connected. 'Perhaps I don't get that across clearly, but I guess it doesn't matter.'

Such an elusive concept is comedy. What makes us laugh? For Carl, an essential part is taking the micky, but not everybody twigs. 'Comedy's about bagging stuff. I did this charity night with a whole bunch of people at the State Theatre and there was an orchestra there. And they had the singers come out and do their bit, and, y'know, part of the comic's job is to take the piss, to break things up, so I walk out after this very nice night—people are thanking everyone on stage—I walk out and look at the orchestra, very straight-faced, and say, "I'm not sure you guys were in key." I look at one violin player and say, "Do you know what you are doin' there? I'm not sure you should be here." Most people laughed, the orchestra laughed, but some people said later, "You ruined the night." One lady was real upset, but I thought, *Do you understand what this is?* As they say, if you're offended by a joke you've missed the point. Comedy is about pushing it.'

Carl doesn't give too many interviews these days. Doesn't have to: his tours sell themselves. Besides, he says he doesn't really want to sit around talking about himself. However, he has a new project on the boil that has livened up his downtime: a movie on the world of stand-up. He and a mate spent three months in 2012 working on the script in Italy. 'It's about the two sides of a person's nature in the stand-up world. A bit of a black romantic comedy. I just wanted to explore all the other stuff that people don't see and understand. The isolation of what comics are, dealing with the crowds, trying to get away.

'And the movie will deal with where jokes come from. The poet Robert Bly wrote about turning your wounds into wisdom, and there's a lot of that. The comics I know are solitary, usually very sensitive. That surprises people, but that's just the way it works. I find that if you get the comics who are loud and gregarious socially, I'll bet you 50 bucks that they're not that funny on stage. A lot of the good comics I know, they doubt themselves. I realised early on what people laugh about—when you are embarrassed or unsure or scared—all the things we have hang-ups about. I just knew early on that they were the things that were the comedy. I love that feeling of starting a new act from zero because then you are talking about where you are at in your life. The real crime about doing old jokes is you are talking about where you were. You're not there any more, so that's why it ceases to be funny. There's no heart and soul in it. A comic I know from England, Stewart Lee, he never does a routine exactly the same way. He says, "You must try and surprise yourself as well."'

And make no mistake—those people with hang-ups include Carl himself. The 50th anniversary of his birth looms, due in October 2014, and he's not real happy about it. 'You're young for so long,' he says, 'in your twenties and thirties and even forties. I dunno, for me there's something in my head about turning 50. Is it game over or what? The marker for me is when you go to gigs and have the young girls flirt with you and say, "Come out for a drink, Carl," and you look at the mothers and even the mothers look too young. You know you're getting old. But then, getting older, the shit starts to drop off, I guess. Less of a drive. You want more good times, want to be around good, happy people. Don't sit there whingeing; let's go have a beer.'

BOB KATTER

Top hat

Tell us it ain't so, Bob. You threw eggs at The Beatles?

'I got international coverage when I was only nineteen,' says Bob Katter. 'But I was a humble little follower, dragged into it against my will. Later on, one of the ringleaders became president of the Bar Association of Australia. Another became a leading doctor in northern Australia, then he became a Catholic priest. When I first told that story he rang the bishop and admitted, "That lying bastard Katter is telling the truth: I was one of the organisers." We said at the time that it was an "intellectual protest against Beatlemania," but, in actual fact, my mates just kicked my door open and said, "Come on, Katter, we're going to egg The Beatles."

'I said, "You're not talking about my car, are ya?" because I was driving a Volkswagen at the time, but one of the blokes started singing "Love Me Do". I asked, y'know, "What are you going to egg The Beatles for?"

'They said, "Ya got anything better to do between now and the milk run?" That was when we used to thieve, er, other people used to thieve the milk bottles from the other university colleges. They used to call it the "milk run". So much for "intellectual protest". Well, afterwards, the lads from Liverpool dared us to meet them alone in their room at Lennons Hotel; they threw down the gauntlet. We sat down for an hour with them. You gotta understand, there were thousands of people in the streets of Melbourne and Sydney and Brisbane when they were here in 1964. In Brisbane, the police cleared Queen Street, but we were like Moses parting the waters. I'm walking through and the sheilas are racing up: "Where are you going, Bobby Katter?" And for years afterwards sheilas would race up to us at campus and ask, "Did you really meet The Beatles?"'

Maybe it is Bob's giant size-59 hat, or maybe it is his no-bullshit perspective on life (he says that a bit of carbon dioxide warming the earth is as likely as a few cockroaches on a glass ceiling blocking out the light). Whatever it is, southern-staters tend to ridicule this motor-mouthed son of the soil from Queensland's far north, and dismiss him as a hick.

'They're probably right about the hick and the boofhead; I wouldn't deny it,' he concedes. But underestimate him at your peril. Fran Kelly made that mistake on ABC Radio. 'She called me the Mad Hatter,' says Bob. 'That did get under my skin. I asked her, "Fran, were you president of your faculty at university?" She said no, and I said, "Well I was. Were you president of the university college?" She said no, and I said, "Well I was. Did you win the science prize for Australia?" She said no, and I said, "Well I did. Have you ever had two books written about you, highly laudatory, that made the reading list at university?" She said no, and I said, "Well I have!" So I told her that when she called me the Mad Hatter, that's a reference to *Alice in Wonderland*, and the Mad Hatter gave a lot of problems to a lot of people. So I told her, "I've just put you in your place and this is where the interview ends."' And Bob Katter walked out.

Fair enough too. Bob is sensitive about his big hat. He reckons there should be one named after him. 'The mayor of Mount Isa "Honest John" Molony, he's got a hat named after him—the "Honest John". Every time I see him he rubs it in. Lee Kernaghan's made it; Kenny Coleman, the great rough rider, has made it.' But not Bob: the Akubra Katter is some way off yet. In the meantime Bob makes do with the wide-brimmed Akubra Arena, $149 off the shelf but valued at $1000 the day it was auctioned off to Wade's Tree Services in Mackay in March 2012 in a fundraiser for Bob's fledgling Katter's Australian Party.

The Bob Katter head has been crowned with a titfer since childhood. 'I'd get a biff off my father if I was seen without one,' he recalls. 'But I should set a good example because skin cancer in Queensland and New South Wales is the highest in the world. And in north Queensland if the sun isn't burning the skin off your face it's teeming with rain, so either way you're going to be using it.'

He calls himself Bob Katter junior, actually: Bob's late father, Bob Katter senior, held the federal Queensland seat of Kennedy for 24 years. Bob senior's father was one of the two dozen original investors who funded Qantas.

Bob junior started his political career in state politics. He held the Queensland seat of Flinders from 1974 to 1992, then got himself elected to his dad's old federal posting and has been there since 1993. For three years—1990 to 1993—Rob Hulls, later to become chief parliamentary head-kicker and attorney-general for the Victorian Labor government, was member for Kennedy, clinching a role in the only parliamentary Katter sandwich in history.

Born in Cloncurry, 770 kilometres west of Townsville, Queensland, Bob junior is a staunch Catholic of Lebanese and Irish descent. He has snow-white hair, a ruddy complexion and a squint from the Queensland bush, although his cattle days are more than 40 years behind him. His family were Cloncurry pioneers. 'Went up by stagecoach,' says Bob, who has a rare ability to rile the hand-wringers of political correctitude.

Check out the scorecard. He has irked feminists by saying that the child support scheme was 'anti-male' and declaring that 'in 90 per cent of cases the bloke has done nothing wrong ... [and] the woman was at fault.' He has tweaked the tail of the homosexual lobby, joking (well, he says he was) in 1989 that there were almost no homosexuals in north Queensland and promising to walk backwards to Bourke if they made up more than 0.001 per cent of the fair-dinkum red-blooded Aussie population. In 1996 he steamed up the goggles of the multicultural mob, defending National Party mate Bob Burgess for describing citizenship ceremonies as 'dewogging'. Bob called howling protesters 'little slanty-eyed ideologues who persecute ordinary, everyday Australians,' but, you see, the joke was on the howlers, according to Bob. 'I got called a racist over that comment, but it is a quote from *Dr Zhivago*. The only paper in Australia that picked that up was *The Adelaide Advertiser*. I hate those people who tell you that you don't think right! The book-burners, Salem witch-burners, the McCarthyists, Oliver Cromwells, self-righteous moralist pricks.'

Friendly fellow that he is, Bob has no hesitation in mixing it with his detractors. 'If you want to pull me up on what I say, I'll take you on,' he says, 'and you'll get it on an intellectual plane you're not used to.' Bob is also a dab hand at rope-a-dope. His new political party set the 'equal love' brigade howling with a gay marriage ad in the Queensland election of 2012, and when he appeared on TV in Ten's *The Circle* during a book promotion tour that year, the panel was anxious to scratch that itch.

PANELLIST A. It's amazing how much compassion you have for the Indigenous Australians. I think the contrast between your feelings for Indigenous Australians and gay Australians is what makes us very confused.

PANELLIST B. I've taken advice on how to approach this with you—I'm curious, Bob, as to where your feelings about gay people come from.

But as the panellists sat, whiskers a-quiver, awaiting an answer, Bob just dead-batted them away: 'The honest answer is, I don't think about it at all. Never have, never likely to in the future.'

Yes, Bob—father of four girls and one son—is unfashionably heterosexual, but he can boast a half-brother, Carl, who bats for the other side. Carl is not at all pleased with Bob's views. 'Bob and his rabble of bigots do bother me, and I worry for the people that receive the hate that is incited by such ads,' says Carl about the TV commercials that showed two bare-chested blokes and some discreet pixilation. 'I don't have a good relationship with him; I hardly ever see him. I haven't seen him for many years, actually.'

Says Bob, who has a brother and sister by the same mother, 'My father married again so Carl's my half-brother. I'm not knocking him, but we didn't have much to do with him at all.'

Bob's sister, Geraldine O'Brien, ten years younger, says the man in the hat has always been easygoing. 'He's friendly,' she says, 'just walks up and talks to people and engages with them very easily, and sometimes they're happy about that and sometimes they're not. The fellow who was the senior on Bob's floor at St Leo's College, he always said the worst thing that happened to him was having the room opposite Bob across the corridor, because there was a constant stream of people coming and going. Day or night, didn't matter. It wasn't so much Party Central but they were always organising something, and I don't think the leopard has changed his spots. My recollection as a little girl, when he came home from boarding school in Charters Towers, is that he always brought someone home with him—kids from New Guinea or whatever, kids who couldn't go home themselves.

'I was very lucky with my brothers. Our mother died when I was only sixteen, and Bob was very protective, very kind. He even used to try to teach me rugby moves by setting up a field with matchsticks—as if I was ever going to play! We had a set of parallel bars in the backyard; he'd teach me kidney rolls and other tricks.'

Bob is big on chivalry. During his Queensland ministerial days a *Sunday Mail* columnist reported an incident in the Queensland bush in which Bob objected to the language one bloke was using in front of women in a pub. After asking the lad to button the lip three times, Bob growled, 'You think I'm a Queen Street powder puff, but you've made a terrible mistake because I'm a Cloncurry boy.' According to the report, Bob and his detractor went outside. Twenty minutes later Bob came back alone. 'True,' says Bob, adding in delight, 'And we were in town for a cabinet meeting! The journalist was there and he killed himself laughing.'

Undaunted by all this, Bob's son Rob Katter also stood for parliament and is the state MP for Mount Isa and a trailblazing member of his dad's new party. Katter's Australian Party won two seats and plans to compete federally, armed with such gumtree-scented policies as higher customs duties on imports, preference for Aussie products with all government spending, and an obligation that all government cars—and uniforms for police, army and prison staff—be Aussie-made. It has not pleased Queensland senator Ron Boswell, who fears the man in the hat's new mob could dilute the influence of the National Party. 'Katter wants to tag every import and say they are not produced under Australian conditions and those imported products could be a risk to your health,' he says. 'But goodness help me if that kind of label went on every piece of red meat, and it would: we'd be retaliated against very strongly in our export markets. Those sorts of things may sound good in the front bar of the local hotel, but they don't sell at all out in the real world.'

Similar sentiment bounced around the Queensland parliamentary chambers when Rob Katter asked his first question as a tyro MP in mid-2012, challenging a change in the school system. Education minister John-Paul Langbroek claimed the younger Katter had adopted the techniques of his father, getting his 'populist views' from people in pubs at night. 'It's like the old One Nation dinner parties and we're not going to have that kind of reflex responses ...'

Bob's reflex response was that it was 'screamingly funny.' However, he cannot figure out why his son would want to go into the political bullring: 'I don't think he'd ever been to a political meeting in his life. I don't know what suddenly sparked him, but I know what it was with me: I got really angry with Gough Whitlam. I just hated him, but I can't figure out why. He really rubbed me the wrong way. Then Joh Bjelke-Petersen, who was the most hopeless, stupid-looking fellow I'd ever seen or heard in my life, he started making Whitlam bleed and suddenly he wasn't so stupid. I was chasing cattle back then, and I came down from the mountains and started going to party meetings and shooting my mouth off. Next bloody thing I'm in parliament. I had been floating my own mining company with Clive Palmer, and I'd be a mile ahead of him today if I'd stayed mining instead of getting mad with bloody Whitlam. It's another reason I hate the bastard.'

He dates his political smarts back to the time he stepped into a lift at a Country Party conference and found himself in the presence of gnarled parliamentary legend 'Black Jack' McEwen. They went for a cup of tea and, in his book *An Incredible Race of People: A Passionate History of Australia*, Bob recalls McEwen outlining his doctrine on trade:

> *If our agricultural industries are to survive and prosper, they need the security of a relatively large home market to allow them to ride the roller coaster of the international trade cycle.*
>
> *To achieve this we need a population and this population must have jobs so we need a protected home market for industry that will provide them with jobs ...*
>
> *I will never see my country plunged into another war without the ability to build a main battle tank.*

The title of the book stems from Bob's days in Queensland's green chamber when he was a minister in Bjelke-Petersen's government. 'During 1988,' he says, 'we had the king of Spain, Juan Carlos, and Queen Sofia out for the Expo, and according to the invitation I was supposed to be hosting a function for them. Couldn't believe it—I hate hosting those things. But they turn out to be very well informed. The queen asked if anyone had read Robert Hughes' book *The Fatal Shore*, and I said I had—how it told of the savagery of the early convict days, the brutish jailers, the violence. She asked if the book was accurate and I told her it was.

'She asked, "So you Australians descended from that?"

'I replied, "No, we *ascended* from that. More than one in three Australians here before World War II had a convict or an Aborigine somewhere in the family tree."

'The queen said, "What an incredible race of people you are."'

Bob backed the Liberal–National Coalition in the 2010 showdown of the Independents that saw Julia Gillard's Labor scrape in. He says that was because the Coalition conceded more of the 'twenty points' that he demanded for his support. Nevertheless, Labor has run strongly in the family veins. Bob's grandfather was a founding member of the party, and his father, a union delegate on the Brisbane wharves, was a Labor official. But Bob senior left the party in 1957 when the Queensland Labor Party split from the federal party, and he was elected to Kennedy in 1966 as a Country Party member. Bob junior remembers well the trauma of the split. Aged ten, he accompanied his father to an federal Labor Party branch meeting in Cloncurry at which the branch president declared it the 'worst day of my life,' claiming that it would be 'ratting' to join a breakaway. After that, says Bob, his father was never the same again. 'It was if his soul had been grievously wounded.'

From 1983 to 1987 Bob was Queensland's minister for Aborigines. 'In those years we delivered title deeds to the blackfellas,' he says, 'but all that legislation was overturned when we lost government. We delivered what Mabo was fighting for—and it was not just Eddie Mabo; there were a lot of people involved who get left out, like Father Dave Passi and James Rice. The thing was, we provided title deeds so you could own your own house, your own farm, your own service station, and you could borrow money from the banks because you had a title deed. Well, that was abolished, and, although Mabo won the land rights in the High Court, no government would issue title deeds. So these great men like Father Passi and Eddie Mabo were betrayed; all of their work has been lost because they never ended up with a title deed. People said, "Isn't that good? You've got land rights!" But what are you going to do? Eat the bloody land? You can't buy any cattle because the banks won't lend you any money. Twenty years earlier people said, "Isn't Bobby Katter wonderful, issuing title deeds?" I would have thought you would be a numbskull not to!'

Geraldine says the Katter clan's links with Aboriginal Australians go back generations. 'Our parents took over the open-air picture theatre in Cloncurry,' she says, 'and at that stage the Aboriginals were segregated from white people. Dad pulled down the fence and said, "No way." There were a lot of Aboriginal kids around back then—we just didn't think about it. I can still remember some of their names. There's no doubt in my mind the Aborigines see Bob as a great champion of their needs and they really trust him.'

On the other hand, you might wonder about this bloke's somewhat daffy 'cockroaches on the glass ceiling' theory on global warming. Even he admits the metaphor is a poor one but says the warmists' claims are silly too. But, with an electorate that covers a major part of the Great Barrier Reef, Bob is ringing the bells about carbon dioxide's effect on the oceans. 'I'm not being stupid about it—I'm not going to pull the reins so the horse bloody bucks—but I do a massive amount of research, so if I say something you can rest assured that I will have the paperwork. I consulted Dr Katharina Fabricius from the Australian Institute for Marine Science, who is a leading world authority—well, I'm not sure about the world, but she looks very good on the beach in a wet suit. I asked her about the impact on sea water; I wanted the lot: molecular structures, valence bonding. She says, basically, if the sea becomes less alkaline, then the shellfish will have less food with which to construct their shells. And the major bottom of the food chain are bivalves, many so small you can't see them, and if they can't form their shells at the bottom of the food chain, then that is a serious problem.'

You would not find a true-bluer Aussie than Bob Katter. The music for 'Waltzing Matilda' was written at Winton, just down the road from the cemetery at home town Cloncurry where his uncles Norman and Bert are buried. Where celebrated Australian poet Dame Mary Gilmore is also burried. For two shillings a week each, Bob and his siblings attended the primary school in Cloncurry run by the Sisters of St Joseph, the order that produced Mary MacKillop, Australia's first saint. Bob visited the old school a few years back and put the kids through their paces on Australian history.

When did the Europeans discover Australia?

'1770? 1788?'

No, said Bob, earlier than that. The Portuguese, with a colony in East Timor from the mid-fifteenth century, sent back a report to the governor of Batavia in 1623 on what is now the west coast of north Queensland. So why didn't they come here?

'Aborigines?'

No, the 6 million 'Red Indians' in America didn't deter the settlers in the wild west.

'Too far?'

No, the Europeans were already in Timor and the Philippines.

'Too dry?'

Bingo! There was no water. So the colonisers, when they did come, sent only convicts. But the early European Australians drilled bore holes and created thousands of billabongs and waterways. The kangaroo population exploded from a handful to millions.

And what about equality? The notion that the average easy-going Aussie does not believe they are better than anyone else, or anyone else is better than them. Where did that come from?

'Convicts? Because they came out in ships together?'

Maybe, says Bob, but he credits the people he calls the First Australians, the Aboriginals. 'People say "Aborigines" as though they are different people,' he says. 'I don't like that. The First

Australians treated each other equally and taught the settlers the same. One of the ideas the whitefellas picked up was how we should properly conduct ourselves. So I reckon we mostly got that idea of being equal off the blackfella Australians—the First Australians.'

PETER RUSSELL-CLARKE

G'day, cobber

Prince Charles was caught by surprise the night that Peter Russell-Clark shut a Carlton restaurant door in his face. It was certainly not the sort of treatment to which an heir to the British throne is accustomed and, in less civilised times, would probably have been sufficient cause for the pioneer TV chef's little bearded noggin to be separated from the kerchief that is habitually knotted around his scrawny neck. However, all these years later, Peter has no regrets. His long-ago restaurant, which had no name and very little publicity, was booked out months ahead, but Charlie and six hangers-on just knocked on the door with the expectation that they would be whisked, noblesse-express, to a table. Peter was quick to straighten them out. 'First, I only have one dunny,' he told them, 'and you'll complain there's not a sheilas' dunny and a separate men's dunny and tell the council and I'll be closed down. And second, you Pommy bastards never pay. You come in, big-note yourselves, eat everything you can, drink everything you can, then piss off and never pay. And to fit you in I would have to kick out seven of my regulars who do pay. So fuck off!'

Sometimes, a bit of colonial shock and awe pays off. Peter and Charlie became such good buddies that the heir invited the hairy one to cook the queen's silver jubilee dinner in Sydney in 1977. Afterwards, the prince—who was in the process of wooing Diana—wrote to Peter for culinary advice. 'He said he was going to marry that sheila,' says Peter, 'and asked what he was capable of cooking so he would impress her. I invented Steak Diana Peaches and Cream. There were two half-peaches, like breasts, with cream around them and a bit of steak that looked like a doodle. He loved it, served it up then probably gave her a good rogering ...'

Actually, there is no empirical evidence to support that last assumption, but Peter is confident his designer dish hit the mark. It is apparent that shock and awe was a Russell-Clarke trademark well before George W. Bush adopted it for international diplomacy. The bearded chef once tried to persuade the ABC to try one of his TV ideas: a variation of the old girl-in-a-cake routine, but he figured a giant pie was more Australian and had a team of chefs carry the monstrous pastry into Aunty's management with him inside, naked. No success there: he fell out before arrival and thus learnt a valuable marketing lesson. 'Gimmicks don't pay; they hide your message.'

Peter had a suitably amazing start in life, born in Ballarat as the offspring of a priest and a showgirl. 'My father was a reader with the Church of England,' he says. 'He did his theology at Ballarat, but they defrocked him. He married four times, and we in the family say thank Christ he married women, because he seemed to want to root anything. To get his own back on the Anglicans he had me brought up as a Catholic and put me in the Sacred Heart boarding school in Bowral, but he never paid the fees. The nuns couldn't afford to keep me so put me in the care of local Catholic farmers, who became surrogate parents. They couldn't afford it either, so would move on every three months. I stayed with a Chinese family for a while:

I had fourteen brothers and sisters and I was the only round-eye, but I learnt to speak Chinese.'

His mother travelled around Australia in a show called the *Three Smart Girls*. 'She was 1.5 metres and my old man was 1.9 metres. I fitted in halfway between. Mum's show was based mainly on fashion and how women could become more independent. At that time it wasn't done for women to drive motor cars, and if they did they had to wear gloves.' Peter's mother later became a dress-maker and designed for the houses of Rome and Paris. 'She was a very clever, arty woman, but she liked a drink and would go on stage pissed as a parrot and shock all the local mayors and their wives.

'Eventually, my father discovered I wasn't wearing shoes, wasn't going to school and that mum was sleeping with a local timber-cutter, so he put me into an experimental school at Melbourne University. I didn't like it. I was virtually illiterate, got beat up half-a-dozen times, so I left home.' He joined George Patterson's ad agency, where he ran messages. 'You got threepence in those days to deliver things,' he says. 'I was a fit young fella so I ran everywhere. I used to pick up tram tickets in the gutter, go back and present the tickets at work and get sixpence.'

At one stage his defrocked father became housing editor for *The Argus* newspaper and wrote articles under a variety of pseudonyms. 'That taught me a thing or two,' says Peter, 'because when I did a bit of writing for the *Melbourne Observer* under Max Newton, I wrote under four different names—Peter Clarke, Russell Granville or whatever—and I also did that as an artist. I started doing cartoons.

'I was freelance from the age of about sixteen but got no work for the first six months. Then I met a Salvation Army bloke named Brigadier Williams. He asked me what I did, and I told him I was a cartoonist but had been out of work for six months. He asked me if I could do some cartoons for *The War Cry*, the Salvos' newspaper, he would give me 10 quid every Wednesday.

'Down the track a bit he asked how things were going. I said, "Great, I've got a few clients and doing well."

'He said, "Well, we've got another kid who needs your job. So thanks and see you later." And that was it. I was shocked, but how I loved and respected that man. I have respected the Salvos all my life. Good on 'em.'

Freelance work, however, was not easy for a single artist. Wiser heads told him that without a grey beard and a heap of experience he needed to join a studio to kick on. 'So I formed one of my own, where the artists were all me: 'Fingers Magee' was one name I used. I gave them all different drawing styles. So the advertising agents would ring up and say, "I want Fingers Magee to do this one," and I would go around and they'd ask, "Where's Fingers?" And I'd go, "Bloody busy, mate."'

Veteran Melbourne columnist Keith Dunstan remembers Peter joining the Melbourne *Herald* as a political cartoonist. 'He turned up at the editorial conference in his usual garb—beautifully cut shirt, open down to the hair on his chest, hand-crafted silver bangles and a nicely sculpted silver ring on a finger. The editor-in-chief looked at him coldly, saying, "Mr Clarke, it is customary to wear a tie to the editorial conference." Next day Peter was back in formal wear, black tie. The editor-in-chief said, "I'm sorry, is there a bereavement in your family?"

'Peter replied, "Yes, sir, I'm in mourning for the loss of my liberty." Peter has always had a curious aversion to wearing neckties. In April 1982 he was thrown out of seven restaurants in San Francisco, one after another, because he refused to wear a tie or a suit. Most of them offered to lend him a tie, but he told them he wouldn't wear filthy ties that had been around other people's necks—they'd have germs.'

It was not long afterwards that *The Herald* ran a campaign against drunken drivers. After a big booze-up in Carlton Peter decided he would do the right thing and hand his keys in at the nearest police station. But, rather than congratulate him, the police contemplated charging him with being drunk in charge of a car.

'I'm not driving a car,' Peter protested.

'Well, how did you get here?' asked the coppers.

'I pushed the bloody thing,' was the reply.

It took some swift talking by the editor-in-chief to extract him from the City Watch House.

In mid-2012, while Peter and his wife, Jan, were on an overseas trip, their home at Tooborac, in country Victoria, burnt to the ground and every possession was destroyed. Caused by an electrical fault, said the investigators. The couple lost clothing, furniture, valuable paintings, a demountable Chinese temple, family memorabilia including his grandparents' wedding certificate: the lot.

A prolific author of books over the years, Peter also saw four manuscripts destroyed in one hit. 'They were all written, illustrated, ready to go to the publisher,' he says. 'A novel called *The Chef*, about a white chef and an Aboriginal chef who maraud around the Snowy Mountains, doing all sorts of terrible things. There was a kids book about diet called *Mr Poo*, fifteen pages of illustrations for a book on Waltzing Matilda, and an encyclopaedia of seafood. I had already brought out the encylopaedia of food.' Yes, he had back-up copies, but they went up in the fire too. The house had been built using 12-metre trusses he obtained from a demolisher mate. 'I couldn't afford walls,' he says, 'so there were two rooms 12 metres square with a 12-by-12 decking outside. I told the insurance company, "We don't need a big house; we'll just have a little house and you give us the money we don't spend," but they said no, it doesn't work like that.'

Despite this massive blow, the little bearded bloke scarcely missed a beat. 'He was designing their new house on the flight home,' marvels business buddy Jack Ayerbe. 'Sketching the plans on a piece of paper. Most people would collapse in a screaming heap. We wondered how he was going to cope. He had Egyptian stuff there going back to 3000 BC. Well, he came bouncing back, better than he was before. The bugger just repainted all the artwork he had lost. Jan was still bright and happy too. Never known anyone to regroup without any hassles like that.'

In fact, the disaster only served to replenish Peter's store of well-honed yarns. 'Fred Schepisi,' says Peter, 'I was with him in the Film House group. Schepisi wanted to buy my Dutch wood-fired oven—beautiful bloody thing, enamel-baked—and I didn't really want to sell; anyhow, he didn't offer me enough money. Bugger me if that didn't get burnt in the fire, so I'm going to send Fred a letter saying, "You can have it now; pay me the money".

'I had one of the original wooden moulds that they used in Paris to make those fish-tailed busts of women propping up the plinths over doorways on government buildings, and a bloke wanted to buy it from me. He only offered $5000 and it was worth $55 000, and when he heard about the fire he rang me up and said, "You bastard, I was going to pay you 40 000; I was just waiting to haggle."

'Let me tell you this. I was in Beijing when I bought that Chinese temple. It had been painted black, but on the way back to Australia it got chipped and I noticed gold underneath. So I scratched all the black off and it was all gold leaf. It had been painted to disguise it when the Red Guards were going through China, smashing up anything that was bourgeois. Bugger me, that's gone.

'And do you know John Hamilton, the journalist? He tried to buy the John Howley painting that was the backdrop behind all those TV episodes of Come and Get It six nights a week for nine years. The most viewed painting in Australia. Bugger me, that's gone too.'

Because of the series he is still a household name, and the couple were bombarded with donated goods after the fire. TV vet Harry Cooper's ex-wife donated one of Cooper's coats—'Probably to piss Harry off,' speculates Peter—and veteran newspaper cartoonist Jeff Hook sent a replacement for a burnt Hook original: it showed Peter in chef's outfit lifting the silver cover on a dish. Underneath was the late Victorian premier Henry Bolte as a rat, belching and eating a piece of cheese. And after a TV report on the fire, a young girl in Queensland sent $5.

While in his seventies, Peter was still managing to stir the possum. Four years before the blaze, an embarrassing blooper tape compiled from the long-finished *Come and Get It* show mysteriously surfaced on the internet, drawing tens of thousands of viewers. Still floating in cyberspace, it shows Peter in unscreened out-takes, swearing like a bullocky on a frosty morning, so the little bloke was chuffed when radio station Triple-J phoned to offer him a regular segment, Peter explained. 'As you get older you get sillier, so I keep away from everything these days except the pub and the missus.' Anyhow, he claimed the show only ran so long—9 years and more than 900 episodes—because 'none of the bosses at the ABC listened to their own radio stations or watched their own TV channels so nobody really knew I was there; and I got away with it. Then one day some silly bugger there turned it on and said, "Hey, what's going on here?" and that was the end of me.'

Triple-J. What have you been doing in the downtime since, Peter?
Peter. Well, the program used to be called *Come and Get It*; now
   it's called *Piss Off You're Buggered*.

Never shies away from a four-letter word, does Peter. But here's the real answer to that question: as always, Peter had been doing plenty in the downtime. This Amazing Bastard is not just a cartoonist who did a TV show; he has been truck-operator, house-builder, veterinary supplement supplier, United Nations food ambassador and much more. To his dismay, what he has not been is canny financial planner.

'I'm a dill,' he confesses, saying that a week before that house fire he and Jack Ayerbe were cleaned out by an unscrupulous associate. 'For six years we had produced a very good product to alleviate arthritis in animals: Dr Jack's Special Formula. We had not taken any money out; we were saving it for our old age. But the bank account was emptied.'

It was not the first time Peter has had his fingers fried. 'Jan and I used to have a trucking business—three trucks carrying sand from the South Australian border to Spotswood for beer bottles. But someone sold our trucks and pocketed the dough. We took him to court and the judge said, "Bad man, give Russell-Clarke his money," but he didn't do it, so we went back to court and the judge said, "Very bad man, give Russell-Clarke his money," but the bloke said he didn't have any money: his wife had it all. So we never got paid.' The upshot of this, and of an earlier financial disaster involving the fruit business that cost him more than $5 million, is that Peter, who has been very wealthy in the past, has been rendered quite poor as he enters the golden years. 'I prefer poor,' he says. 'You see, I used to confuse wealth with intellectualism. But I was dopey when I was rich, and I'm dopey now I'm poor. There's no difference.'

Peter eventually reunited with his father, Peter Russell-Clarke senior, in Sydney, where son found father living in luxury with a nubile blonde. Told that Peter senior was sleeping and could not be disturbed, Peter junior picked up a brick and threw it through the window. Peter senior appeared, naked, called him a bastard but invited him inside, where, still naked, he opened a bottle of claret, lit a cigar and put a record on the record player.

'He kept squirting the record with a soda siphon,' says Peter junior. 'Said it was to get the dust off. It wasn't what I expected—it was incredible—but we became the greatest of mates.'

Peter senior died in 1965, after a fight in north Queensland. He had been a late-life yachtie, and his fellow salts held a wake. 'About 3 a.m. they decided they couldn't leave him lying in the morgue, so they drove there, broke in, squeezed the body through a small window, popped him onto a yacht and buried him at sea. And they did it properly. Because he was English, they draped him in a Union Jack.'

So many years, so many stories. At one stage Peter was founder of a venture called Doctors TV Network, which supplied a TV set to every medical waiting room in Australia, and then sent a three-hour tape to play on it. 'We made our money from selling ads,' says Peter, 'but Paul Green and his partner then got rid of me—threw me out of the business—and we've been mates ever since.'

According to one old pal, Peter 'has the ability to upset people. He can be abusive and crack the shits, but you can ignore it because the next day he's over it. People shouldn't take it personally.' Paul Green is a director of a film company called Horizon and produced 350 of the *Come and Get It* episodes. 'Back then,' says Paul, 'Peter was a partner in a backyard restaurant in Middle Park where they used to do chocolates and things like that. He was wonderful on TV. Cooking shows went crazy after that.'

Business buddy Jack Ayerbe is a Melbourne veterinarian and a bit of an Amazing Bastard himself, having gone to Ireland in his younger days to spend a year or two shoving his arm up cows' bums and attempting to keep up with the Guinness consumption of the Celtic cockies. He played a small and sometimes messy role in the national program to eradicate tuberculosis and brucellosis in Irish cattle, and then wrote a book about it all called *To Ballina & Back: An Aussie Vet in Ireland*, in which he diarised daily life with startling frankness. Sample: 'The testing process then began with most animals managing to kick me, tread on my feet and defecate in my pocket'.

Jack, who has since had the sartorial problem dry-cleaned, says that few people know his mate Peter was once a state-level hockey player. 'He played in a golf pro-am at Noosa years ago and brought his hockey stick along. They objected, but he said there was no rule against it and proceeded to out-drive the pros. They were so pissed off they voted that night to boycott him. He had to play next day— again with his hockey stick—with a politician.

'And never argue about history with him. Knows all sorts of stuff. He told me once that, the night before the Burke and Wills expedition left Melbourne, either Burke or Wills won a bet by going around the picture rail in the Melbourne Club dining room using just their hands—feet off the floor. In fact, Peter wrote a book about the Melbourne Club at one stage.'

Jack, whose Spanish-born father was maitre d' at the Hotel Australia, is a fair hand at cooking paella and says he once challenged his old chum to a paella competition over two weeks, with a large table of friends giving the verdict. 'It was at my place at Geelong,' says Jack. 'I cooked mine first, and the following week he did his. Peter loves the grog as much as I do, but he didn't touch a drop until he had finished cooking. In the end the guests voted for mine, but Peter just said they were wrong: said they didn't understand paellas. But his cooking is superb. I often ring him up—because I love having black-tie dinner parties—and ask his advice and he is always spot-on.'

Like any self-respecting Amazing Bastard, Peter has a robust disregard for mere rules and regulations, a stance that cost him dearly as a schoolboy swimmer. As a youngster he was a fair type of breaststroker and represented his country school in the state championships. 'He was miles ahead and touched first,' says Jack, also an accomplished swimmer, 'but when the judges came up to advise the placings he was ignored. He said, "What about me?"'

'They told him, no, he had been disqualified because he touched with one hand. "You are supposed to touch with both hands; they're the rules."'

'Peter said, "No one fucking told me!"'

'He's never forgiven them.'

Jo Stewart

TIM JARVIS

Life in a deep freeze

In Antarctica, the gap between survival and turning into a permanent two-legged ice block can be wafer-thin—the sort of mini-measurement that larrikin Aussie Rules footycaster Rex Hunt used to call a 'poofteenth'. That razor's edge of survival even applies to the speed at which you can pull a sledge full of tucker. 'If you travel too slowly,' says South Australian explorer Tim Jarvis, 'you don't generate enough body heat to keep your extremities alive. If you go too fast, you sweat, and that sweat freezes and you start losing fingers and toes. So you travel at a speed you feel comfortable with.'

However, Tim's idea of 'comfortable' and yours are probably very different. This Amazing Bastard was aged 34 when he and fellow adventurer Peter Treseder completed a record 47-day and 1580-kilometre unsupported trek to the South Pole, in 1999. About 300 kilometres short of the destination, he lost sight of his travelling buddy. 'Visibility was zero and wind speed was picking up,' says Tim. 'You often get a double whammy with these things, because the faster the wind blows, the more unsurvivable the conditions, but also the worse the visibility, because it whips things up.'

Amid this maelstrom Tim stopped to fix the broken harness on his sled. That meant removing three of his four layers of gloves: an outer mitt, a vapour-barrier glove that stops sweat from the hand going into the outer mitt, and a thick wind-stopper glove. Only a small woollen glove remained to protect the skin. 'You have to pull off the outer gloves,' says Tim; 'you have no dexterity otherwise.' But on this occasion he took too long on the repair. 'I lost all sensation up to the elbows—similar to how it feels when you go to sleep leaning on an arm—and the feeling has never returned in the tip of the right thumb.'

Similarly, the nerves died in the large toe on his right foot in a later expedition, when one of the hobnails on the sole of his left boot scuffed the side of the right boot, cutting a 5-centimetre gash. By the time he was able to erect a tent and suture the cut shut, the pinkie maximus was doomed.

Tim carries an array of polar war-wounds. He has three molars missing from his mouth—metal fillings froze, shrank and dropped out, destroying the teeth—but such things are mere trifles in the icy south. This is a bastard of a place, even for Amazing Bastards like Australian explorer Douglas Mawson, whose two companions, Xavier Mertz and Belgrave Ninnis, perished on an expedition in 1912–13. Britain's Robert Scott and his four-man team also lost their lives in 1912, in one of world exploration's great tragedies. Antarctica, 14 million square kilometres and the fifth-largest continent on earth, is unforgiving; although, paradoxically, it is the sheer brutality of the place that safeguards humans against the germs that contaminate the outside world. 'There are no germs there,' says Tim, 'it's too cold. The rule of thumb is that if you are not ill in the first week you assume you are safe. You have not caught anything off one another, and most of the food is freeze-dried so the chances of getting sick through eating that are virtually nil.'

But let's wind back a bit. Even as a kid, Tim Jarvis was pushing his physical limits, climbing trees, breaking the odd arm, cutting the occasional knee, a boy with dog exploring a kid's world but simultaneously cutting his teeth for an outdoor manhood. Now a long-time resident of Adelaide, Tim was born in Britain but spent most of his youth in Malaysia and Singapore. His father, a businessman who moved the family to Kuala Lumpur, sent Tim to the Singapore campus of the progressive United World College, which boasted scores of different nationalities among its students.

At a school camp in Malaysia, small groups of kids were sent into the jungle on what today would be called a 'geography field trip'. There was a twist. Members of the group had to play roles, and one was cast as a spy trying to sabotage their navigation. As Tim told ABC interviewer Richard Fidler in 2011, the spy did his job a bit too well. 'We got lost, completely lost, it got dark, and it became serious very quickly. We went around in circles and soon the jungle became increasingly thick. We started to get very concerned, but as a ten-year-old I thought to myself, *Well, I know what direction we should be heading in, I know what direction the sun should be setting in, let's just try it and see if it works.* The rest is history. We moved to the coast, then south—all in the middle of the night, mind you—and eventually found the camp. It was one of those defining moments where, if you trust your instincts, you can get yourself through.'

At age nineteen Tim moved back to Britain with his parents. He was growing into a giant of a man—eventually to be 196 centimetres tall and 104 kilograms—and was more than handy on the rugby field. But it was a leg injury from five-a-side soccer that was the unlikely trigger for a life of exploration. As part of his rehabilitation he began using a rowing machine at a local gym and, to his amazement, within weeks he was outgunning the fair-dinkum rowers. He was urged to enter the national indoor titles, where, he will tell you modestly, he did 'quite well.' In fact, records show he won the British title of 1996 against competition that included local Olympians. He was 29 and had trained for six weeks but beat men who had been rowing since childhood.

Tim's delight at the victory, however, was mixed with regret. 'It was fantastic to discover something like this about yourself,' he says, 'but I felt intense disappointment that I had not pushed myself to discover it before. That really hit home and has been part of my philosophy ever since. You can't rely on an aunt or uncle or father to suggest you might be good at something. You have to cast the net yourself and see what comes back. People are not necessarily going to spot it and nurture it for you.'

But the seed had been sown. What other capabilities could he discover within himself? 'If you really want a challenge,' a friend suggested, 'try polar!' The suggestion lit a fuse.

In 1996 Tim set off with an old school pal to cross 500 kilometres of crevassed ice sheet on Spitsbergen, an island between the Arctic Ocean and Greenland Sea. No dogs, no machinery: this was man-haul only, with sleds weighing 100 kilograms apiece and packed with provisions, fuel and equipment, plus a .303 rifle, explosives and trip wires to deter any polar bears. The journey took a month, and by the time they arrived in Longyearbyen, on the west coast—the world's northern-most town and a former mining settlement originally called Longyear City—Tim was hooked.

Three years later he and Peter Treseder headed for the other end of the planet and completed their record-breaking journey, for which Tim wore the famous balaclava used by Douglas Mawson, an item lent to him by Mawson's grandson.

At this stage Tim was still single and had been working as an environmental scientist, but, even away from his polar sled, adventure seemed to seek him out. In 1994 he was returning to the United States after a year working with remote Indian communities in Guatemala, helping them build gravity-fed water systems. In his airline seat somewhere over the Atlantic he had a stretch, rubbed his hand over his chest and was startled to feel a serpentine shape under his skin. Back in Guatemala he had been bitten by an unseen beastie while sleeping on the ground deep in the jungle, which had caused a wound to his abdomen, but now something had grown inside him and was eating his flesh. The unwelcome stranger was the thickness of a ballpoint pen and about 15 centimetres long, stretching from navel to chest. 'I still had five hours to fly,' says Tim, adding, rather unnecessarily, 'that was a really bad flight.'

When he arrived at Heathrow, the customs official asked him if he had anything to declare. Er, actually, yes!

'We can't help you there, mate,' said the startled official, and he was shooed away to the tropical diseases hospital, where biopsies were taken. But testing takes three weeks: Tim had to return home with the parasite still on board and a hole developing in his chest. He went to bed with that thing every night, and every night he noticed the hole was getting larger. 'It got to about 5 centimetres across and a centimetre deep,' says Tim. 'They never did identify the parasite, but it was so aggressive they treated me with a biological kill-all drug called amphotericin.' It killed the parasite but knocked Tim around badly too, damaging his liver function. 'It was a close-run thing,' he says.

So explorer Jarvis had broken the ice both north and south, been lost in the Malaysian jungle and become a weird sort of take-away snack for a tropical bug. Now he set about organising three more expeditions, starting with a 1100-kilometre trek across Australia's Great Victoria Desert, in June 2001. He wrote later, 'The team experienced visitations by dingoes, as well as disturbing several snakes during the hotter weather in the second half of the trip, and temperatures ranging from the mid-thirties during the day to as low as minus 5 degrees at night'. It took 29 days, one of the longest unsupported journeys undertaken in Australia.

Just a year later Tim was at it again, trekking 400 kilometres across the frozen Arctic Ocean to reach the North Pole. Two years after that, he and Australian adventurer Ben Kozel paddled 200 kilometres down the Warburton River, in South Australia, which is usually dry, then man-hauled their supplies 100 kilometres across the salt crust of Lake Eyre to a road and a waiting vehicle.

Another three years passed as Tim prepared for his next challenge—and the greatest to date—replicating part of Douglas

Mawson's 1912–13 Antarctic expedition. This was the mission on which two men had died, leaving the survivor, Mawson, so emaciated that upon his return to base he was unrecognisable. After he stumbled into his hut at Commonwealth Bay, Mawson was asked, 'Which one are you?' Tim knew well the hardships he faced on this one, having read Mawson's own words: 'My whole body is apparently rotting from want of proper nourishment—frostbitten fingertips festering, mucous membrane of nose gone, saliva glands of mouth refusing duty, skin coming off whole body'. On this Jarvis expedition a film crew was to capture parts of the journey for a TV documentary that also became a book: *Mawson: Life and Death in Antarctica.*

This was the original story: late in 1912 Mawson, British army officer Belgrave Ninnis and Xavier Mertz, a Swiss doctor, set off as one of several sledging parties from main base, Cape Denison, to explore uncharted territory. It was the sort of work that later established Australia's territorial claim over 40 per cent of Antarctica. However, on day 34 of the expedition, Ninnis, with his sled and dog team, fell through a snow bridge that Mawson, on a sled, and Mertz, on skis, had already crossed. Ninnis and the dogs plunged down a crevasse towards an ice ledge which, measured by Mawson with a plumbline, was 46 metres below. 'No sign of Ninnis,' noted Mawson in his diary; 'must have struck it & been killed instantly then gone on down. Our ropes not long enough to go down'. Most of the food had been on the lost sled, along with such essentials as tent, pick, spade and sail. They had their sleeping bags, a spare tent without poles, a cooker, kerosene and food for about ten days. There was no feed for the remaining dogs.

From this point in the story, Tim, 'playing' Mawson, with Russian-born Evgeny 'John' Stoukalo filling the role of Mertz, set out to retrace the earlier explorers' journey back to base, using the equipment of the day and allocating themselves the same amount of food, although without dogs (no longer allowed in Antarctica) the meat Mawson acquired by killing his sled dogs was substituted with kangaroo jerky. 'Hoosh' was the name early explorers gave to the broth they made from every ingredient available. In Tim's case this was beef jerky, lard, broken whey biscuits and the ground-up roo. Tim wrote later, 'The resultant mix was acrid, oily, bitter and incredibly unpleasant-tasting—even worse than its unpromising individual ingredients, if that were possible. It made me retch. John was apparently something of a lard connoisseur, shaking his head disapprovingly and claiming that it was of poor quality. We washed it all down with a mug of weak tea fortified by a small amount of sugar'.

For Mawson and Mertz, day 14 of their return journey was a turning point, the day they had to shoot their last dog, Ginger, for food, dining that night on brains and thyroid, using the dog's skull as a bowl. Mertz started to deteriorate, and so too at this point did Tim's companion, who was beset by fatigue. Stoukalo was wearing the same type of clothes as Mertz, had eaten the same amount of food and had pulled a sled of the same weight. But he had not been consuming the dog livers Mertz had eaten and was spared the hallucinations and fever attributed to an overdose of vitamin A that such organs are reputed to generate. Whatever the cause, Mertz died on day 25, about 160 kilometres from their destination, and thus Stoukalo was trucked out at this point, leaving Tim to hoof it home alone.

What happened next with Mawson has been the subject of dark rumours for a century. Had he, with little remaining food and with 160 kilometres still to travel, solo, to reach safety, eaten parts of his dead companion? The cannibal question was one Tim wanted to tackle on his expedition: could he, with the same available food, make it home without the 'extra' that might have sustained Mawson? There were 21 days' trekking ahead of Mawson and only 450 grams of food available per day. Surviving would have been difficult, even at peak fitness.

'I think I got inside Mawson's head,' says Tim, 'and I think he definitely had it within him to eat human flesh. Mawson was very scientific in his thinking and would have thought it would be a terrible waste not to make it back and tell people what had happened, to bring back all the data they had gathered over the previous few months, and it would have been somehow disrespectful to their memory if he had not made it and told everyone what had come to pass. I think he would have gone to the extreme of eating Mertz to make it. But by doing what I did I think I proved it can be done without that; and he and I were physically similar—Mawson was 1.93 metres, I am 1.96 metres—but he was six years younger than me.' In fact, it was the emaciated state of Mawson when he arrived back at base that Tim sees as the clinching evidence: 'His far greater weight loss than me means that I simply don't think he could have eaten Mertz's flesh.'

The film crew, roaring in occasionally on tracked vehicles to record the journey, proved far from a welcome link to the outside world. 'They wanted all the drama they could get, so they were actually antagonistic—not conciliatory, not "It's great to see you, mate"—it was all about dwelling on the dangers. Trying to cause issues between you and the other guy. When I was on my own it was probably worse, because I had no one to talk to about that.'

Tim began his expedition at 104 kilograms and finished at 79 kilograms. A series of before-and-after tests showed that all his vital measurements—cardiovascular function, bone density, hearing function, body-fat levels—had gone through the floor.

Long-term damage?

'Definitely,' says Tim. 'They said, "Don't do that again!"'

But he did. In February 2013 he and fellow explorer Barry Gray reached an old whaling station at Stromness in the Antarctic, completing a recreation of Ernest Shackleton's great survival saga of 1916. Tim and Barry, with four companions, had spent twelve days covering 800 nautical miles in a lifeboat from Elephant Island to South Georgia. They wore the same kind of clothing as Shackleton's team. Tim said he hoped his latest sub-zero adventure, risking crevasse falls and howling blizzards, had inspired a few people to find their inner Shackleton.

Why would a bloke want to do that to himself?

'I do it to plumb the depths of my own personality and to see what's there,' he replies. 'You have a completely unique relationship with the planet. You are just a human walking across a vast unpopulated continent on the bottom of the planet that spins on its axis as it moves through space and you get that appreciation of the enormity of it all. Your insignificance forces you to re-evaluate who you are and what your place in the scheme of things is.'

Tim has both British and Australian citizenship, having moved to Australia in 1997 to set up home in Adelaide for work as a soil scientist on the Murray-Darling Basin. That is where he plots all his expeditions and where he acts as Australasian chief of innovation and environment for Arup, a global engineering firm whose first Australian project was the Sydney Opera House. 'The company is owned by the staff, which allows us to do all sorts of things you would otherwise not be able to do. That's why I joined. I spend a lot of time advocating about the environment, ways to change things for the better.'

Concern for the environment has played a role in all Tim's polar exploits. In his latest book, *Mawson, Life and Death in Antarctica*, he declares that the 'debate is over' on human-caused global warming and that Antarctic ice melt is the most significant result.

> *The Larsen B Ice Shelf (3250 square kilometres in area and 200 metres thick) broke up in less than a month in 2002. It's a good example of the glacier acceleration problem. Ice shelves like the Larsen B form the floating edge of ice sheets that extend into the sea. When they break apart they do not directly cause sea levels to rise but they do dramatically increase the speed of ice loss from glaciers behind them.*

Such ominous signs are even more concerning to him since he became a father of two sons. Back in 2007, out there on that wild Antarctic plateau during the Mawson adventure, Tim's thoughts had turned homewards and he decided he would propose to girlfriend Elizabeth, a teacher, upon return. The marriage clinched a friendship that went back to their childhood in Kuala Lumpur, where Liz's brother was in Tim's class—Tim was seven, Liz was four. Now they have toddler sons, Will and Jack, too young yet to realise their old man is a walking, talking *Boy's Own Annual*. But it can't be long before they do.

ALAN HOPGOOD

Seconds in time

Achilles Jones was one of the greatest footballers Aussie Rules has ever seen. He was discovered out in the Victorian bush by a talent scout named Wally, who had been alerted by rumours of a beefy young farmhand who could kick a bag of wheat 10 metres in bare feet. Turned out to be Achilles, and, sure enough, when he got hold of a Sherrin he could boot the tripe out of it like some sort of mixed clone of Travis Cloke and Buddy Franklin. This bloke Achilles was a sure-fire premiership flag on two legs, and the devious coach-manager of the Crows, J.J. Forbes, was intent on signing him. Forbes had to do a heap of haggling—even bribed Achilles' girl-friend, Lil, with a fur coat—but in the end he was recruited for the team and the Crows made the grand final the same year.

But that's not the Adelaide Crows. We're talking here about the team in the first fair-dinkum stage play about the great Australian game, *And the Big Men Fly*, written way back in 1963. Tasmanian-born Alan Hopgood delivered Achilles Jones and the Crows to the Melbourne stage that year, and it was a smash hit. 'It was booked solid for the whole twelve weeks,' recalls Alan, 'but no one paid on the opening night. They were all comps. No one thought a play about football would work, but the crits next day were tremendous and we had sold 2000 tickets by lunchtime. By the end of that week the season at the Russell Street Theatre was booked out. We could have run forever, but another show was already locked in to follow.' Ten years later *Big Men* was made into a mini-series for the ABC and then was revived for the stage in 1988, probably the last show staged at the now-vanished Russell Street Theatre.

However, there's a fair argument that none of this would have happened without actor and showman Frank Thring. Fact is, in 1963 the flamboyant Frank was topping the bill in *The Man Who Came to Dinner* at the same venue for the Union Theatre Repertory Company, a guaranteed long run in the view of producer John Sumner, who used the opportunity to take off overseas. But not even movie star Frank, son of Melbourne impresario F.W. Thring (supposedly the inventor of the movie clapperboard), was able to draw enough bums on seats for this one, and the box office dried up.

'Sumner came tearing back,' says Hopgood, 'but there was nothing around to replace it. Back then they didn't have the twelve-month seasons they do today. John asked me to have a cup of coffee with him.

'"You write plays, don't you, boy?" he asked.

'I said I had written a few.

'He asked if I had one they could use, and I said yes, but told him he wouldn't understand it as an Englishman, because it was about Australian Rules football. I told him it was about a bloke who could kick wheat bags with his bare feet—so what wouldn't he do with a footy?'

Sumner was desperate. 'When can I see it, boy?' he asked.

'In a week,' said Hopgood, who had a good reason for the delay: he hadn't written the play yet. 'I just had the idea,' he says, 'so every night after my tango on stage with Frank—because I was in the play with him—I would rush home and write into the wee small hours. I gave John Sumner the script and rang him nervously a day or two later. He said, "It's being typed up now, boy. We go to rehearsal next week!" I was in it, playing J.J. Forbes, but I didn't want to be. I wanted to watch from the audience.'

Funny how such serendipities can set your life course. Alan calls them 'seconds in time', and in fact his career in theatre began with one. He was the youngest of four children raised in Hobart, and one evening he tagged along as a pint-sized chaperone to sisters Margaret and Denice when they played piano at an ABC revue at the Hobart playhouse. 'I was sitting in the dark when a comedian there was looking for a fall guy in his act, spotted me and beckoned me up. All I had to do was wear a Yankee cap and eat a cupcake or something, but, after that, whenever a touring company would come to Hobart and needed a kid, and they couldn't bring one with them, they'd get me because they knew I wouldn't pee in a corner or something disastrous. Between the ages of six and eleven I was in five or six plays, then when I was fifteen I had the title role, of Ronnie, in *The Winslow Boy*, so I had acting credits and a bit of experience.'

Alan's father, Herbert, a woodwork teacher, died aged 65, leaving wife Ella with limited income to support their four children—Alan, the two sisters and brother Bruce. 'God knows how she did it,' says Alan, who was aged five at the time his father died. 'I do remember she took in boarders; we had a big house. I think we were quite economically poor, but as a family we were rich. I never for one moment thought we were lacking anything: it was a very happy childhood. The house was always full of music with my sisters playing the piano. Hobart was a wonderful place to grow up in as a kid. We just walked everywhere, no need for a car. For something to do on a Saturday we would just walk up Mount Wellington. We had the Yankee invasion during the war, of course. All the troop ships had to come around Hobart because Bass Strait was mined. So through the local church we would have American soldiers at home for tea on Sundays.'

When Alan was fifteen, Ella decided to move to Melbourne, where his brother and sisters had already gone to find employment. However, Ella died two years later, at age 57, leaving four orphans, and Alan the youngest at just seventeen. He had won a scholarship to Wesley College (where Bruce later taught for 21 years) and still claims to have introduced the school to hockey. 'A student named Jack Hoadley, from the chocolate family, and I were the only boys who played,' he says. 'I'd been in the Tasmanian schoolboy hockey team.

'I was in the Wesley school play, of course, and the school's famous English teacher, A.A. 'Tosh' Phillips, made me editor of the school magazine, *The Chronicle*.' Alan won another scholarship, this time to Queen's College, and, to supplement the rest, enrolled with the education department and obtained a secondary student-ship. 'I was at Queen's for five years and acted my pants off,' says Alan. 'All the college productions plus the Melbourne Uni dramatic society. Had a great time.'

The problem with the studentship was that it bound a bloke to teaching later, at a school of the education department's choosing, and when it was time to settle the debt, honours-student Hopgood was assigned to teach in faraway Stawell. However, he was saved from his bush posting by another serendipity, this time with bite—a car accident. 'It was 1956,' he says, 'and the Olympics were on. I had been driving Japanese officials around as a volunteer but I was alone in the car when it rolled over. My hand went out the door and was crushed, and I finished up in St Vincent's Hospital needing plastic surgery. I couldn't go to Stawell. Went to Preston Tech instead.'

He juggled his teaching with acting at the Union Theatre Repertory Company and then wrote his first play, *Marcus*, which the leading critic of the day, Harry Standish of the *Herald*, reviewed with backhanded praise. 'Harry said that one day, when I wrote about real people, I'd make a playwright,' Alan remembers.

By this time he was married to Gladys Rayner, a dancer and choreographer with the Channel Nine ballet in Melbourne, but he decided life was getting 'too comfortable' and took off to Sydney to play in the Phillip Street Revue with Mary Hardy and Gordon Chater. It proved a bad life choice. The show was a turkey, but, because the producers had spent so much on the previous show (with Bobby Limb and Dawn Lake) they couldn't afford to reload. 'They kept us going for six months,' says Alan. 'Couldn't get out of it. My stocks were really low. The marriage broke up—she didn't want to come to Sydney and I couldn't escape.'

When Alan did return to Melbourne as a devastated divorcee he went to an audition for narrator in a show called *The Fantasticks*, but his confidence was so dented that he decided to go home. 'I was halfway into Russell Street,' he recalls, 'when a voice said, "Oh, Hoppy, you're on next!"' Not only did he land the role, but a lady in the audience one night also took such a fancy to him she went to see the show eight times. That was Gay, now his second wife. The theatre giveth, and the theatre taketh away.

By the early 1990s Alan was a familiar name on the Australian theatrical scene. He had turned out a welter of new plays, including *And Here Comes Bucknuckle*, *The Golden Legion of Cleaning Women* and the oddly named *Private Yuk Objects*, the word 'objects' being a verb, not a noun. The *Yuk* play was the first in Australia to tackle the Vietnam War, and Alan is proud of it, despite the fact he now thinks the title stinks. During the 1990s he was also in much demand as an actor, and a familiar face to TV viewers, with roles in *Bellbird*, *Neighbours* and *Prisoner*, and to patrons of the Melbourne Theatre Company, with which he was a regular cast member. Alan and Gay had two kids—daughter Finski and son Sam—and life was rolling along just fine.

Then in early 1994, when Alan was aged 59, a blood test picked up a possible problem; and a second blood test three months later, showing a rise in prostate-specific antigen from fours to sixes, prompted more tests, which confirmed it. Prostate cancer. Alan was stunned. 'I then had two months to think about it, to make a decision about an operation, and that's a bloody long time. Gay told me to go ahead and get it done, but I thought, *Jesus, this is wrecking my career*, y'know? All very well for everybody else!' So Alan had what he calls a 'conversation with myself,' talking into a tape recorder most nights as he weighed up the grim options that face many a male today—decide against the operation and risk death by cancer or have surgery to remove the prostate gland and risk impotence and incontinence for the rest of your life.

The tape reveals some dark moments. 'Driving down here,' he said on 29 April 1994, recalling a trip to Pascoe Vale, in Melbourne, to give a speech, 'the hardest thing was to ignore the feeling that I could aim the car off the road and in a split second this would all be over, except that it wouldn't solve the main problem that the family would feel cheated. But, as I've thought so many times in my life, if I jump would I actually kill myself? You almost dare yourself to do it, not wanting to but fascinated by the possibility that in a split second, you would jump in front of a train or jump off a cliff.'

In Alan, such self-destructive thoughts are unexpected. He is a most engaging bloke with an amiable and friendly manner, but he confesses that the early loss of his parents prompted him to put up a 'protective shield.' When his doctor suggested he talk to his best friend about his medical dilemma, Alan replied that he did not have one. 'I have lots of acquaintances,' he says, 'but I really don't have a best friend. I don't think, *Oh, I must call up Joe Blow*, or something. Of course, my family are my closest friends, but I was destroyed by the break-up of my first marriage. With all due respect to my second wife, you never quite give that same love again. I think I've put up this huge barrier to protect myself.'

At least the scans showed the cancer had not spread, but the post-surgical outlook did little to brighten him up. After visiting a urologist Alan wrote, on 24 May,

> *A deep depression hit me. It was more the thought that there is an alternative. I could take a punt and do nothing, retain the quality of life I've got at the moment. Even if I had two to five years those years will not involve me being reduced to*

a bloody shuffling old man with a catheter sticking out of his dick. What depressed me was the doctor spelt out the details of the catheterisation and how long it would be in and when I suggested that I had been asked to do a play in Tassie he said: 'Oh no, you won't have bladder control for about six to seven weeks and you'll be wearing a nappy.'

Alan says his tape recorder became his confidante and, as he neared the date of surgery, he finally tired of fretting and accepted his decision. 'From that moment on I became absolutely positive, and that's when the doctor asked how I was handling it so well. I told him about the tapes, and he said I should consider putting this into a book because there was no literature from the patient's point of view. He said he had done hundreds of these operations but did not know how a patient feels.'

So Alan continued his taped diary for a full twelve months, and in 1996 published the book *Surviving Prostate Cancer: One Man's Journey*, with a medical section from Dr Mark Ragg, through Reed Books. In a post-surgical entry in July, he noted that, 'I am coming to the end of one of the most important experiences of my life. A flirt with death has to be considered pretty important although I have had that before as a kid. I had one when I was eleven. The doctor told Mum that I very nearly died when my appendix burst'.

The book led to invitations to speak about prostate cancer at men's health nights. 'Back then men did not really discuss health,' says Alan, 'but there seemed to be what I term a "quiet revolution" going on. One of the first I did was out Burwood way, in Melbourne. They told me they might get 200 if they were lucky, but 500 turned up; they were knocking them back at the door. I thought, *Hang on, something's happening here. And I'm a playwright—I should make a play out of this.* And because it was my story I could make jokes about it, turn it into a bit of a comedy, because it's a scary enough topic and if the blokes are having a bit of a laugh at the same time, the message is getting through. So I wrote *For Better, for Worse.*'

For two years on and off he toured the play around Victoria, South Australia and Tasmania. In South Australia their transport broke down and they hired a school bus with driver. 'On the road the driver turned to me and said that I had saved his life,' says Alan. 'I replied that, no, he was saving our lives getting us to the next performance, but he told me he had been at a health night at Ouyen where I had spoken. "I went off to have my tests," he said, "and sure enough I had prostate cancer. I had surgery and I'm all fixed." So that was the start of the feedback.'

Thus did the curtain go up on a new phase of Alan's stage career. At the suggestion of people who had suffered other health problems he began writing further medical comedies. His former 'screen wife' Maggie Millar (Alan and she were Dr and Mrs Reed in *Bellbird*) inspired him to write *A Pill, a Pump and a Needle* after she contracted late-onset type 2 diabetes. 'When we toured that,' says Alan, 'everyone asked, "What about the blokes?" so I wrote another play, called *Six Degrees of Diabetes*, about three journalists. And each play led to someone knocking on my door suggesting a new one.'

He wrote *The Empty Chair* about dementia, *My Dog Has Stripes* about the 'black dog', depression, and *Four Funerals in One Day*, about palliative care. There is one about life after death, *Wicked Widows*, one called *Hear Me*, about patient care, and he even tackled the ticklish subject of geriatric sex, with *Never Too Old*. The restless Hopgood mind is still hunting out new topics. 'The stories I look for,' he says, 'are positive and allow a bit of comedy.'

That first play on prostate cancer was full-length with a cast of seven but this proved too expensive, so Alan trimmed it down to 40 minutes with a cast of three. 'The formula now is that each play is 40 minutes, followed by a forum with an expert in that particular problem or issue,' he says. 'Then we have a cup of tea and a scone.'

The plays are packaged by Alan's Bay Street Productions under the name HealthPlay, which by 2013 had staged almost 500 performances since 1997, drawing from a pool of 28 professional actors. In 2012 the tour was backed for the first time by philanthropic sponsorship and staged 65 performances, starting with three differ-ent plays staged in three different states within five days. Alan appears in all of his plays except the all-female *Wicked Widows*.

So, two decades down the track, with his 80th birthday approach-ing, Alan is as busy as ever. He avoided one of the twin post-op curses of prostatectomy—incontinence—but had his machismo somewhat dented by impotence, although, he says, he was able to overcome this by injection. 'It just meant I couldn't throw the local lollypop lady down behind the hedge without some warning,' he jests.

He has become a go-to man for others stricken with the same disease and has been able to offer advice from the battlefront. 'Look, one can't generalise', he wrote to a friend overseas faced with the same medical crisis.

> But from my experience if you've been caught in time, as it would seem, then you can go down on bended knee and thank whatever you thank. Yes, it's a bloody inconvenience and who wants to lose two months (especially if you're self-employed like me) but I have to say—once 'cancer' was a dreaded word that spelt only death. Now, for me, it has just meant a major health crisis.

For Alan and his play *For Better, for Worse*, life as a cancer survivor turned out for the better, with a reinvention of his stage-craft that simultaneously amuses and informs his fellow citizens. And the HealthPlay program gives him regular paid work—no small consideration for a mature-age thespian. Back in 1995, after he had made a successful recovery from surgery, a counsellor told him he had been lucky, that he had 'obviously been saved for something.'

He remembers replying, 'Yes, I've just got to find out what.' Now he knows.

Earl Carter

SHANNON BENNETT

The world's the limit

Early one evening in March 2012 four blokes in business suits were among the patrons sipping cocktails at the bar of Melbourne's 55th-floor Vue de Monde restaurant. Once they had finished their Negronis, they strolled out to the balcony, jammed the door shut behind them and jumped over the guard rail, 243 metres above the ground.

'They waved to me through the glass,' says the owner, Shannon Bennett, who was understandably freaked out, having failed to see the small BASE-jumping chutes on their backs. Nor did he notice the helmets with cameras that the kamikaze quartet strapped on as they leapt off the ledge. One small comfort: they left 100 bucks on the counter. The foursome lived to test gravity another day; but, in an allegorical kind of way, their perilous leap into the abyss off the Rialto's south tower was a bit like the career path of chef Bennett himself.

Go back to the year 2000 and you find him in his first small cafe, in Carlton, barely making a buck. His vocational BASE-jump had scared the dickens out of his Swedish-born wife, Linda, who walked out on him two weeks before opening, leaving the chef at home with nothing to sit on but milk crates. 'She said she wasn't cut out for the restaurant life,' he says. 'We still keep in touch but it was a hard apprenticeship.'

At 24 years of age this son of a marine engineer had ploughed his entire savings into one of the riskiest trades going around: cooking food for picky diners. However, this was what he had wanted to do since age fifteen. For years he had been taken regularly to London to visit family and had enjoyed cooking with his uncle Tom, the eldest brother of his mother, Bridget. 'Uncle Tom was a chef,' says Shannon, 'and loves kids, loves inspiring kids. He worked nights so he could spend time with me during the day. He started teaching me French, took me to some great restaurants, showed me cooking. On Sundays, his day off, we would cook a big breakfast together. He did his apprenticeship in Galway then moved to London. He's retired as a chef now. Teaches chess and guitar.'

Shannon got his start as an apprentice in the kitchen of chef Roger Leinhard at Melbourne's Grand Hyatt and then moved to Europe, where he worked with such names as Marco Pierre White in London and Alain Ducasse in France. His finances were tweaked by a remarkable fluke: the long-haired, dark-browed apprentice had that Leonardo DiCaprio look just when it was fashionable, and he was stopped in the streets of London one day by a modelling agency talent-spotter.

'I made ads, travelled—it was great,' he says. 'I made some quick cash for seven or eight months.' He eventually saved $50 000, not quite enough to launch his own Melbourne restaurant, so he and father Ben went to an old family friend named George and asked to borrow $70 000. 'George had lent money to Dad 30 years earlier to enable him to start a business. I hadn't seen George for ten years but we rocked up at his door in Port Melbourne and he lent me the money. I paid it back—with interest that he didn't expect.'

Shannon's Vue du Monde restaurant opened in Carlton with a $4500 blunder—the cost of printing business cards and stationery. When the stuff arrived he found there was a misprint in the name. It was supposed to be Vue *du* Monde, 'view of the world', but it had been spelt Vue *de* Monde throughout, as uncouth to a French ear as a Brit dropping his aitches. It was ironic, considering mother Bridget at one stage had worked as a proofreader, but what the hell; Shannon rode with the punches and renamed his restaurant Vue de Monde. 'It's a bit risqué but I like it,' he says.

His cooking skills back then were a trifle raw. 'Bistro fare,' he confesses. 'When I think of some of those dishes ... I was mad. One was grilled sawfish on lentils with beer-battered onion rings!'

Within five years the once-threadbare chef had cashed up sufficiently to move his operation to the city and set up a $1.3 million fine-dining oasis in Little Collins Street. It was an eye-opening contrast: one piece of white-leather furniture there cost $70 000, the same sum he had borrowed to start up the business. But this venture, in the grand surroundings of the historic Normanby Chambers, was not enough. Shannon soon added Café Vue at the same location, aimed at catching the lunchtime crowd. Still not enough—there was more space adjoining the cafe, and the whisper was that a fast-food joint was sniffing about. 'Can't have that,' said Shannon and set up Bistro Vue, part-furnished with the fittings from a 140-year-old Buenos Aires restaurant that he had found on the internet: a wooden bar with a zinc top, a weathered wine rack, an original front door. They oozed history: all had previously been part of a restaurant in Paris.

Shannon's new trio of Vues quickly proved a winner in a part of Little Collins Street that foodies had previously shunned. Saturday nights were soon booked out months ahead. There was no dinner menu; the waiter noted each patron's likes, dislikes and dietary needs, then suggested courses to suit.

There were five years of success, but it was still not enough. In 2011 Shannon took his biggest leap so far. Keeping his cafe and bistro in Little Collins Street, he moved Vue de Monde restaurant to the top of the Rialto's south tower, a step that cost him around $10 million.

'It was the biggest gamble I ever took,' he says. 'A big chunk of that $10 million was debt. I had to put guarantees in place on my house, but I was confident everything was going brilliantly there. We had to reinvent ourselves. At that stage it was either let Vue de Monde go sideways, just keep trying to cook good food, or really stretch myself and say, "Let's really go for it." I still really love French cuisine, but over the years I was becoming more and more knowledgeable about Australia's culture and food relationship. I was starting to tell a story but the restaurant space wasn't. I needed a view that said, "Hey, you're in Melbourne."'

Twelve years down the track, that struggling Carlton chef now had a restaurant empire: along with Vue de Monde atop the Rialto, the Bistro Vue and Cafe Vue in Little Collins Street were another five cafes, two of which were at Melbourne airport. Another was at the Heidi Modern Museum of Art, in an east Melbourne suburb, where Shannon had started a garden for organic vegetables. As the empire grew, the garden proved too small, so Shannon and a business partner bought Burnham Beeches, an art deco mansion in the Dandenong Ranges, 35 kilometres east of Melbourne, where resident gardeners tended an organic crop.

Shannon's younger brother Liam says their father has always been an enthusiastic vegetable-grower. 'That's where it all started,' he says. 'Dad still grows lots and lots at their place at Mount Macedon—some of it goes to the restaurant. Dad's right into gardening. He helped Shannon build a vegetable garden on Shannon's garage roof a while back.'

Shannon says that his biggest role is sourcing the best ingredients. 'You get this sixth sense that radars in on a rumour. For example, I heard chef Rob Marchetti talking to someone about a guy in the bush who roosts hens in two double-decker buses. I said, "Hang on, what was that story again?" Turned out there is this guy in New South Wales who moves the buses from location to location on a very large property. Rob knows people who have got the eggs and they're the best ever. The hens get no supplementary feed at all; he just moves to beautiful pastures. Then he gets a grader and rips up the ground and lets the hens go for it. So, fully free-range. Then a year later they put a crop there.

'It's the same with our oyster farm. There were rumours that there was this guy who hand-turns every oysters each morning. I tracked him down: Steve Feletti on the Clyde River at Batemans Bay. Calls his business Moonlight Oysters. He's the pioneer of the native oyster farm—I've been up there quite a few times. We've become good mates.'

And Shannon's fish? Caught on a line and a hook by a fisherman with a satellite phone. 'He's got six boats. We ring him directly, and he tells us what we are going to have; we don't tell him. It's what's in season, what he's caught—and not in a massive net. You can imagine dredging. Would we allow it if there was a big hill with one bulldozer on one side and one on the other and a huge rope between them, basically going up the hill dragging that rope and ripping everything out of the ground and making a bare mountain? Well, that's what we are doing in the ocean.'

There's more. Shannon found a Japanese master in brain-spiking fish. 'There are only six in the world. It kills the fish instantly, as soon as it comes off the boat. We regard fish the same as the way we regard meat: if you are prepared to pay $50 for a piece of the best beef you can buy, knowing where that beef has come from, you should do the same for the fish. And the taste is so much different. With fish that are caught in a net there is a very distinctive and horrible metallic taste: that's a stress enzyme. The fish caught in a net could take four or five hours to die.'

One of Shannon's best mates is writer and filmmaker Scott Murray, son of Gillian Helfgott, the wife of *Shine* pianist David Helfgott. The friendship dates back to the Carlton restaurant days, when Scott rang to cancel a table for two. 'I said, "You can't do that," and told him what he would be eating. So he turned up, and we sat him in front of the kitchen and we've been mates ever since.'

The Scott and Shannon show soon became a literary partnership. The boys did a guide to Paris, then a guide to New York and a guide to France, and then returned to France in 2012 to do a sequel. 'It's for a specific demographic of foodies who really enjoy travelling around gastronomic-wise to little towns in France,' says Shannon. 'The Michelin Guide is pretty confusing, so we have summarised where we think the Michelin is good and where it's not. We also invite other people who are passionate to write in the book about their favourite places, hotels, how to get there, little journeys. The books have been popular; we do rewrites every year and a half.'

The two mates set a cracking pace, eating in three cafes or restaurants a day for ten days, Shannon having plotted the journey in advance. There is plenty of creative friction. 'Shannon and I have not exactly crossed swords,' wrote Scott in *Shannon Bennett's France: A Personal Guide to Fine Dining in Regional France*. However, referring to Le Louis XV restaurant, he said

> *there has always been a little edge in our voices when we discuss its merits. I guess I should have taken into account how Shannon worked here and how it, and mentor Alain Ducasse, still mean so much to him. I should have gone easier on my complaints. However Shannon's spirited rejoinders made me realise how much he is not only a chef but an astute restaurateur ... Shannon sees a much wider picture. He understands what difficult tasks are silently being achieved, how the magic of a great restaurant experience can be the buzz in the room and the way people are greeted, the gleam of the polished wine goblets.*

Judging by the preface in the same edition, Shannon has a fair philosophical streak too. 'Everybody has two lives,' he says.

The first is pretty obvious. It dies for most people pretty much at the same time as their heart stops beating—or maybe a few months later when everybody has mourned their death and moved on. However for a select few there is a second life. That life is your legacy, it's your name. It may be the book you wrote several years earlier or the money you helped raise for the local football club. When people leave this world fulfilled that second life may never die. It lives on through the people they have influenced or who are reminded of them every day. I use France to extend my second life. I have this strong belief that nature designed us all to have one.

There is another book too: *28 Days in Provence*, published late in 2012. It records the four weeks in which Shannon, his wife, Madeleine West, and their children stayed in the famous French region on a self-imposed culinary challenge. 'For the whole 28 days I couldn't visit a supermarket; I had to cook from local village ingredients and farmers' markets. I loved it. In the end our eldest daughter, Phoenix, was speaking French. She was six then but she was ordering breakfast at the bakery. Put me to shame.'

Shannon and Madeleine chose the name Phoenix after the Melbourne restaurant where they were introduced, by actor Daniel MacPherson and photographer-councillor Serge Thomann at a Jamie Oliver dinner. Back then, Madeleine, an actress in the long-running TV soap *Neighbours*, was a vegetarian. 'She didn't tell me,' says Shannon, 'and I was accusing vegetarians of missing the point. I was wondering why she was kicking Daniel under the table. He knew about it.' They met again six months later and the heat was on. By 2012 they had started their own version of the X-factor— Phoenix, Hendrix, Xascha and the latest arrival, Xantha. 'It means little golden one,' says Shannon.

Marriage to one of the best chefs in Australia soon led Madeleine away from vegetarianism, a philosophy that Shannon still sees fit to challenge. 'We are designed on this planet to use its resources but to use them smart. Animals eat each other; vegetarians are trying to go against nature. Madeleine was always sick as a vegetarian, but now she hasn't looked back.'

It is only in recent years that Madeleine has fully recovered from a nasty accident in Sydney, in which she was clipped by a bus as she stood at the kerb. 'Sent her flying,' says Shannon. 'She had to have two metal plates put in her head. She had pretty bad migraines for a few years and couldn't work. She was lucky not to be killed: she was in hospital for two and a half months. To make it worse, she was robbed when she was lying on the ground. Someone nicked her handbag. It was outside a supermarket.'

Madeleine says her husband's highly trained palate is daunting when it comes to her own cooking at home. 'We used to make pizzas together. He would make the dough and I'd make the sauce and was very proud of the fact that I roasted up all the vegetables, reduced this and caramelised that. But one day the tomatoes were not terribly ripe so I put one tablespoon of tomato paste in what would be 2 or 3 litres of sauce. Shannon dipped a finger in, took one taste and said, "There's tomato paste in that."

'I said there wasn't; he insisted there was.

'I said, "You bastard! How dare you question my integrity? I'm never cooking for you again!"' But of course she did.

Liam, younger than Shannon by seven years, says the whole family pitched in to get the chef started. 'I was in Year 12,' he tells me, 'and I'd been a dishwasher at Rockman's Regency. I came back to help at Carlton. It was a pizza shop that turned into a restaurant overnight. That first night everyone stayed up to get it ready: Mum was painting floors! Even now Mum and Dad are helping out. Dad's quite handy, so he's always up there fixing bits and pieces.' Cooking was always a vital part of family life. 'Mum was always a good cook,' says Liam. 'One of her favourite dishes is what she calls Dublin coddle, a sort of Irish casserole made from sausages and potatoes. The whole family loves cooking.'

Liam, no mean achiever himself as a pilot with Virgin Australia, says his energetic elder brother originally wanted to be an archaeologist. 'We lived in Westmeadows, near parkland, and Shannon was fascinated with animals. At one stage he collected cow bones and got Dad to bleach them and wire them together so he had a little skeleton in the backyard.'

For an Amazing Bastard yet to reach 40, Shannon has set a cracking pace. As a former Essendon Grammar schoolmate of Essendon Football Club veteran Dustin Fletcher, Shannon has his eye on the fast food at Aussie Rules football grounds. 'I'm not sure why we go to the football and eat French fries,' he says. 'So that's another thing we do now: food for the footy club.' His restless mind clicked into environmental gear when his high-rise Vue de Monde was being designed, and he is not averse to taking you for a 'sustainability' tour.

Let's start with the restaurant lift: the power to take you to the 55th floor is generated by the energy created by the subsequent descent. 'Going down,' says Shannon, 'the brakes trap all the kinetic energy.'

'Over here,' says Shannon, gesturing at an area resembling a large domestic lounge room, 'is where people come up for a drink. We are recreating old-world cocktails from the 1880s. Back then, after the gold rush, Melbourne was so wealthy that it would bring its own ice. It was lake ice from Massachusetts, believe it or not, brought in by the Melbourne Patent Ice Company in Elizabeth Street. They cut it into practical-sized blocks and every day they'd deliver ice to the hotels, restaurants and hospitals. The company was run by the Tudor family—they were known as the "ice kings". So we now have big ice blocks here and hand-carve the ice blocks for each drink. And all this furniture we bought second-hand off eBay from all around the world then had them re-upholstered.'

So what's the story with the unusual leather tables? 'We got a bootmaker to make the tops out of kangaroo leather,' says Shannon. 'We tried to replicate what the tables were like in the gold rush.

All our chairs are made from recycled telephones, and we just put kangaroo leather on top. All lighting is LED, which uses only one-tenth the power of a conventional light bulb. I've cut my power bill from about $3500 a week to $1800. See these tiles? They're made of biochar from furnaces in Japan. The furnaces run so hot there are no emissions, and the remaining powder is the biochar. The Japanese build all their hospitals out of it because it absorbs bacteria and carbon. It also absorbs odours.' All the plaster is eco-plaster, recycled magnesium oxide board.

Shannon used a Danish engineering company based in Melbourne to implement many of his plans. 'They worked on the Spencer Street Station project,' he says, 'and I heard that they wanted to do a lot of environmental stuff there but weren't allowed. Well, the extra I have spent here, I am saving. That's what I like about it.'

The cloud-like artwork on the ceiling over the bar, the first thing you see upon arrival, is made from recycled plastic Coca-Cola bottles. Even the feature artwork, a collection of scientific squiggles in multicoloured neon light tubes on one wall, has a story behind it. 'There's this guy, Joseph Kosuth, who comes to Melbourne every year for the tennis,' says Shannon. 'He used to come in here in white shorts and Dunlop Volleys, such an eccentric guy, and I thought, *Who is this nut case? I've got to talk to him.* Turned out he's a famous American artist, a professor of art with one of the famous pieces in New York's Museum of Modern Art, *One and Three Chairs.* Andy Warhol was his best mate, and in his will Warhol left him a sketch-book belonging to Charles Darwin that he bought at an auction. This artwork is one of the pages in the book. Joseph thought neon was underused as an art medium.'

You finish Shannon's eco-tour at the chemical-free kitchens, which use what he calls 'e-water'. 'It's electricalised water,' says Shannon. 'Water with a pH of 10.6, and sanitising water of pH 2.3. It kills all rhinovirus, all E. coli, any bacteria whatsoever. See those taps? We wash all the knives and forks under those. There's 1000 litres of water collected on the roof, mixed with 10 kilograms of salt in a tank with titanium membranes. It splits the solution into acid and alkaline. You have to keep reinventing yourself in this business. You can't rest on your laurels. You have to keep getting better and better.'

And so he does. Early in 2013 Shannon moved his family into a $5 million four-bedroom Victorian mansion in South Yarra, Barwon, complete with pool-house. Meanwhile over in Carlton, in the building that housed his first restaurant, there is now a pizza joint—again. Shannon Bennett has come a long way.

NEIL JENMAN

The case of the golden eggs

Considering its lamentable contents, Neil Jenman's Form 2 report card from the Builth Wells Secondary School, in Wales, seems an odd thing to find in a frame on the wall of his rambling family home in Sydney. 'Sixtieth out of a class of 61' was his ranking back in July 1966. 'No practical ability. Makes little or no effort. Difficult to assess.' His marks include 10 out of 100 for general science, 8 out of 100 for rural science and 0 for history and metalwork. He scored 4 per cent for Welsh, although, all these years later, Neil says he can still say his prayers in that lyrical Celtic tongue.

It was wife Reiden's idea to frame this dismal report card, and it seems to amuse her husband, because, by any business estimation, this secondary-school flop—born in England of Australian parents, Rodney and Ruth—has been a stunning success. Neil is a millionaire many times over, a quietly spoken bloke who turned one Sydney real estate agency into a seminar-driven agent-training system and then launched a nationwide consultancy network.

Then he wrote books about the lurks and perks of the real estate industry, one of which—*Real Estate Mistakes*—has sold more than 300 000 copies.

Across the hallway from the school report card you will find another unusual piece of framed memorabilia: a weathered copy of W. Somerset Maugham's novel *The Summing Up* with a note recording the fact that Neil bought it at Brisbane airport at age 21. He says it was one of the major events of his life. 'This is the actual book,' he says. 'It created a lifelong love of literature and philosophy. I read Cicero, Plato; I read Aristotle's *Ethics*; and I read Socrates, about how to lead the good life. I remember being so excited about discovering these sorts of things. I remember being excited about Somerset Maugham, because there is much wisdom in his stories. At 23 I said to my father, "Hey, Dad, have you ever heard of a writer called Somerset Maugham?"

'His reply, "That fucking poofter!" That was my father.'

Regardless, Neil went on to become one of the world's biggest collectors of Maugham literature and memorabilia. One wall of his huge library is all Maugham: every edition he has been able to find over the past three decades. In his fireproof safe is the original manuscript for Maugham's 1902 novel *Mrs Craddock*, written entirely with fountain pen in longhand, with the author's own corrections and notations.

If you push a section of the bookcase on another wall, a hinged partition swings open to reveal Neil's inner 'writing room', where he has an autographed picture of Maugham looking down on his desk. There is a chart on which Neil logs the number of words he has written each day. His latest book is about achieving success. He shows me the first page of the manuscript. The opening lines read thus: 'In the English summer of 1954 my father tried to kill me. But fortunately, after being persuaded to have two earlier abortions, my mother refused to have a third so I was born in the English winter of 1955 weighing barely five pounds [2 kilograms]. A narrow escape. I was very lucky'.

Neil's late father was a dark force in his life, a hard-headed businessman and the sort of rogue that Neil now pursues as a consumer advocate. 'I have a friend, a child psychiatrist,' says Neil, 'who said to me in 2006, "When are you going to stop chasing your father?" In fact, I didn't know him very well at all. I was estranged for a long while. What upset me most about him was that he used to beat up my mother. He was the managing director of a publishing company. At his 60th birthday there was no one who had known him for more than a year. At his funeral there were seven people, and that included himself. I wasn't there, but I didn't know he had died. He had ordered my mother not to tell me and she didn't—that's the power of domestic violence. He made my mother swear not to have any contact with me even after he died.'

Rodney had moved his family back to Australia in 1967. Twenty-seven years later Neil finally confronted him with an ultimatum. 'I told him I would hit him if he hit my mother again. So my father forbade my mother and sister to see me again.'

In 2006, after his father had died, Neil used a private detective to find Ruth, who was in a retirement village in Mackay, Queensland. Neil sent a son from his first marriage, Lloyd, to see Ruth, but she still obeyed her late husband's command—no contact. Neil then sought the help of the Salvation Army and an officer flew up from Sydney. After talking to the Salvo for an hour Ruth relented and rang Neil. 'I went up to see her,' he says. 'She then moved down to Sydney in a house near us. She died in my home here, aged 83. That was 2008, so I had just over two years with her. She is buried in a small village near our cattle property in Queensland, well away from my father. She has finally escaped him.'

During his long estrangement from his mother, Neil had launched a rescue service for abused women; it was set up in Chatswood, on Sydney's North Shore, under the control of the Salvation Army. Despite having experienced domestic violence firsthand, he is still astonished at the power that brutal men can exert over their wife or girlfriend. 'Police officers will tell you that they have had women jump on their backs and pummel them as they arrest their husband, and they'll turn around and say, "What are you doing? He's just broken your nose, love!"'

The Salvos' Lieutenant-Colonel Colin Haggar was in charge when Neil first approached the organisation with the idea of a women's shelter. 'Neil is a great genuine bloke; there are not many people like him,' says Colin. 'He totally underwrote this venture from the start. It was felt there were enough women's refuges around and in a way they were counterproductive, so we established the Northside Women's Services, totally underwritten by Neil. Over the years he has probably paid in close to $1 million. Northside is a two-pronged service: education and alternative long-term housing if necessary. It has been a very innovative way of addressing the problem.'

Neil and Reiden chalked up seventeen years marriage in 2013. They met at Hyatt Regency Sanctuary Cove, on the Gold Coast, where Reiden worked in hospitality. 'Married within six months,' Neil says proudly. 'Reiden and my mother are the two finest women I have met.' It is his third marriage: the first lasted eighteen months, the second fifteen months. 'There's no point in hanging around for years if it's not going to work,' says Neil, who has one child from the first marriage, two from the second and three with Reiden.

On the wall over the marital bed is a large photograph of Alchera, the Queensland cattle station. The family spends much time there, and it is of particular significance to Neil: it was the property his parents bought when they returned to Australia in 1967. 'They sold it in 1972,' says Neil, 'and I bought it back in 2005. It's beautiful.'

So the boy who made 'little or no effort' at school, who scored 10 per cent in science, ended up with wealth enough to buy back the family ranch. And that was also after a substandard performance at Queensland Agricultural College, from which he was expelled. 'Low academic performance and tomfoolery,' says Neil with a cheerful lack of concern. 'I was sixteen then, so I went back to my parents' cattle station. As soon as I got my driving licence I took off and worked in the cane fields. I wanted to get as far away from my father as possible. Then a fellow called Joe Lowe, a friend of my dad's, suggested I get into real estate. He told me, "Don't worry what your father says. If they can make penicillin out of mouldy bread, I can make something out of you." He told me to clean myself up, get a haircut, and he would help me.'

At age seventeen Neil landed a job in a real estate office at Yeppoon, on the central Queensland coast. But, with a knack for writing, he had a yen to be a journalist and headed for Melbourne to see if his great-uncle, prominent broadcaster Ormsby Wilkins, could help. 'Ormsby was my paternal grandmother's younger brother,' says Neil. 'He died of cancer in 1977. But on the way down to see him I stopped in Brisbane and asked the ABC about getting a job as a cadet journalist. The pay was $23 a week and the cheapest rent I could get was $25 a week. I kept travelling but ran out money in Sydney, and basically that's where I stopped for 30 years.'

There was little choice but to return to real estate, and he joined an agency. By 1984 he was able to open his own office, Jenman Real Estate, in Auburn, Sydney. It was not your typical property office: he did not do auctions; he did not do open-for-inspections; he did not charge up-front for advertising. He declared that those methods were wrong and were designed primarily to benefit and promote the agent rather than the customer. 'When I was training as an agent,' he recalls, 'I attended one auction course, and I remember, on one of the breaks, walking up the street almost in tears, thinking to myself that if this was what I had to do in this industry I would rather get out. They taught you the whole bag of tricks, the whole kit and caboodle: how to bully the people, cajole them, twist facts, how to use dummy bidding. This was regarded as normal practice. It was despicable.'

Neil's unorthodox approach proved successful, and his office did such good business that in 1989, during an economic slump, he was able to tell an inquiring property reporter that he was having his best month ever.

'That's not what other agents are telling me,' said the newshound.

'You're not ringing other agents; you're ringing me,' said Neil, insisting that 'we opened in 1984; it is now 1989, and this is the best month since we opened.'

The newshound sent a photographer and wrote a report about the real estate agent who was making boom-time sales in the economic gloom. 'At that stage I was part of a franchise network of 75 offices called Combined Real Estate,' says Neil. 'I was number one every month in dollars and property sales. Other agents started coming to see me, asking how I was doing so well, and I was happy to tell them, because I believe in helping people, particularly those younger than me. I benefited from the advice of an older, wiser man named Alec Shev; in fact, I named one of my sons after him.'

Neil's explanation to other agents was this: 'First, I don't treat my staff like dirt; I pay them good salaries, not commission-only. I also give guarantees to my customers: if they don't like me they can sack me. With other agents, if you sign up you are stuck with them. Another thing: I open seven days till 7 p.m.; most buyers work from nine to five. Most real estate agents are open from nine to five. The buyers come home from work; the agencies are closed. We do most of our sales between 5 p.m. and 9 p.m. Our busiest time at Auburn is around 7 p.m.'

The demand on Neil's time grew. There were agents coming to see him daily, learning how he worked his inquiry log, how he handled contacts, how he used canvassing letters. 'Eventually, it was such a demand that I struggled to do my own work,' he says. 'So I said to our receptionist, "Instead of seeing the agents individually, I'll book a room and speak to them all at once." She booked, and next thing I know we had 96 people turn up. I spoke for two days and charged $24 to cover the drinks and sandwiches.'

The demand increased and Neil did more seminars. At one of them an agent sidled up to him, claiming Neil had a hidden agenda. Said the agent, 'You're going to go all around Australia teaching agents about this, aren't you?'

Responded Neil, 'Not at $12 a day I'm not.'

Said the agent, 'You could charge thousands for this.'

The suggestion turned on that metaphorical light bulb. *Really? Could I?* thought Neil, and he went away to consider it. Settling on a fee of $595 a ticket, he put some brochures together and booked some venues. He issued the challenge: 'If you come and hear me and pay me $600 you'll make lots of sales, and if you don't make lots of sales I'll give you your 600 bucks back.'

Hundreds of them came, eventually thousands. Neil travelled Australia, enjoying the gratis accommodation provided by the seminar venues, which were happy to see their function rooms full. Then some of the agents began asking, 'This is the sales part of the business; why don't you do an office management seminar?' Again, Neil went off to think about it, wrote a management seminar, then really pushed the envelope by charging $10 000 a ticket. The seminar was attended by 118 people, some with discounts because they came as couples. But the startling fact was that he earnt over $1 million in a week.

'I was earning so much that I decided to sell my real estate business in 1993–94,' he says. His long-time mentor, Alec Shev, advised against it, saying the business was like a goose that laid golden eggs: you don't sell the goose. Neil showed him the figures from his new seminar business and Alec quickly changed his mind. 'Neil,' he said, 'you have a new goose!'

The seminar business brought in $2 million a year, but some of the agents he trained began to complain. 'We've paid you all this money, and now you train our competitors.' Neil proposed a deal: he would introduce a consultancy service. A real estate office would pay him $1500 a month, and he would train its agents exclusively. By the year 2000 he had 300 real estate offices paying him a total of $450 000 a month, with each agent in those offices paying him an additional $2000 a year. 'Sounds easy,' he says, 'but I did do a lot of work.' The kid with 'no practical ability' was doing okay.

Such revenue streams brought Neil back to his earlier interest in philosophy. 'There is a "doctrine of enough",' he says. 'When our stomach fills up we say, "That's enough, thank you." When we fill the car with petrol, the pump clicks off when it's full. But when it comes to money we never know when we have had enough. Reiden and I decided we had enough, and I had to decide what to do next. More than anything else, I wanted to be a good man. I wanted to try to do something decent.'

He performed unpublicised acts of goodwill, including the purchase of a collection of Don Bradman letters, which were controversially put up for auction in 2002 by Greg Chappell and since donated to the Bradman Museum in Bowral, south of Sydney. Neil also anonymously bought two Victoria Crosses to stop them leaving Australia, and now both are on display in the Queensland Museum: one permanently donated, the other on loan. Friends say that Neil stepped in to finance a national children's swim-safe program after a sponsor dropped out, put $300 000 into a favourite Melbourne bookshop to prevent it from closing and ploughed $1 million into the Chatswood women's refuge.

On the real estate front Neil became a bloke whom the Australian press dubbed an 'ethics-in-real-estate consumer advocate'. In 2000 he told his 330 Jenman-trained agents that he wanted to set up a public-assistance service to help people who had been duped or dudded in property transactions. 'I said we could be the place where the public can come for real help,' he says. 'I suggested that we all throw in $10 000 each towards a Home Sellers and Home Buyers Protection Fund—and I would go first. That got rid of 100 of them right away. But we raised enough to hire a barrister, a former police officer, two secretaries and a consumer advocate.'

It was a noble quest but one that cost him and his family dearly. This new crusade baffled the high-rolling real estate trade. He was told he was 'insane', that he was 'commercially unrealistic.' His training business shrank so much that he sold it.

Undaunted, Neil ploughed more of his own wealth into the

cause, conceding that 'my wife says I'm a sucker for a sob story and that I chase too many lost causes.' Even the winning causes came at huge cost. The fund backed one case that ran for seven years, all the way to the High Court. Sydney solicitor Geoff Roberson, who led the case on behalf of three naive property investors, says the costs covered by the fund totalled more than $1 million. 'It was hard,' he adds. 'We were up against the big end of town, but we finally won with costs, in June 2012. Hopefully we will recover a good deal of that money, but the legal process to do that is extremely expensive and cumbersome. Maybe another $100 000. Over the time the fund has required extra financing from Neil personally. He has been extremely generous. He and Reiden have backed this all the way.'

In 2006 Neil went further, setting up Real Estate Monitors, which provides a vendor advocacy service that helps Joe Public find a suitable agent and then oversees the sale process without any cost to the vendor (as the agent pays a percentage of their fee to the service). However, while consumers have welcomed these unexpected support schemes, Neil soon found he had a tiger by the tail. Those who made big bucks out of property and financial schemes began to feel the pain, and the internet—a defamation Wild West—started to bristle with abuse and anti-Jenman slander. He was sued, and he was physically and verbally attacked. His family was threatened to the extent that Reiden posted a message on a Jenman Fights Back website:

> On a recent television biography about my husband I told the reporter that sometimes I'll cry. Neil's critics have somehow twisted that comment, inferring that Neil mistreats me or that his consumer work hurts his family. Neil never mistreats me. To the cowards who make these claims and to one coward in particular (who places our home address on the internet and puts my family at risk) I say this: Your type disgust me. You lie, cheat and deceive the public for your own financial gain.

*When my husband stands up to protect the public, you then
lie about him. I am proud of what my husband does. I am
especially pleased when he threatens your crooked schemes.
Of course, as any wife would, I'd prefer that my husband not
take so many risks. Yes, I worry about him.*

And with good reason. Neil spent a week in hospital after being
punched in the face and kicked in the shins while confronting a
spruiker for a TV current affairs show. 'He eventually apologised, but
it was not the punch that caused the damage; it was the kick,' says
Neil. 'I said to Reiden the next day, "I think he has broken a bone."
We went to the hospital later that night and the doctor said I would
have to be admitted: there was a risk of losing the leg to cellulitis.
In fact, he said I could die without treatment.

'Then there was the time a guy spat in my face. I was a bit stupid
really. I sat in front of his car while a TV crew filmed him, so he
backed into the garage and ran for the office. But his hand was
shaking so much he couldn't get the key in the lock. That's when
he turned around like a snake and spat. It was so disgusting. I got
the flu a few days later.'

The vehement backlash did not surprise Neil, who went on the
front foot and posted individual rebuttals to the many unfounded
claims against him. In another Jenman Fights Back posting, adult
daughter Ruth conducted a 'personal interview' in which her father
explained, 'The fact that bad people don't like me is a good thing.
It would only bother me if good people said bad things about me.'
But it has been a long, expensive and traumatic journey for 'the man
who chased his father'.

Fact is, for all his extraordinary success, all Neil ever really
wanted to do was write bestselling novels. 'If I could have been
certain of succeeding as a writer, I would have,' he says. 'There has
been virtually no financial reward in what I have done since 2000,
but there has been a huge personal reward. Would I do it again if
I knew what was ahead of me? I'm not sure.'

Real estate writer and analyst Terry Ryder is among the many who are glad he did. 'Neil Jenman is dogged and determined,' Ryder told *The Courier-Mail* in 2007, 'particularly when he knows someone is a villain. It is a shame there are not more people speaking out'.

Simon Schluter, Fairfax Syndication

COLIN LOVITT

Don't mention Crete

News bulletin: Melbourne Queen's Counsel Colin Lovitt has been hit by an ice truck. Mind you, it was more than six decades ago and he was aged seven, but, as with many things in life, there have been consequences. The accident, in which his left thigh was shattered and his right knee broken, left him with a 'stretched' left leg that is almost 2 centimetres longer than the right. That gave him an uneven gait, which in turn caused his left knee to wear out. So in 2007 this fierce advocate for the defence had an operation that put him out of action for six months.

The surgery marked the sort of *annus* that Her Majesty once dubbed *horribilis*. Colin's 88-year-old mother, Bonnie, died that year, and so did his 91-year-old mother-in-law, Maisie. His father, Ron, pictorial editor of Melbourne's *Age* newspaper (which explains Colin's media debut at age three—a photo taken by Ron of his naked son under a hose that illustrated an *Age* report on a heatwave), had died at his desk of a heart attack in 1971, at the age of just 52.

So Colin has chalked up almost two decades more than his dad, surviving an operation for prostate cancer on the way. It was a close shave. 'No symptoms at all,' he recalls. 'It was just that my prostate-specific antigen reading doubled in a year. (I am one of those rare males who has an annual check-up.) The GP sent me to a urologist, who fisted me! I said, "Jesus Christ, the engagement's off!" They took the whole prostate out and found one-third of it was a tumour. Had I opted for anything less than complete removal it would not have worked. But I'm lucky—no incontinence.' Opportune indeed, considering the giant wine rack inside the front door of his Carlton apartment, not to mention the two giant wine coolers he keeps in the spare bedroom and the wine cellars that he says are downstairs. 'It's my magnificent obsession: I'm a wine collector,' says Colin, then, as if to excuse the quantity, 'I give a lot away to friends.'

Perhaps he was conscious of the startling claims made in 2007 by fellow silk and reformed alcoholic Peter Faris that drugs and drinking problems were rife at the Victorian Bar. 'I think he's talking through his blurter when it comes to hard drugs,' says Colin. 'I've never seen anything at the bar remotely suggesting that. But Peter's always been controversial, when he was a left-wing rabble-rouser and now, when he's right-wing. It has been a 180-degree turn.'

Colin has a wry view of his barristerial brethren. 'I knew that I would probably cop a lot of shit about the prostatectomy from my idiotic colleagues who see you as nothing more than a means of satire. I've thought of writing an article about this because I thought someone might listen and a few more blokes might go and get checked. Blokes are so ignorant about their bodies. Pathetic. Women are fantastic in comparison. They're used to going to doctors, used to being poked and prodded and invaded.'

He has a bit of a dicky ear, has Colin. Well, that was his excuse in 2003 when he narrowly escaped jail. He claimed that his congenital deafness made him a 'loud whisperer,' and that is why, two years earlier, in a case before magistrate Bruce Zahner, one of his whispers to a solicitor regarding Zahner had been overheard. Yes, that's the one: 'This bloke is a complete cretin; surely they can't all be like this?' He later retracted the comment, but the manner of the retraction left a bit to be desired: 'I take it back. He's not a *complete* cretin.'

After Brisbane's *Courier-Mail* conveyed all this to a chortling public, Zahner disqualified himself from the hearing. Colin was soon up before Supreme Court judge Richard Chesterman, charged with contempt of court and being told by the beak that his 'statements were calculated to impair public confidence in the magistrate' and that he should be 'punished by the imposition of a very substantial fine … or a short term of imprisonment.'

Colin, who was fined $10 000, confesses it was a foot-in-mouth but believes some traditional interstate acrimony was at play: 'My remark was supposed to be sotto voce. But the Queensland media was dying to send up a silk from the southern states, from below the barbed-wire fence, and were onto me like a flash. It was an old sessions court, and the reporters were using the old jury box, right next to me.' He says he has not used the word 'cretin' since then, 'not even when I'm referring to someone from Crete.'

That Lovitt mouth, which has pulled so many defendants out of trouble, has done an equally good job of dropping its owner into hot water. A month after the contempt case Colin was irking another beak during the trial of Gypsy Joker Graeme 'Slim' Slater. Colin was back on thin ice. 'I'm frankly getting tired of Your Honour ruling that the Crown can ask things that, frankly, if I had asked and the Crown objected …'

Supreme Court justice Robert Anderson cut him short: 'Be very careful.'

Colin persisted and copped a judicial rebuke for being 'sarcastic and discourteous,' but he insists that he lauds the bench more often than not. 'It's just that I don't get quoted when I'm sticking up for judges.' As opposed to sticking it *up* judges, one might observe.

There was a time among his Carlton footy club mates when he was nicknamed the Embarrister. In 2005, as president of the

Carlton Cricket Club, he told a meeting of 100 at the club awards night that the Carlton Social Club was giving the cricket club a hard time. The problem was the embarristerial way in which he explained it: that the cricket club was being 'raped' by the social club and that 'if you are going to be raped you may as well lie back and enjoy it.' Colin reckoned he got a good laugh, but there were at least three who did not join in. One woman wrote a letter of complaint, and another opined, 'I'm disgusted. There were probably about 30 women there and four or five young children'. A male in attendance was also aggrieved: 'It was a terrible comment and if I was a woman I would have walked out. But I know the type of character he is, he was trying to make an eccentric point and it was just very poorly made'.

Colin, often gruff and particularly so in the face of the behaviour gendarmes, snarled at the time, 'Political correctness gone haywire. You can't say anything without someone taking exception. I was talking about the treatment of the cricket club by the social club. It's an old expression and no way, shape or form supposed to be serious.' He then stepped down as president. 'After 25 years on the committee it has been a bit of a life sentence.'

Colin and his wife, Margaret, were born ten weeks apart at the Sacred Heart Hospital, Brunswick, in Melbourne's north, and met at the beach when they were twelve. At fifteen they were sweethearts and dated for two years before going their separate ways.

The sudden death of Colin's father reignited the flame. 'Margaret sent me a card, and we started going out again. Then we got married. We've always been close.' They have two sons in their thirties: Marcus, who lives in Tokyo with his Japanese wife, teaching English; and Zane, who made documentary films before gaining a law degree. In 2012 Zane published a crime novel called *The Midnight Promise*, which Colin, paternal bias aside, says has 'wonderful perception.'

Colin and Margaret live in twin apartments. 'That way we don't drive each other mad,' says Colin. 'A lot of people think it is the perfect arrangement.'

He is a man of wide-ranging interests. Cooking is number one, and only the previous night, he says with some excitement, he made and froze the base for a chowder. He used to be a madly enthusiastic golfer, often playing 36 holes a day, and once played 57 holes at Brighton Public Course, southeast of Melbourne. 'When I get involved in something I take to it with passion,' he says.

In 1967, during the final year of his law degree, he taught maths. 'I needed the income,' he says. 'It was at Hadfield High School in Pascoe Vale, north of Melbourne. Helluva drive from our house at Highett, 30 kilometres to the south. I was form master of 1A, and I was only there three days a week. It was a remedial class for kids who did worst in the tests, but because it was 1A all the parents thought it was for the brightest of the bright.'

Then there is Lovitt the singer. 'I learnt it seriously as a kid,' he says. 'I was once called on at a private soiree in one of Melbourne's more luxurious neighbourhoods to sing a duet with a woman from the opera. She played key roles like Violetta in *La Traviata*. She chose 'Summertime', and we sang harmonies—no one could believe we hadn't rehearsed it. Learning singing has helped in court. You speak from your diaphragm so you can always be heard.'

There have been many descriptions of the burly Lovitt QC over the years. Stuart Rintoul in the *The Australian* likened him to a rhinoceros: 'large, disconcertingly quick and nimble-minded'. John Silvester in *The Age* declared Colin was the 'sort of lawyer you would want on your side—passionate, ruthless, pedantic yet generous'. Fellow silk Philip Dunn has lauded Colin's willingness to 'take on lost causes,' and Chris Dane says he is a 'valiant, good-hearted, devoted fighter.' There have also been less complimentary views. Justice Philip Cummins once observed (although he is said to have modified his view since) that Lovitt's 'continual misconduct' had brought disgrace upon the bar, the bench and Lovitt himself.

Nevertheless, late in 2012 Colin's legal brethren named him and his colleagues Philip Dunn and Robert Richter as the three first 'Legends' of the Victorian criminal bar, an honour which—according to Susan Brennan in the *Victorian Bar News*—reflected 'an absolute commitment to acting in their client's interests and not being deterred from standing up to irascible judges'.

Back in 1978, Colin, peeved at the pecking order that seemed to cast criminal barristers in a dimmer light than their colleagues in other specialties, organised a meeting at his modest chambers and founded the Criminal Bar Association of Victoria, despite being the most junior of the five barristers present. 'We didn't have a voice on the bar council back then,' he says. 'And we were being treated abominably by the court listings system. Criminal lawyers are generally regarded as the poor relations. Equity lawyers look down on us; the civil lawyers barely tolerate us; but criminal lawyers are the experts on examination and cross-examination because we do it day in, day out. In fact, when most people think of barristers they think of us.'

For the public, the stamp of QC has the sort of mystic kudos that 'Sir' carries for a knight of the realm. Both, of course, are vanishing breeds, with no more knights created in Australia and Senior Counsel, or SC, having replaced Queen's Counsel as the title of the nation's barristerial elite. Remaining QCs can switch over if they wish, but Colin, though an avid republican, has not. 'Had I been a younger man, in my Peter Faris phase and full of angst,' he says impishly, 'I probably would have made the switch; but you have to change everything: your stationery, letterheads, notepaper. Too much trouble.' Colin became a QC in 1989, but he says he does not trade off the rank. 'My bank manager asked, "Would you like us to add the QC to the name on your chequebook?"

'I told him, "No bloody fear. It's the last thing I want."'

Colin is a man so practised at interrogation that he is often credited with near-mesmerising skills. His style is one of systematic analysis. 'There are various ways of asking questions,' he says. 'You can ask something like, "What do you feel about such and such?" Or you can sort of prise things out of people. The best way of cross-examining is to scout around the edges than go straight to the nitty-gritty. If you say, "I put it to you that it didn't happen," what do you think they are going to say? But if you snipe away at what appears to be small print about their version of events, you often find it doesn't stack up, that effectively it is made up. When you are making a story up you might be consistent about the bare bones, the basic allegations, but the small print is more troublesome.'

Yet the courtroom skills of an advocate like Colin pose a thorny question: is the Australian court system fair when the likelihood of acquittal is enhanced by hiring a top gun? Can you buy a better justice?

'Yes,' concedes Colin, 'it is an innate weakness in the system. It would be ridiculous to say anything other than that if you have the best representation you have a much better chance of being acquitted. When I was young I used to hear people in the law say that it really didn't matter who represents you, but I strongly disagree.'

Colin says much of this disparity has arisen through changes in Legal Aid. 'In the first 100 murder trials I did, all bar 1 of them was legally aided. Of the last 50 I've done, only four or five have been legally aided. That's because Legal Aid won't brief silks any more like they used to in all murder cases. They would brief QCs with juniors, which meant that younger criminal barristers, as happened with me, got tremendous schooling in murder cases by being junior to the best in the business. I was junior to George Hampel, John Phillips, Frank Vincent, Austin Asche—great barristers. But clients have become more and more like file numbers. If people want a QC they have to pay for it themselves and that means it is extremely expensive. A trial might run two weeks and, just plucking a figure, a QC might cost you more than $20 000 a week. And there's got to be a solicitor too. The average man can't afford it.'

It was the murder of Moe toddler Jaidyn Leskie, in 1997, that thrust Colin into both the limelight and notoriety. In the Victorian Supreme Court the following year he successfully nibbled away at the prosecution's case against Greg Domaszewicz. Colin says he charged no fee for the case, because, 'to put it bluntly, Legal Aid fucked Greg Domaszewicz up the arse. There was the Crown spending oodles of money, it seemed a bottomless pit, on their preparation. On the other hand, Domaszewicz didn't have two bob. At first he was represented by Legal Aid, but when it came to the committal they weren't prepared to spend any money. His counsel wanted an independent observer at the autopsy and arranged for a former government pathologist to be there and do a report. But because the counsel had not got approval from the grants section, Legal Aid said he was at risk of having to pay that expense himself. Bear in mind the autopsy was on New Year's Day. The people they were talking about were not contactable; the office was closed. The counsel had to make an executive decision himself and was pilloried for it.'

Colin was holidaying on Castaway Island, in Fiji, when the Leskie case erupted. 'Our son came to join us and brought the Sunday newspapers,' says Colin. 'I read this double-page spread written by Andrew Rule and read his description of Moe, which was pretty scathing. That is the first I heard of it. When we got back home the Domaszewicz solicitor rang me and asked me to act for him. I spoke to Domaszewicz several times before he was charged. I told him they would bug all his phones, his house and so forth, but Domaszewicz is such a complete chatterbox. He's not very bright. I am quoted as saying in my opening remarks that I am here to defend him for murder, not for being an idiot. Because he had said some extraordinarily silly things. For example, his made-up story about the baby being in hospital.'

The subsequent acquittal angered the police and the prosecution, and enraged much of the public, which had already deemed the odd and bumbling Domaszewicz guilty. As with the ice truck, there have been some consequences of that verdict. Some viewed Colin as a veritable con artist who duped the jury, and for a time his success with jury verdicts dwindled. 'There might be a connection;

I don't know. It's almost as though people thought, *Well, you're the bloke who got D off; if you can do that then you are obviously a bullshit artist and why should we believe anything you say?'*

But the Domaszewicz case has defined his career, a case that will not go away. On 7 November 2006, the front page of the *Herald Sun*, the biggest-selling daily newspaper in Australia, carried the screaming headline '"Greg Did It"'. There were quotation marks around it, thereby passing the buck to the SC responsible—coronial counsel Jim Kennan, a former Victorian attorney-general—but the effect was to confirm the entrenched view. Acquitted in court yet still convicted in the press. How is this possible?

'That's a media headline,' says Colin. 'The coroner can't find that Domaszewicz, having been acquitted, did it. That's the media headline, not what the coroner said. The coroner found that he couldn't say who had done it but found Domaszewicz assisted with disposal of the body. Certain arms of the media have encouraged the view that Domaszewicz got away with murder. The day after the acquittal one front-page headline was "Not Guilty", but the first paragraph was the jailhouse confessions that were never led by the Crown and deliberately not led because they knew they weren't worth a pie and that they would only blow up in their face. Which is what happened at the inquest anyway when they tried to use them. Two of the supposed confessors refused to give evidence, and the third one you could drive a truck through. The case against him was pathetic. There was virtually no evidence against him apart from a lot of innuendo, which went nowhere. He's a bloke who would almost have shouted from the rooftops if he'd done it. He would have given a hint, would have played games, because he does that.'

You may ask why a barrister would want to do criminal law. In Legal Aid cases the stock daily court fee for a QC is about a third of what some silks earn in big corporate cases. And, worse, in criminal law the dirt tends to rub off on the learned friend. In 1984 Colin was the silk defending the publicly loathed paedophile priest Michael

Glennon on a charge of sexually assaulting two boys. Glennon, now in jail until at least 2018 for other sex crimes, on this occasion got off. 'That doesn't mean he was innocent,' says Colin. 'It means the jury found him not guilty.'

When broadcaster Derryn Hinch breached the law by naming Glennon and giving details of his previous convictions, it was Colin who drafted letters of complaint to the solicitor-general. The complaints eventually led to Hinch being jailed. Ironically, around the same time, Colin was engaged by the Melbourne media to fight attempts by former lord mayor Irvin Rockman to suppress publication of testimony in a drug case. In Glennon's case, Colin was fighting against media disclosure of his client's prior convictions; in Rockman's case, he was fighting for media disclosure. But he sees no contradiction. 'The law says you can't reveal priors, and the reason is that a jury will be prejudiced to the point where they won't really bring a verdict according to the evidence.'

Nevertheless, in the eyes of the public the criminal defence counsel is often tarred with the same brush. 'Sometimes you're almost as bad as the client,' says Colin. 'It's almost as if you committed the offence.'

After more than 200 murder trials Colin has mixed with some of the worst villains and rogues you can imagine, but, to quote from *The Godfather*, it's 'business not personal'. 'Just because I've acted for people doesn't mean I have to believe them or like them. You've read the depositions. Just because someone walks in and says, "I didn't do it" ... I often suspect they're lying to me. You'd have to be an absolute cretin if you didn't.'

A what?

Never mind, the well-read and well-lubricated Lovitt QC has moved on, dipping into his collection of memorised lyrics to pay qualified homage to his brethren. 'The Lord High Chancellor from *Iolanthe*,' says Colin. 'That's Gilbert and Sullivan.'

And away he goes:

When I went to the Bar as a very young man,
(Said I to myself, said I,)
I'll work on a new and original plan,
(Said I to myself, said I,)
I'll never assume that a rogue or a thief
Is a gentleman worthy implicit belief,
Because his attorney has sent me a brief,
(Said I to myself, said I!)

I'll never throw dust in a juryman's eyes,
(Said I to myself, said I,)
Or hoodwink a judge who is not over-wise,
(Said I to myself, said I,)
Or assume that the witnesses summoned in force
In Exchequer, Queen's Bench, Common Pleas, or Divorce,
Have perjur'd themselves as a matter of course,
(Said I to myself, said I!)

Ere I go into court I will read my brief through,
(Said I to myself, said I,)
And I'll never take work I'm unable to do,
(Said I to myself, said I,)
My learned profession I'll never disgrace
By taking a fee with a grin on my face,
When I haven't been there to attend to the case,
(Said I to myself, said I!)

JOHN HOERNER

The blind photographer

Life as John Hoerner had known it ended one terrible morning in 2003 when he awoke with a splitting headache at his apartment in Melbourne's South Yarra. 'It was about two o'clock,' he says. 'I've never known pain like it. I'd been working ridiculous hours, seven days a week, fourteen hours a day.' The pain came from a stroke, which was followed quickly by two others that left him physically shattered but, more critically, virtually blind. 'The blood supply had been cut off to a section of the optic nerve and I lost all peripheral vision.'

John's eyesight had been reduced to a pinprick of light, the sort of view of the world you get if you clench a hand and peer through the curled-up fingers. 'When I was in the hospital I thought I was going mad. My remaining vision was kaleidoscopic. I just got snippets—someone's eye or ear or leg—and it didn't make sense. I was doing what everyone else does, looking around quickly, and the therapy people had to teach me to scan slowly so I could put the pieces together. The rest of my body was okay, although I could no longer write and, oddly, I couldn't whistle. It devastated my mind.'

At that stage John and publicist wife Alison Waters, who slept beside his bed while he was in hospital, had been living in their apartment for over twenty years, but he did not recognise it when he returned home. 'At first, when I walked into the room I would be convinced there were five walls. I couldn't figure out where one wall finished and another started, couldn't get the shape of the thing. To this day, if you asked me to draw a design of this small apartment I could not do it, yet I used to have excellent spatial relations abilities. My vision was so limited that if I looked at your shirt collar, I couldn't see your face. If I looked at one eye, I couldn't see the other. And that has not changed.'

It was a grim irony that sunlight became an enemy, due to the glare blocking out what little visual input he had. Here was a man who had pioneered a unique 'solar village' at Victoria's Cape Otway, who had founded an annual race for solar and electric cars. Here was a man who had been flexing his inventive mind since childhood, developing high-fidelity amplifiers before they became the staple of rock bands, patenting a small bottle for wine that is sealed with its own drinking glass, a concept that later took off worldwide (albeit, unfortunately, through someone else). Alison will proudly show you his crude but effective 'lightbulb remover' for ceiling lights: a simple stick with a rubber suction cup at one end and a wad of Blu-Tack inside the cup. It was a similarly ingenious use of an everyday item that brought John back to the sighted world and, incredibly, allowed him to become a photographer who, less than ten years after the strokes, had already had two exhibitions. He's probably the only 'blind' photographer in the world.

However, to appreciate John's fall to earth and his unexpected salvation, you first have to know something of his Icarus-like flight towards the sun. That flight began early, as a student at Melbourne's Trinity Grammar, where he was dux of science in Year 10. His German-born father, Hans, previously in the German merchant navy, was an electrical engineer, who encouraged John's natural feel for science and technology. John won a cadetship in electronics with the Defence department and studied at the Royal Melbourne Institute of Technology, where he built electronic equipment. That led, at age twenty, to his opening a store in Little Lonsdale Street called John H. Hoerner Hi-Fi Stereo Salon, selling amplifiers for classical-music lovers. 'But nasty little kiddies would knock on the door, saying, "Mister, build me an amplifier for my guitar," and I'd say, "Piss off, sonny," not realising that rock'n'roll was about to take off, so how stupid was that? I walked past the opportunity of a lifetime!'

Business boomed, nevertheless, until one day he noticed a report in the newspaper that mentioned something called a 'credit squeeze' and went to his bank manager. 'He told me not to worry, that I'd be fine,' recalls John. 'But the problem was that, to grow my business, I had invested every cent I had, and then some, in the best of the available equipment, and the amount of stock was huge. Suddenly, my sales went from thousands a week to a few dollars a week. It came to an abrupt stop, cleaned me out completely, and I spent a couple of years paying off the creditors.'

Around that time he attended a bottling party, a suburban ritual involving the group purchase of a wine keg that is decanted into empty wine bottles saved for the purpose. 'We had a hand-corker,' says John, 'and I was watching one guy having trouble and offered to help. Actually, I used the fateful words "Let me give you a hand." He hit the cork as I held the bottle, it exploded, and my hand was driven down into the shards. I had seven hours of microsurgery and spent the best part of a year with that right hand strapped up to my chest.' During his rehabilitation, John devised a simple hand exercise using a sheet of newspaper, clasping it in one corner then slowly scrunching it up into a ball.

As therapy, John began painting and then taught himself to frame his better works, but he soon realised that he was a lot better at the framing side. Before too long the John H. Hoerner Art Dealers and Picture Framers business had been launched. It eventually employed 30 people, catering to fine-art collectors and dealers.

'It helped that I had gone to Prahran Mechanics Institute to study industrial design,' he says. 'Everything I've done has been a visual interpretation.'

Successful business, good income—it would seem a basis for a lifetime career. But another Hoerner passion, surf fishing, was about to change his life course again. Whenever he had a chance, John would take off westwards along the Victorian coast to the furthermost tip of Cape Otway, a route that past Lorne became a bumpy dirt track, to where he had found an old shack that he was able to use.

Again, he saw a better and faster way of doing things and devised a spring-loaded flange to replace the screw-on variety that attached the reel to his surf rod. He also started thinking about his transport. 'To get there from Melbourne you really had to have a four-wheel drive,' he says. 'But driving my old Range Rover along that winding road was like driving a truck. So I got the motor enhanced, what they called "blueprinted", built to the finest of tolerances to get the maximum performance. And during a trip to England for my art business I had met a fellow who had an agency for Schuler transmissions, which were especially suited to towing and cross-country driving, and I obtained the agency here in Australia and started rebuilding a Range Rover for myself.'

His new company was called Quadramotive, based in South Yarra, and produced what John called 'automotive architecture,' tailoring Range Rovers to order. There was no workshop: Quadramotive put the vehicles on the back of a flat-top truck and carted them around to the various specialist tradesmen. 'I would tear the vehicle apart in every way you could think of,' says John, 'used it as a kit.' Business grew, and Schuler Range Rovers began appearing on the streets.

John was by this time also getting to his fishing spot a lot faster, the original aim of the exercise, and while he was at the Cape Otway retreat one weekend he received a phone call from a representative of the crown prince of Abu Dhabi who wished to test-drive one of the Schuler Range Rovers—the crown prince was interested in a vehicle that would allow him to go falconing with his sons. As John told ABC Radio's Terry Lane in an interview on 3LO,

> We saw a real opportunity. The envoy told me that if His Highness liked it, he would not order another one; he would order five or six. In the end he bought another ten. For that first one we set a maximum price of $45 000. They supplied a left-hand-drive Range Rover which was flown in on the crown prince's Boeing 707. After we had finished the job the only authentic parts of the Range Rover left were some axle housings and the steering. We used a Group 3 Brock motor, stroked it out to 6 litres, with gas-flow exhaust systems. It went from 200 to 400 horsepower. The grille was 0.6-centimetre steel on edge and immensely strong.

Lane was intrigued: 'So what he got was an English Range Rover body, an Australian Holden engine and some German transmission components?'

Replied John, 'Plus Australian design and craftsmanship.'

The crown prince's Range Rover had a flat floor and open roof to allow the passengers to stand while releasing their falcons. The birds, the Arabs told him, were worth as much as the vehicle. The car could accelerate to 100 kilometres per hour from a standing start in 8 seconds and was capable of running up the side of 100-metre sand dunes.

As well as the crown prince's fleet, Quadramotive produced about 150 vehicles for the Australian market. 'What I was producing then was today's Range Rover Sport.'

During this period the shack John had been using at Cape Otway, plus the 180 hectares of land it stood on, had come up for sale, and John bought them. He still loved the surf fishing and the wilderness, but the feeling grew that he should do 'something useful' with the property. The decision was made to separate out 65 hectares as a unique solar village called Otway Park, a sixteen-lot subdivision using a cluster-type body corporate that would control use of the land. 'For instance, no cats on the site and no cutting down trees,' he says. 'What you got was a patch of land to build on and the wilderness around you. There was no power on the site so energy had to be solar.'

John built the first solar house, but, as with his hi-fi salon, his creative skills were not quite matched by his marketing and he had difficulty in explaining the concept to potential buyers. And the Ash Wednesday bushfires did not help. 'Who needs all-glass houses in the wilderness in bushfire season,' says John. Eventually, he and Alison sold the estate and moved on. 'I had too many balls in the air,' he says. 'The framing business, the car business, the solar village—and Ali and I were building her publicity and PR business, the Waters Group.'

A call to this branch of the family business in 1993 set John off on his next project. A group of Ford engineers in Geelong wanted to build a solar vehicle to enter the triennial solar car race from Darwin to Adelaide and needed help to raise funds. John drove to Geelong, where the engineers were assembling the vehicle in a shed. 'I was blown away by this beautiful machine,' he says. 'It joined all the dots for me. I was passionate about building cars and design and solar energy.'

The Waters Group took it on and the engineers' Aurora solar racer emerged from the drawing board. However, John saw a problem with the Darwin to Adelaide race's three-yearly schedule: 'With that gap in between you are off the radar and we were trying to create awareness of solar energy in the minds of the public and industry.'

And so began Australia's annual SunRace, in 1994. Entry was free—all that competitors had to do was assemble a solar or electric vehicle—and the route each year was strategically plotted to generate as much media exposure as possible. In 2003, the last SunRace before John's illness struck, the nine-day route ran from Adelaide to Melbourne, Canberra and Sydney, and eleven solar, electric and hybrid cars competed. The winner was the Aurora solar car built by engineers at the Royal Melbourne Institute of Technology, which averaged 77 kilometres per hour over the journey, slower than the previous year, when Aurora won with an average 94.5 kilometres per hour.

As usual, the media were all over this late-summer road marathon. According to the *101 Quarterly*, a publication for tenants of 101 Collins Street in Melbourne, this was the 'brain sport of the 21st century', and these 'visually spectacular high-tech "cockroach" vehicles have been demanding media and public attention for quite some years and along the way making some outstanding contributions to sustainable energy and transport technology'. *The Buloke Times*, in regional Victoria, reported that the race tackled the 'petrol dilemma', pinpointing the highlight as 'the battle between RMIT University and the University of New South Wales'. Meanwhile, the *Illawarra Mercury* in New South Wales reported that the cars could 'travel at 100km/h using the amount of energy it takes to make a slice of toast', while the *Plains Producer*, in Balaklava, 100 kilometres north of Adelaide, declared that SunRace 'inspired Australians to see the potential for inventing "green machines" that could easily become cars for the future'.

Riding on this success John plotted a SunRace 2004, to be what he dubbed 'the world's most challenging solar car circuit,' over 2000 kilometres from Melbourne to Sydney and back. At the same time he launched a company called Etek Australia to design road-going electric cars and built three 3-wheeled electric race cars, which he lent to Australian high schools to lubricate the minds of the students. One went to his old school, Trinity Grammar, another to a school in Broken Hill. 'Once they had got their minds around the concept they could then go off and build their own electric or solar cars,' says John.

And then he woke at two o'clock that morning with the strokes that knocked his life for six. 'It wiped out everything,' he says.

An estimated 200 million people worldwide watched the SunRace in 2003, but there was no SunRace 2004, and John, robbed of his sight, faced a bleak future. However, technology came to the rescue. 'It was just after I got home from hospital, and a friend brought along one of the then-very-new digital cameras. He suggested I fiddle around with it.' John turned it on, the digital screen lit up and suddenly he was readmitted to the world of sight. 'I couldn't believe it. It was absolute bliss. The little screen could frame scenes that I could not see myself.' Using the telescopic function he could zoom in on faces. Once again he was able to enter a crowded room and do what everyone else takes for granted: look around to see who's there. 'I can't see it, but my camera can,' he says.

In his frequent travels through the arts scene with Alison, whom he has called his 'life guide,' he began snapping faces along the way. In January 2012, at son Jake's Kick Gallery in Collingwood, central Melbourne, he opened an exhibition called *Out of Sight—Faces in the Arts Crowd through the Lens of a Blind Photographer*. Dame Elisabeth Murdoch, MP Barry Jones and former Victorian governor John Landy were among familiar faces on display when he told the gathering that his rediscovery of life had been a wonderful journey. 'Alison and I try to what we call "bottle the moment," those fleeting times when you see someone in the crowd and you think, *Gosh, that's an interesting face, I just want to capture that.* So that's what I'm trying to do with my work. You could probably call me an indoor street photographer.'

John, with more panoramic vision than he has now, first set eyes on the petite and pretty Alison Waters over three decades ago. 'It was at the Georges store in the Jam Factory shops in South Yarra,' he recalls, 'and I thought she was most beautiful woman I had ever seen. She was working at Hunt Leather, but I was heading off to the United Kingdom to do my Schuler deal and I thought, *This is no good; I'd better do something about it now.* I had some fine stationery at the time from one of my art galleries—it had fancy hot-stamped gold lettering—so I wrote Ali a little note then I went to the florist around the corner and told them to send the note and a giant bunch of flowers.'

When John returned from his trip he asked her for a date and she agreed, but it didn't happen. 'I asked if we could try again and she said she couldn't do this, couldn't do that, and I was getting sick of it. So I said, "Look, I'm going fishing next weekend; do you want to come?" and she said, "Oh, okay!"'

John says that people often ask whether he is angry about losing his sight. 'What's the point?' he asks. 'You simply get up in the morning, see what's written in the sand. And you get on with it."

On the other hand, ask him about solar and watch him fire up. 'It's amazing how quickly times have changed. Back in 2003 practically no one in the community could spell "greenhouse"; they certainly could not spell "solar". The media still can't spell "solar"; the manufacturing world can't spell it either. And if you want the classic example of how dumb this country can be, we had the situation in the University of New South Wales' photovoltaic faculty under Professor Martin Green where a Chinese student was having real troubles getting funding for his PhD activities. He ended up going back to China with the technology he had been working on— developing and improving Martin Green's solar cell—and I think he is now about the fourth or fifth richest man in China. We just have a history of doing stupid things with our technology. We get shot of people at a rate that is unimaginable. We let brilliant people slip through our fingers again and again. I hear politicians to this day talking about being "empowered with opportunities"—what bullshit this is.

'I would say to people, "Don't think for a moment that solar cars run on sunshine." They are like everything else in life: they run on money. If science isn't funded with enough money it simply doesn't happen. That was what SunRace was all about.'

Danièle Kemp, a French presenter on SBS Radio whom he met during the SunRace saga, opened John's 2012 photography exhibition and said his life had turned full circle: he had started with pictures and now had embraced photographs. 'And there is the journey,' she said.

Scientific research on the plasticity of the brain shows there can be incredible results and raises the hope that we can rebuild. But there is a price—you have to work at it. After his three strokes John became not only a photographer but also a philosopher. These are his words: 'If the hand of fate strikes, you can either give in or you can decide that you are going to survive—and perhaps go in a different direction.' And as you can see, John has done that.

The amazing thing is that he has a tiny ray of vision yet you look at the photos and see that he has managed to capture a moment that most people would find difficult to capture. And with a special inner space as well. Each picture seems to be taken from a different angle and shows something very different and deep about each of the characters. I think what comes through in these pictures is John's philosophy of life: of endurance, of fighting back, of not giving up, the courage to ask for help. He believes life is about choices and that happiness is one of these choices. And that it is a good life if you don't weaken.

TIM COSTELLO

The gold jacket

For seventeen of the eighteen warring tribes of the Australian Football League the sight of a gold jacket triggers only abhorrence and despair, for it evokes memories of Joffa, grand chieftain of the Pie people, whipping out the garment from under his tearstained seat in the Collingwood jeer squad and putting it on to signal a victory is nigh. Joffa's jacket was retired in 2010 but, just for a moment, let globally roaming preacher Tim Costello (an Essendon Bombers man) whisk you away to another world, that of Nagaland, in India, where the gold coat carries a quite different message. 'The gold coat is worn there by someone who has given a feast of merit,' says Tim. 'That means hosting a feast for the entire village, particularly the poor, which might go on for weeks until the person involved has liquidated all his assets. When everything is gone you have a gold coat placed on your shoulders in a ceremony of great respect. Then you start again with nothing.' The kicker to his story is that some of these same people, divided into more than 40 different tribes, were headhunters as recently as two generations ago. Skulls can still be seen dangling from the doorways of huts. However, they were converted to Christianity by the missionaries.

Tim, World Vision Australia chief since 2004, travels for three months of the year and has seen many curious—as well as heart-breaking—things. In the Sudan, for example, there is the tradition of the Alok Toch. 'It is a party thrown by a wife's family, who give the husband gifts of money and a feast. Hundreds attend and the highlight is when the wife feeds her husband with a spoon of food and pours a glass of milk down his throat.' Until then, hubby is in virtual purgatory—he cannot eat, drink or even go to the toilet at any meal or party hosted by the wife's family. And family acceptance can take time. 'One Alok Toch I attended was ten years and three children after the wedding!' says Tim.

When we meet he is just back from Niger, where refugee camps are packed because of drought—and desperate men are going 100 metres down dangerous disused mine shafts on ropes, searching for scraps of gold. 'The mines are going to cave in; people die. You see some awful things.' Costello turned 58 in 2012 and is feeling the load. It was a 26-hour economy flight to Niger, and he went straight from the airport to the field. 'The older you are, the harder this gets,' he says.

Tim's middle name is Ewen, and, depending on your point of view, Australia probably owes the name a great debt. 'Dr Ewen was the man who saved my mother's life,' says Tim. 'Mum had rheumatic fever at the age of nineteen and was in hospital for weeks and told she was going to die. Finally, Dr Ewen decided to use some new drugs which were just on the market and she pulled through.'

Some years later, having married fellow teacher Russell, Anne delivered unto the world the high-achieving Costello brothers, poverty crusader Tim and former federal treasurer Peter, and their sister, Janet, who leads a lower profile life as an educator. Russell and Anne turned 92 and 81, respectively, in 2012, still astounded at the national prominence of their boys. 'Mum sometimes looked at us and asked, "How did all this happen?"' says Tim. 'She was quite bewildered by it. We were raised in Blackburn. Mum and Dad were not political at all.'

The Costello parents may have been even more astounded had Tim made the political move that he considered in the 1990s. The Democrats offered him a safe Senate seat, which he accepted at first and then turned down. He later explained to Karen Kissane of Melbourne's *Sunday Age* that it might have been impossible for the family to accept. 'My parents would have found it just too painful. We discussed how, once under a national spotlight, where potentially the Democrats would hold the balance of power on Peter's Budget, the strains would be so great they'd blow family relations apart.' However, Tim's analysis of Don Chipp's bastard-busting organisation gives an insight into the bloke himself. The Democrats served the role of prophets, he says. 'They're not the priestly caste who governs and makes the laws. The prophets are always the ratbags who come from the margins and shake up the system.' Yes, Tim would like to have been a Democrat ratbag.

A few years earlier I had met him at a Melbourne cafe. He was looking thin and wan, having been stricken with malaria in the Congo. 'I was admitted to a hospital there,' he says, 'but a nurse came at me with a hypodermic syringe the size of a cricket bat and I told them, "Just leave me with malaria!" I was so sick the cameraman who accompanied me on the trip bought me a crucifix. In my delusional state I saw this figure approaching me holding a cross and I thought, *This is it! The last rites!* But the difference between me and the Congolese is that I could get medication and I got better. Tens of thousands of them can't and they die. And in a global village in the 21st century why should one child die for the lack of a tablet?'

Tim's job is not for the frail. In 2008 he travelled to Burma to supervise delivery of relief supplies after the Myanmar cyclone. He returned home with an illness that left him exhausted and stripped

15 kilograms from his body over the next two months. Doctors had no answer until a specialist finally identified a rare virus and zapped it with targeted medication. There was a bonus outcome: all that testing had revealed that Tim was gluten-intolerant, and when he altered his diet accordingly his health surged. 'Only problem was,' says Tim, 'I discovered that gluten seemed to be what makes food taste good.'

His job takes him to some of the most bereft and desperate places on earth. Every year tens of thousands of Congolese children starve to death: one in four does not see his or her fifth birthday. 'Four million people died there between 2001 and 2005,' he says, 'mainly through conflict. It has been chaotic, the world's great historical ongoing tragedy. King Leopold II of Belgium personally owned the Congo from 1890 to about 1908. Ten million slaves died digging out the rubber to pay for Brussels and all the magnificent architecture. It wasn't Belgium that owned it; he owned it. It has been a tragic place and it is not even on the radar. There are many reasons, but for a start it is a long way off and it has no oil. This is what we know about humanitarian disasters: if they are not playing to an Australian voice of suffering, they don't touch the heart. But I have hope. Ten years ago, 50 000 kids under five died each day in the world; today it is 30 000, so we have made progress. But I think we are technologically connected and ethically disconnected—we haven't risen above our tribalism. Why are the deaths of kids in East Timor, only 40 minutes' flight from Australia, not personal? What changes with the continental shelf?'

Since his teenage years Tim has kept a diary of his life journey, which, since taking on the World Vision captaincy, has been an adventurous one. In New Delhi he was pulled over in his car by police for 'overspeeding', incurring a fine of 1500 rupees. Tim's Indian companion offered 300 rupees then haggled a sum somewhere between. 'And your tyres are bald,' said the cop as he departed, 'so you are lucky it is not Tuesday because we do bald tyres on Tuesday.' It was corruption, says Tim, but not unexpected.

In Mozambique he was buttonholed by two armed cops and asked for his passport while on a walk near his hotel. The document was back in his room, but his protests were ignored and they threatened to take him to the police station, where he would be locked up for 24 hours. Again, baksheesh came to the rescue and US$100 saw him walk free, with one of the cops shaking his hand and declaring that 'God will bless you!'

However, Tim got lucky. 'It was amazing. A bloke down the road saw me looking furious and asked what the matter was. When I told him the police had stung me he said he was the nephew of the police chief of the village, Maputo. How odd is that? He made some phone calls and the officers brought the money back. I said, "I forgive you; now, what are you going to do tonight?" and they replied, "We are going home to bed; it has been a bad night."'

Not surprisingly, given the horrors he sees on a regular basis, Tim has had bad nights himself. In 1986, even before he took on his World Vision post, he found his faith being tested like never before. He was a Baptist minister in the Melbourne suburb of St Kilda, an area then infamous for street prostitution, drug addiction and social despair. He noted in his diary that he was starting to feel uncharacteristically depressed and lacking in vision, but by chance he and wife Merridie caught a TV program that week on Martin Luther King, a fellow Baptist minister. The program finished with King's famous and inspiring 'I have a dream' speech, and Tim says he felt his heart lift. When his and Merridie's next child was born—which was only a matter of days later—the choice of name was easy: Martin.

'I don't know whether it is my faith or my DNA or psychological make-up,' says Tim, 'but I do find hope resurging. And in surprising places. The curious experience I often have is that the places I fear going most, thinking, *This is going to be terrible*, invariably have shafts of light of hope. It's actually a wonder and a theme in my life. In the Congo, for example, you see women who have made order out of chaos to protect their young. There are militias which plunder and loot and rape, but the women smile, show hospitality and are concerned about me, a man who comes from a First World country that has everything. It is utterly humbling and makes me ask myself, *Where's your perspective, Tim?* Human spirit is extraordinary. In moments of deepest, darkest pain there can be laughter.' And here is a further paradox: the happiest people, says Tim, are the poorest. 'Those who literally have nothing by our standards have this well-spring of joy and it bubbles up and there seems no rational reason. It is extraordinary.'

The concept of the Nagaland gold coat—giving away all your accumulated wealth to your community—is baffling to First World Australia, but Tim says it works only because there is 'the surrounding culture that reinforces and celebrates it. I don't think we have that culture in Australia. I think the Americans do it more. I think our rich are let off the hook relative to American rich and even British rich.' Not that Nagaland is some sort of utopia; it has been at war with India for decades. 'The tribes were promised independence by Ghandi, but he was killed and the Indian army just annexed them and said, "No, you're part of India." I was there doing some peace negotiation. Even between the Nagas there is dispute. Some want to fight, some don't; some want independence, others don't.'

Tim pulls no punches as a poverty campaigner. In Timor he took the military to task for being 'invisible' and failing to protect food convoys. On Aboriginal Australians, he says the 'irony is that almost all the Aboriginal leaders today were trained by the missionaries. They may have been part of the Stolen Generation, but they had education at schools. Now we have gone back to the Indigenous languages in remote communities, that next generation can't read, can't write, can't get jobs.' He has attacked Australian pokies tycoon Bruce Mathieson over the way his machines siphon cash from the population's pockets, saying Mathieson 'has to face up to the social consequences.' As head of the Australian Churches Gambling Taskforce Tim was called a 'wowser' by some sections of the media for opposing the first temporary casino in Melbourne.

But in 2012 he declared that public opinion had changed since then, swinging against the proliferation of these machines. 'Look, I want maximum freedom for people to live a good life but I find this "nanny state" charge really superficial. Was it a nanny state for a Liberal government to introduce seatbelts, or for Kennett to make you have fences around your pool? I find this an extreme libertarian argument—we will continue to prey on people and our defence is "freedom".'

Tim started working life as a solicitor. He was in family law, immersed in its often-spiteful human wrangling, and admits that he sometimes felt like slitting the proverbial wrist. 'I did law because I had a great passion for justice,' he says, 'but I found that the law was not necessarily just. That was part of my disillusionment. God knows all, but a judge doesn't, so you are going to have an imperfect system. It's who can afford the best lawyer.'

He eventually changed tack and trained as a minister with the Baptist Church, with Merridie training as a pastor. From 1987 to 1994 he was the minister at St Kilda Baptist Church, where the congregation was so sparse the church could afford to pay him only $80 a week, so he supplemented his income running a legal practice out of the church, charging only those who could afford it.

He was elected to St Kilda Council and was mayor in 1993–94, during which time he was the same squeaky wheel for the oppressed as he is today. When new Victorian premier Jeff Kennett ordered suburban councils to impose a $100 levy on Victoria home-owners, Tim rode out to battle. 'St Kilda, with the highest population density in Australia, has many privately owned bedsits and one-bedroom flats', he wrote to *The Age* in January 1993. 'This $100 tax, imposed irrespective of property value, has produced enormous anxiety for poorer owner-occupiers … It represents an encroachment on local government independence in turning them into a collection agency for a state tax.' His protest got nowhere, as did his strenuous objection to the government's amalgamation of councils. St Kilda Council was swallowed by Port Phillip Council, and Tim went down in history as the last St Kilda mayor.

Around this time he published the book *Streets of Hope*, which he described as 'a diary of observation of the struggle to build an integrated model of community.' In 2012 he published another book, *Hope*, based on 40 years of diaries, which he says he wrote in five days.

Tim is the first clergyman to head World Vision's Aussie organisation, but he does not wear the clerical collar, saying it can be both a help and a hindrance. Some people will be on their best behaviour in front of a man of the cloth, but for others it can be a negative. 'Those people have a judgmental, authoritarian picture of God and of a reverend who makes them feel guilty. Besides, if I wore a collar I wouldn't hear any good jokes!'

The World Vision annual budget is more than $250 million. 'It comes from mums and dads; we have 400 000 child sponsors,' says Tim. 'We've analysed our donor base and it's very telling—more than 1 million people have donated to us over the years, and overwhelmingly it comes from the poorer postcodes: the least comes from the richer postcodes. The way the model works is that we put together those child sponsorship dollars in what we call an ADP—Area Development Program—typically, that is anywhere from 30 000 to 150 000 people. And we do the education, the agriculture, the health, the microfinancing with small loans to get businesses going. And we move out after fifteen years. They have to be self-sustaining. They mustn't go on with the handout, which is what I think people fear with Australia's Indigenes. But the most beautiful thing for me is being stopped in the street every day by parents who say their sponsored child on their fridge has made a huge difference to their family life, that they have been given a window into the world. They write letters, they visit: it's wonderful.'

The job has seen him mixing with the celebrated as well as the impoverished. He featured in a memorable episode of *MasterChef* with the Dalai Lama, in which one contestant refused to call the Tibetan leader 'Your Holiness' and the program was stymied when the Dalai Lama refrained from taking up his role as a judge. As a Buddhist, that contravened his beliefs. So the onus fell on the Reverend Costello, who earnt a laugh by declaring that as a Christian he was 'more than happy to judge.'

Similarly, as a man of the cloth, he earnt the respect of the late Kerry Packer, once Australia's wealthiest man, and was given a personal rendition of Packer's famous declaration on the afterlife: 'Son, I've been there, and take it from me—there's nothing fucking there.' Packer, of course, was able to call on his own experience, having been revived after he was declared clinically dead from a heart attack.

Tim noted in his diary, 'I respected Packer's honesty that said to live now and refuse any deathbed confession of convenience', recalling the remark attributed to French philosopher Voltaire after being urged to renounce the devil while on his deathbed: 'This is no time to be making new enemies.' However, Tim has no doubt that the 'work of the devil' is a constant in the world. 'I try not to trivialise the fact there is evil in the world,' he says, 'and there are things you fall silent about because you have no answers. I try to be honest about that.'

Security is always an issue in the more perilous areas to which he travels. 'World Vision has security briefings as soon as you land because you don't actually have the cultural fear gene. It's like someone telling me they are walking down Grey Street in St Kilda at two in the morning: I'd freak, but they don't know. Wherever we work overseas our staff is always local, so they do the security briefings. They may say it's fine to walk there, not after this hour, not in this area, here's a phone number, when you see police and think they're here to help, think again!'

Surprisingly, all that globetrotting, through 60 countries, seems to have given him more time with his family than he had as a cleric. 'I can have Sundays to myself now,' he says. 'I can watch my sons play footy.' Tim and Merridie have two sons and a daughter, all in their twenties. Ironically, the favourite TV fare for this crusader against selfish consumption is *Seinfeld*, the American sitcom which is devoted to that very subject. 'It's my turn-off zone,' he says. 'You know there won't be any moralising. In my world you are overwhelmed with the big ethical issues. *Seinfeld* is as superficial and superfluous as they come.'

BOB McMAHON

Pulping that pulp mill

It takes a rare mix of courage and madness to be a rock-climber. In just one recent edition of *Rock*, the Aussie climbers' Bible, you find these three telling signposts. First, a sad tribute to one 51-year-old Brisbane bloke who tumbled to his death off Mount Lindesay on the Queensland–New South Wales border; second, a cheerio to another who was in a coma after a BASE-jump gone wrong in the French Alps; and third, an interview with an eccentric named Crazy John who is infamous for videotaping his own vasectomy (30 000 YouTube views and rising for the right knacker alone).

Crazy John is an American climber who was lured to Tasmania by Cupid and stayed on, even though that particular arrow fell harmlessly to ground. Why did he get a vasectomy? 'I see seven billion people on the planet as a scourge,' he told the magazine. 'Some people get tattoos or wear a T-shirt in protest, I got sterilized. I reckon if everyone followed my example, all of humanity's ecological and social problems would be solved in less than 100 years.'

The bloke critically injured in the French Alps, who had renamed himself Lucky Chance, broke his pelvis, jaw, leg and foot, and suffered a collapsed lung and head injuries. He still calls himself Lucky—the accident didn't injure his sense of humour—and appreciative friends and admirers have chipped in more than $30 000 towards his medical bills.

Want more? The same magazine tells of a so-called Suicidal Beginners Club, an international organisation founded in the 1900s when a Pom named John Laycock used to scale big rocks in England's Peak District in a tweed suit and hiking boots. This club is for people 'wanting to start climbing, regardless of their lack of experience or safety equipment'. Yikes.

So far, Launceston's Bob McMahon, a veteran on the ropes and the author of a swag of rock-climbing books, has not cracked anything serious, even though he has been swinging off steep verticals for decades. Nor has he allowed a surgical scalpel anywhere near his golden apples. But, like Forrest Gump, Bob's been walking. He just started out one day, determined to walk the entire coast of Tasmania, beach by beach, cove by cove, stretch of scrubland by stretch of scrubland. Although, unlike Gump, he is doing it in stages. 'More than 1500 kilometres so far,' says Bob cheerfully, 'but it is something I never want to end, so I am getting distracted now by the islands. I'll see one from the shore and think, *I just gotta go there.* So I fly out. Latest has been Cape Barren Island. I was ten days out there. I just take a tent. I've spent most of my life in a tent. You get the most beautiful sunsets in Tasmania.'

Bob started off in Coles Bay, on the east coast and by 2012 had made it to Strahan. He told *Wild* magazine's Ross Taylor that the inspiration for this personal walkathon came one night when camped on Mount Parsons, in Freycinet National Park.

'We were looking down across Flowstone Wall. It was a full moon, the sea looked like a piece of velvet and those wonderful whipped toffee slabs dropping—what would it be—500 metres into the sea? I just loved that freedom.'

So you are guessing by now that Bob is a quiet sort of bloke, a fella who likes his solitude. And you'd be half-right. Bob confesses that he was a nervous sort as a kid, had a bad stutter, and, yes, he loves the space of the great outdoors, far from the chattering crowds. But then there is the other half of Bob, the fierce, campaigning Bob, who was a key player in one of the longest and most bitter public campaigns in Australian history, which rocked the state of Tasmania for more than eight years. We're talking here about the infamous Gunns pulp mill project, which tore the Tassie community apart and, according to Bob, hampered the progress of the state for almost a decade. 'But the campaign is often misunderstood,' he says. 'Everyone thinks it was environmental. It was actually a community campaign, a socioeconomic campaign that began because of a great sense of injustice, because the costs and the risks were going to be borne by the community, and the benefits, if any, were going to be gained by private enterprise with massive government support.'

When Gunns first announced the project, in 2004, it was to be a chlorine-free mill using plantation trees, and it was welcomed by federal government and Opposition alike. Prime minister John Howard pledged $5 million as a pre-election sweetener, and Opposition chief Mark Latham hailed the project as you-bloody-beaut for both the environment and the economy. But only a year later the company conceded that chlorine would be used and that trees from native forests would also be pulped—and concerns grew. In December 2005 more than 2500 people rallied in Launceston to protest, despite the view of the Tasmanian Chamber of Commerce and Industry that the mill was of 'vital public importance.'

And so the arguments raged, for seven years, until in March 2011 federal Environment minister Tony Burke gave the nod: the plant could be built. It seemed to be the final green light but wasn't. By then Gunns was in financial strife and a year later told the stock exchange the mill might not go ahead. Tellingly, the company accountants began listing the $250 million already spent as an 'expense' rather than an 'asset' and, despite a squeak of hope from

premier Lara Giddings, Bob and his Tasmanians against the Pulp
Mill campaigners were claiming victory.

'They've got no hope,' says Bob, who virtually saw six years of
his life disappear for the cause. 'At the height of the campaign my
phone would start ringing at 6 a.m. and wouldn't stop till midnight.'

How Bob was swept up into this marathon struggle is a story in
itself and takes us halfway across the world to Chile and a moment-
ous fluke. In January 2005 Bob was heading south on a flight out of
Santiago to sail some yachts, climb some rocks. By chance he was
seated next to a young bloke named Paul, who was headed for the
Chilean city of Temuco to see his girlfriend. Paul was reading a newspaper, and there was a report in it that caught Bob's eye concerning
widespread pollution caused by a new pulp mill in the wetlands at
Valdivia, in southern Chile. It was an environmental cock-up of the
first order, with wildlife dying and the communities in uproar. Calls
had been made for the mill to be shut down, a reaction which left
Paul feeling no small pang of guilt, for he was an architect with the
firm involved in the mill's design and construction.

'Of course,' says Bob, 'there was a similar pulp mill planned for
Bell Bay, in Launceston's Tamar Valley, and when I returned home
I discovered that it was not to be a chlorine-free mill; it would be a
standard mill, right in everyone's backyard, on the banks of the Tamar
River and adjacent to the woodchip mountains at Long Reach.'

Now here's the thing: Launceston and Valdivia are almost
geographic twins. They both are on the same latitude, are located
at the confluence of two rivers (South Esk and North Esk for
Lonny, Calle-Calle and Cruces for Valdivia) and are subject to
tidal changes (3 metres for Lonny, 1 for Valdivia). It was no coincidence that two reps from the Tasmanian government's pulp mill
task force visited the Valdivian wetlands in 2005, releasing a report
on the mill early the following year that mentioned a dramatic loss
of bird life due to the 'severe and widespread decline of an aquatic
plant' but stating that the cause was 'inconclusive'. Bob thought
this was hogwash.

A little earlier in 2005 a Chilean forestry student, Marianela Rosas, had visited the University of Tasmania's Launceston campus and given a lecture on this growing Chilean scandal. There had been violent protest from local fishermen about effluent pumped into the sea by the pulp mill, she said. The mill had been forced to shut down three times by regulators because of environmental concerns. And, most tragically, all the beautiful black-neck swans of the area had died or departed. In scenes more befitting a horror movie, some of these graceful birds had even fallen dead from the sky, a number crashing through car windscreens.

It was evidence Bob could not ignore. With the huge $2.3 billion Gunns project seemingly rubberstamped, he flew back to Chile to see for himself. His only contact was Marianela Rosas, but the cabbie who drove Bob in from the airport, a bloke named Luis, was the first to raise the red flag.

Luis heard why Bob was there and began waving his arms. '*Los cisnes mueren! Los pájaros mueren!*' he shouted, words that sent a shiver down Bob's spine. He knew enough Spanish to recognise *cisnes*, the word for swans; *pajaros*, birds; and *mueren*, from the verb *morir* (like the French *mourir*), death.

'Luis took his hands off the steering wheel and flapped his arms like a bird flying,' recalls Bob. 'He was almost in tears. It was obvious that something awful had happened there.'

Marianela introduced Bob to Eduardo Jaramillo, professor of ecology and marine biology, the man who had traced the cause of the pollution in the Valdivian wetlands. He explained that the area had been flat agricultural land until 1960, when the Cruces river valley dropped up to 2 metres after a massive earthquake. The epicentre was 570 kilometres south of Santiago and a consequent tsunami sent waves of up to 25 metres surging against the Chilean coast, killing 5700 people, flooding the valley and creating the wetlands. Two months later the Riñihue Lake collapsed and also flooded the valley, the first time it had done so since 1575. In his blog Bob noted that the first environmental problems were noticed early in 2004 when *luchecillo* (egeria densa), an aquatic plant that is a main food source for the swans and other bird life, began dying. Soon afterwards brown water began flowing down the river into the city. Aerial photos showed a stark difference between the clear waters of the Calle Calle river and the brown Cruces. Later that year the number of black-neck swans fell sharply because of migration and unexplained death.

Residents in Valdivia suspected the pulp mill 50 kilometres upstream, which produced around 560 000 tonnes of pulp a year, and an $80 000 study was commissioned. The culprit was pin-pointed—wastewater from the mill. The aluminium sulphate being used to treat the water had produced aluminium hydroxide that caused damage to the aquatic plants. The *luchecillo* plants just turned to mush. Dead swans were found to be 2 kilograms lighter than healthy birds and their stomachs were found to contain nothing but sediment and parasites.

Horrified by this ecological nightmare, Bob returned home and threw himself into the campaign against the Gunns plant. 'We organised river rallies,' he recalls, 'big flotillas of boats. We had up to 15 000 people protesting in the streets of Launceston. Although Tasmanians against the Pulp Mill had only small numbers in Tasmania, about 1600 on our email list, we had vast numbers of hits on our website. We managed to turn both the West Tamar Council and the Launceston City Council against the mill with sheer public pressure.'

By 2007 the man with a childhood stutter was addressing public protest meetings, telling one gathering in West Tamar that the region had been set up to be a sacrifice zone. 'But the sacrifice zone is not restricted to the Tamar and its 100 000 people,' he said.

> It extends into Bass Strait, where the Bass Strait fishery could be wiped out. Who would want to catch, buy, let alone eat fish that is contaminated or perceived to be contaminated? Would you?
>
> And it gets even worse. The sacrifice zone extends to all the farmland of Tasmania, especially the farmland in

*the north of the state. The area of plantations required to
feed this pulp mill, one of the biggest modern pulp mills in
the world, will gobble up our farmland. Tasmania will have
to sacrifice food production for tree plantations: perhaps all
our food production if this dumb project is allowed to run
its course. That is not a fair exchange. That is suicide. You
can't eat trees. Tasmania produces 70 per cent of all Australia's processed vegetables. Already more than 20 per cent of
our farms have gone under trees. The pulp mill, if it were to
last 100 years, as pulp mills do, requires just about all of our
farmland.*

Bob threw up some figures, and losses outweighed gains. For every
dollar the pulp mill generated, Tasmanians would lose 3 dollars
through loss of food and wine production, fishing, tourism and the
rest. 'We are told the pulp mill would generate $6.7 billion over
30 years. In that time Tasmania will lose something in the order of
$20 billion.'

Bob was as surprised as anyone when he became a firebrand
orator, but it was not the first time he had surprised himself. 'I found
myself years ago lining up in a queue at the arts school down in
Hobart,' he says wryly. 'I don't recall making a decision to do that.
I suppose I must have signed up to be a teacher. The only way to get
a tertiary education in those days was to get a studentship. We had
no money. Not a brass razoo.'

Yes, living in Stanley, population 700, the McMahon household
was heavy on numbers and light on cash. Bob had seven brothers
and didn't meet his father until he was 23. His English-born mother,
a former sailor in the Royal Navy, married again to a waterside
worker named Keith. 'Good bloke,' says Bob. 'I don't count the
blood thing—it's the person who does the work and brings you up.
I regard Keith as my father.'

His biological father was in the Australian navy. 'He met my
mother at Portsmouth when his ship was over there. He was a classic

naval pisspot: when he came home on leave from Korea he just went up the bush and got pissed, didn't bother coming home to see his wife and kids. There was just me and two brothers then.'

Five more boys came along with the second marriage and they were all big lads. One broke the Australian powerlifting record at age 40; another was at the London Paralympic Games in 2012 with the Australian weightlifting team. 'But there are only six left now,' says Bob. 'One brother died young, and my 57-year-old brother, Tommy, who had been a policeman, dropped dead recently. He was a big fellow; he'd been feeling unwell and been checked by a cardiologist the previous day. Was told his heart was fine.'

Bob's time at the Hobart art school provided both an education and a romance. At age eighteen he met Susie, a sixteen-year-old art student and now his wife of over 40 years, who makes dolls for customers all over the world. They were still at school when they wed, in 1971. 'We hitchhiked up from Hobart to Launceston to get married in the registry office,' says Bob.

'I had to extract him from a bunny boiler first,' says Susie.

Now the couple have two children, Andy and Iseult, and five grandchildren. The pulp mill campaign stole much of their lives, both private and professional. The Tamar mouse that roared started off as the Tamar Residents Action Committee, but dissolved and reformed as Tasmanians against the Pulp Mill, or TAP, before evolving into TAP into a Better Tasmania because members 'didn't want to sound negative.'

Lynn Hayward, one of the Tamar campaigners, said Bob was hesitant at the beginning to take on the leadership. 'He didn't like the idea of getting up in front of large crowds,' she says. 'I remember encouraging him to take it on because I always thought he had great leadership qualities and he's an incredibly intelligent bloke. He is very knowledgeable about the history of Tasmania. It took enormous courage to do what Bob and Susie did, which is why it has been bitterly disappointing how some of the mainstream environmental movement behaved towards him. They do deals, but Bob never did—he doesn't fit the organisational mould. He held the line, never wavered. And he and Susie were sometimes criticised and attacked for it, often by people you might think would be on their side.'

Bob concedes that he and Susie eventually grew weary of the fight. 'I did hundreds and hundreds and hundreds of speeches and interviews,' says Bob. 'I spent half my life on the phone.' Protesters stopped short of chaining themselves to trees or bulldozers, but Bob says they were 'keeping their powder dry.' The group had contingency plans ready in case the mill ever materialised; says Bob, 'They could not imagine what we had in store.'

Susie says Bob became the group's go-to bloke because he could think on his feet. 'The media would be ringing here at 6 a.m. for an interview when we were still in bed, and Bob would just open his eyes, start talking and make sense.' Their house became a campaign headquarters, with callers providing a continual flow of information. 'No one to this day can work out how we were so far ahead of them,' says Bob. 'A typical call would be something like, "I can't tell you how I found this out, Bob, but …".' Then, having passed on a useful tip, the caller would hang up.

And so, in September 2012, Gunns, the 137-year-old timber company crashed to the ground like one of its chainsawn trees. It was $900 million in debt; its shares (once as high as $16) worth 2 cents. The protest campaign, the falling pulp prices, the high Aussie dollar: all had combined to send the company into administration. By then the McMahons had had enough. Susie went back to her internet doll-making business, and Bob, named by *Rock* magazine as one of Australia's 50 top climbers, was back to clawing his way up impossibly steep cliff faces as an instructor. That David and Goliath battle must now seem like some crazy and exhausting dream. Strange thing is, Bob never planned to get involved; he just happened to sit next to a bloke on a plane to Chile.

Postscript

Bob McMahon, climber of mountains and conqueror of pulp mills, died suddenly as this book was about to be published. Seemingly fit and robust, Bob passed away in his sleep. Wife Susie told me: 'We are all in shock, but it was mercifully quick and pain-free—how he would have wished it. He just went to sleep and didn't wake again.'

Bob was 62 and you had to suspect that his marathon fight against the pulp mill had taken more out of him than anyone suspected. However, he left a priceless Australian legacy—a Tamar Valley unsullied by the sort of problems that devastated the Valdivian wetlands in Chile.

His drive and energy helped slay a corporate giant yet Bob remained a modest man to the end. When I flew to Launceston to meet him late in 2012, he picked me up at the airport, genuinely perplexed that I deemed him worthy of this book and a little embarrassed to find himself among the better-known names. 'Are you sure you want to talk to *me*?' he asked.

His story speaks for itself.

GARRY BARKER

War and peace

The top of Che Guevara's large mahogany desk at the Cuban bank was bare apart from a gourd of *maté*—a kava-like narcotic brew—and a 9-millimetre Browning pistol, which the guerrilla chief kept spinning on its side with a finger.

'Each time the pistol ended up pointing at me,' says Garry Barker, 'he would look up and smile.'

Garry had been taken there around midnight by two toughs in a Chevy. 'Guevara had become president of the Banco Nacional after the revolution,' says Garry, who had travelled to Cuba as New York correspondent for the Herald & Weekly Times group to seek out Guevara, Fidel Castro and a former American soldier named Murphy who had fought for Fidel and now claimed to have become a frog farmer. By chance, Garry had got Ernest Hemingway into the bargain after wandering into the brutish wordsmith's favourite Havana watering hole, the El Floridita, a few days earlier.

'That stool's reserved,' the barkeep had said, and Garry had moved over just before a hangdog Hemingway, with grizzled beard, came lurching through the swinging doors wearing a sailor's cap. Garry wrote later, in the *Melbourne Age*

> *The rest of the evening is hazy. If I said that Hemingway and I swapped stories I would be gilding the lily but we, and mostly he, spoke of derring-do, the Australian outback, manhood, bulls and the fighting of them (not, I assured him, yet done in any formal way in Tennant Creek). Others came in and the conversation veered and turned again and all the while the bartender fed us his potent mixture.*

That was the high-octane Papa Doble, a frozen daiquiri named in the author's honour and constituting what Hemingway would have termed 'a man's drink': 90 millilitres of Bacardi or Havana Club rum, the juice of two limes and half a grapefruit, and 2 millilitres of cherry brandy, all blended with ice. Garry says it is somewhere between a Boilermaker (a double shot of neat Scotch drunk in one gulp, followed by a beer) and neat nitroglycerine but it tastes better: 'Strong, citrus-tart, icy-cold in the mouth, richly warming in the blood.'

Hemingway was in decline back then, his former drinking pals both unable and unwilling to keep pace. He was morose—he had the genetic disease haemochromatosis—and two years after Garry encountered him he killed himself, as his father had done, with his favourite 12-gauge shotgun. He talked to this Aussie stranger of 'things past and things not done,' remarking that he had long wanted to visit Australia, a 'man's country.'

It was more than daunting for Garry—here was the literary giant, the Nobel laureate author of *For Whom the Bell Tolls* and *The Old Man and the Sea*, towering over him in full alcoholic flight. 'I was trying to keep up with one of the greatest boozers America has ever produced,' he says.

Hemingway's fourth wife, Mary, eventually turned up to guide the great man home. 'She ignored most of us and waited while the bartender filled a quart-sized Thermos jug with icy-frothy pinkish-white daiquiri mixture—Hemingway's nightcap—then they left.'

Garry's hangover the next day was monumental, but he managed to front up and hear, through a struggling interpreter, Castro give a feisty address to the nation that 'went on forever.'

The adventure continued. A Russian engineer whom Garry met at his hotel let slip that he had been brought in to work on proposed missile sites, the Cold War project that eventually provoked the thirteen-day Cuban Missile Crisis between the United States on one side and Cuba and the Soviet Union on the other. Garry filed a story and Castro threw him out of the country 24 hours later, never to return.

Garry was a correspondent in the days when newspaper chains spent big on foreign bureaus. He was four years in New York, where he 'covered the United Nations, saw Khrushchev bang on the desk with his shoe, that sort of stuff,' then spent eight years each in Singapore and London. He met Cambodia's Prince Sihanouk, watched the fall of Indonesia's Sukarno, reported coups and counter-coups in Thailand and covered the Vietnam War. And, yes, this is the same Garry Barker who, in his eighties, is now a leading Melbourne-based commentator and podcaster on IT and technology, having accomplished one of the great career reinventions of modern journalism by becoming Macman. His new media persona earnt him the inaugural Pearcey Media Award, in 2001, when, at 68, he was hailed as 'one of Australia's most prolific generalist IT writers.' Says Garry, who survived prostate cancer in his late seventies, 'Never retire. Age needs purpose and activity. Ergo, reinvention of oneself.'

As Macman, he has chalked up further notable interviews, including tech-head super-hero Steve Jobs. Garry says he first laid eyes on the Apple chief at his company headquarters, at the wonderfully geeky Californian address of 1 Infinite Loop, Cupertino, where

Jobs—in customary jeans and black turtle-neck shirt—chowed down with the rank and file in the staff canteen. Garry met him face to face a year later, in a giant suite atop a five-star Tokyo hotel. 'Jobs was an intensely private person,' he recalls. 'I was soon to learn just how private he wished to be. He was sitting at a desk with two or three computers, playing with a new font design for Apple, typing the names of his kids, Reed, Erin and Eve. I asked if he missed them and he said yes, he resented the travel that took him away too much.' Garry then commented on the Apple chief's suit—a 'terrible grey one with pink stripes'—and Jobs explained that his wife, Laurene, had told him to wear it because the Japanese were so formal. 'I thought all this was too good to leave out,' says Garry, 'so it led my story.'

The Apple grapevine later told him, 'Steve thinks you intruded on his family life—don't expect a Christmas card!'

It has been an extraordinary eight decades so far for Garry, and it all started in New Zealand, where his parents, Arthur and Marianne, were farmers in Canterbury. Arthur killed himself when Garry was seventeen. 'Cut his throat with a razor,' says Garry. 'I found him one day in the milking bay at the farm. Terrible for my mother. We had no money; things were pretty tight. My brother, Roger, and I have never really forgiven him. You know, I never had a conversation with my father, not a proper one. I think it was part of the generation at that time.

'He'd falsified his age to go to World War I as a sixteen-year-old. He never spoke about it, but in the top of the wardrobe he had a German Luger and a wide webbing belt of badges—cap badges, shoulder flash badges, British, Australian, German, you name it. Even an Iron Cross. Looking back, I think he was one of the guys assigned to go out into no-man's-land to see if there was anyone left and possibly decide whether they could be brought back or dispatched.

'He gave up as a farmer. I think he was damaged by the war. You wonder about the torments he was going through. He was only 48.'

Garry sometimes feels a bit guilty about leaving home a few years afterwards and moving to Australia, leaving his widowed mother behind. He had started at university in Christchurch to study engineering, but the maths stumped him and he signed on as a cadet journalist with the Christchurch Press, on 32 shillings and sixpence a week. Roger, an accountant, later became the newspaper's general manager.

After a couple of years at the journalist's craft Garry sent a story to the Melbourne *Herald* about a 'mad Kiwi bastard' on a motorbike setting a world speed record on a country road, and it was published. 'The Herald regularly sent blackbirding parties to New Zealand looking for journalists,' says Garry, 'and I was offered a job and 10 quid a week: big money then. I stayed in a boarding house in Jolimont, East Melbourne, run by a woman whose husband was a dipso. He used to ricochet along the walls of the hallway to shake hands with anyone who came through the front door. They had a motto on the wall in a frame: "It's a permanent personal pleasure to please you".' Then he moved into a rented house with four others, a bachelor dive they dubbed the Heartbreak Hotel. 'Grace Brebner, the first senior woman police officer in Victoria, lived next door,' says Garry, 'and used to disapprove that Saturday nights were a bit noisy. When we ran out of funds we'd go out the back and collect the empty bottles to get the seed money to start the next party.'

Nothing wrong with Garry's memory: that was over half a century ago. 'Somewhere up there, someone must be forgiving my sins,' he says. 'God knows how, but I became the *Herald* motoring writer and had a ball testing cars for two years, before the editor came over one day in 1958 and asked if I would like to go to New York. I thought for a nanosecond and said yes.'

Four years later he moved to Singapore, where he met and married Jenny Smith, of the British foreign office. Her brother, in the Royal Navy's Fleet Air Arm, was flying helicopters in Borneo. Garry by then had learnt to fly and was vice-president of the

Singapore Flying Club. 'I invited Jenny's brother to the club. He brought his little sister, and that was that,' he says.

'The club had a contract with some Singapore banks to run "pay drops" to rubber plantations in Malaya, today's Malaysia. There were bandits on the roads around the plantations who could have ambushed a car. All we had to do was drop the money in a big leather bag onto the football field at each plantation and enjoy a couple or so hours of free flying. My instructor Bob Harrington was a Royal Air Force pilot who flew a Hastings in the Berlin Airlift. His tailfin number was 555, so his call sign was State Express, a brand of cigarette that had 555 on the packet.'

No, nothing wrong with Garry's memory at all. In 1995 he was one of 68 Australian journalists to be awarded service medals for reporting the war in Vietnam. He had been there when the Buddhist monks launched their protest and witnessed an elderly monk douse himself with petrol, light a match and collapse in the flames. Reports out of Vietnam were heavily censored, but the newshounds found a way. 'We set up a pigeon system,' says Garry. 'One of us would gather everyone's copy, film and audiotapes into a suitcase and, surrounded by a posse of shouting, gesticulating reporters, he would race through Tan Son Nhat terminal at the last minute to catch a Pan Am flight to Hong Kong or Singapore. The police knew what was going on, but no one got shot or arrested. Besides, it was worth the risk to get a night of luxury at the Peninsula Hotel in Hong Kong.'

In contrast, Garry recalls spending a night in an 'ancient and diseased establishment' in Da Nang, the only accommodation available after he returned from a patrol with the South Vietnamese army. 'The sewer pipes had long given up the fight,' he wrote later, 'and evil effluent from the bogs ran sluggishly along an open drain in the floor on the veranda. In a shop I found a large bottle of very cheap eau de cologne, soaked a towel in the perfume, hung it over a pedestal fan and tried to get some sleep'.

Reaching the war zones was almost too easy: correspondents could take a cab to the Tan Son Nhat airport and, equipped with a military pass, hitch a ride on an aircraft flying out. Garry saw a lot of the war 'over the shoulder of a machine-gunner slouched in the open doorway of a Huey helicopter gunship.' Sometimes the correspondents were able to hitch a ride right out of the war, because the military aircraft went everywhere: the United States, Hong Kong, Manila, even Australia.

In a piece for *The Age* in 1995 Richard Yallop said Garry 'had gone to Vietnam against the background of the communist insurrection in Malaya, and it had seemed that he was reporting the West's last stand against the rising communist tide'. Garry said he felt back then that there was some sense to the conflict, and he respected and identified with the Australian troops. 'I tried not to take sides, and simply report what was going on. For me the war was a great adventure. I think it was for most correspondents. It was the adrenaline run. I enjoyed it thoroughly, even though I was scared witless.'

He revisited Vietnam for a newspaper feature in 2000 and wrote,

The Vietnamese never seem to throw anything away. All over the country great heaps of stuff—metal, wood, barbed wire, packaging, vehicle parts—are to be seen, a good part of it the debris of war. On a visit to the Korean Tiger division that had supported the American effort, I spoke to Colonel Chung whose father had become rich buying and selling the shrapnel, wrecked vehicles and other detritus of the Korean War. 'Some day,' he said, as we sat on the hill sharing his bottle of excellent single-malt whisky, 'someone will get rich from scrap metal here too.' They're still picking up metal from the battlefields of Vietnam. People are still losing legs and arms, too. Unexploded shells and bombs do that. Occasionally even unwary tourists get hurt among the thousands of tonnes of weapon debris still littering the demilitarised zone and many battlefields. Neil Davis, who was the war's most celebrated TV news cameraman, played patron to a legless urchin beggar boy whose patch was the sidewalks near Lam

Son Square in Saigon. Most mornings he would accost us on the terrace of the Continental Hotel or at Givral, the corner café where many of us ate breakfast. The kid got around on a skateboard—just a board, a cushion, four caster wheels and two short sticks with which he pushed himself along. Watching him cross a busy street was truly awe-inspiring. On this trip I met a legless beggar man of maybe 50 scooting around outside the Paloma café and the Grand Hotel, a couple of hundred metres closer to the Saigon River from the Continental. I tried but could not confirm that he was the same person. Some expatriates had recently chipped in to buy him a wheelchair. He used it for a week then went back to his old skateboard. In the streets of Saigon today, a man with a wheelchair is seen to be rich and not in need of alms—but a beggar on a skateboard can scratch an existence.

Garry survived seven years of the Vietnam War unharmed, but he saw numerous colleagues killed and wounded. 'The worst thing that happened was during the Tet Offensive, in 1968. A cadet on *The Herald*, Bruce Piggott, came to Vietnam thinking that war was fun. One day at the Australian Associated Press office he heard that a North Vietnamese army unit was in Cholon, in the other half of Saigon (today's Ho Chi Minh City), and like idiots he and some others got in a Mini Moke and drove over there. They ran into the North Vietnamese and were shot dead.'

Eventually, Garry grew weary of the futility. 'I didn't think killing people and blowing them up was the answer.' He was aged 28 when he first reported from Vietnam, as one of about a dozen correspondents. When he finished, at age 35, there were 600 correspondents, and the American forces had grown from 1000 to 600 000, with no victory in sight. 'We fool ourselves,' he says, 'because it's not one country; it is Cochin and Tonkin, and the war that we pay so much attention to is but a chapter, maybe just a couple of paragraphs, in a conflict that has been going on between the two for 2000 years. They call it the American War; we call it the Vietnam War.'

Garry returned to Melbourne and became foreign editor, responsible for handling the likes of talented but wayward Bruce Wilson, the buccaneering correspondent with a taste for the Hemingway life. 'Bruce would ring me and say things like, "There's a great story in Mongolia," and I would ask what it was then say, "Well, I guess we should cover it," and he'd reply, "I'm already here."'

After two years of increasingly itchy feet, Garry was asked if he would like to head up the London bureau. This time cogitation took only half a nanosecond. He and Jenny, at that point expecting a child, were off and the adventures resumed. Garry travelled to Northern Ireland during the Troubles, meeting some of the Sinn Fein and at one stage spending a few days in the barracks of one of the Royal Marine commando units. 'The saddest part was when the IRA kneecapped a dog that the British had befriended. Some arsehole shot its back legs out. It had to be destroyed. The hatred was unforgiving, unrelenting.'

As a correspondent, Garry 'scraped acquaintance' with all sorts of people: former prime minister Ted Heath, the 4-minute miler Roger Bannister, even Enoch Powell, the 'Rivers of Blood' MP who damned the mass immigration of the 1960s. 'I followed him when he was campaigning for votes through Wolverhampton,' says Garry. 'He was interesting, a brilliant historian. He would run from house to house, knocking on doors. It was exhausting. The whole media would run after him. I got sick of it after a while, watching ladies in pinafores shutting the door in his face, so I took a break and bought a drink at a corner shop run by a Pakistani. I said to him, "Suppose you won't be voting for Mr Powell," but he said he would.

'"Any more people like me come to this town," he told me, "my shop gets burnt down."

'And suddenly you understood at grass roots the pressures—and that was way back. You would find most people in England would agree with Powell now.'

Garry met and drank with Nobel Prize–winning German chancellor Willy Brandt. 'A friend of mine was Willy's speechwriter and sort of shuffled me into the inner circle. We were having a drink at a bar in Coburg one time—it was on top of an old fort that overlooked the East German border. From there you could see the dogs running the wire, the VoPos, or East German police, in their towers, the searchlights and whatnot. Willy liked a beer. He emptied his stein then absent-mindedly picked mine up and drank that. We didn't argue: my friend just bought me another. And one for Willy.'

Garry covered the Middle East at the time of the Lebanese Civil War, when militia shelled the Holiday Inn; and he flew to Saudi Arabia after the assassination of King Faisal. 'I met his successor, Prince Fahd, on an aeroplane going back from London to Riyadh. He and his wife, very glamorous and expensively dressed, were sitting across the aisle. This was a time when Australian senior correspondents travelled first class.' Indeed, no expense spared. When Garry and Jenny—by now with two daughters, Victoria and Charlotte—eventually left London for Fiji, where Garry was to manage the *Fiji Times and Herald* for 'four horrible years,' they flew the United Kingdom to United States leg on Concorde, courtesy of the Herald & Weekly Times. 'Fiji was great socially,' says Garry, who had the use of a 6-metre cabin cruiser and an open invitation to the Fijian governor-general's private island. 'But I'm a journalist, not a businessman.' On the day the family moved back to Australia the Herald & Weekly Times won a court judgment in a defamation case brought against it by the prime minister, Ratu Mara. 'We had won, but sometime after that, Ratu Mara sacked the judge who brought down the decision, appealed before another judge and won. Fiji's a bit like that. It's a sad, sad place.'

Upon Garry's return to Melbourne after so long away, it was quickly obvious that office life at *The Herald* had moved on. 'I went up to a board lunch,' he says. 'All the senior journalists were there. When I came in you could see the body language: they all moved up and left no space. It was caution, I suppose. Worried someone might be going to lose their position. And, of course, I had no network. Stacks of friends in the United States and London—but no one here.'

He was posted to suburban newspaperland as editor-in-chief at Standard Newspapers. 'The most interesting thing that happened there was a five-week strike,' he says, 'and I ran all the group's newspapers pretty much on my own. Then we were taken over by News Limited, and Standard was amalgamated with Leader. I was sent to one division as the toecutter, a role I hated. I moved to Leader's headquarters, in Blackburn, where I interested myself in printing. We were among the first papers in the country to do good offset colour photographs on newsprint. That's where I really met the Macintosh. I learnt about printing and technology. That's where it all began.'

After 37 years he left the Herald & Weekly Times group and, after a brief hiatus, joined *The Age*, first as a production subeditor on the computer section, then writing for it and starting the Macman column. In 2013, Garry and former *Age* business journalist Leon Gettler were into their third year of podcasting *Talking Business* through the Royal Melbourne Institute of Technology. They had a second podcast too, called *Talking Technology*. 'We interview people doing interesting technological things,' says Garry. 'A man who rejoices in the name of Igor Pasternak is one. He's developing airships that he hopes will replace fixed-wing freight planes and trucks.'

And so, the man who used to drop cash on Malayan rubber plantations, who downed high-octane Papa Dobles with Ernest Hemingway and saw eight years of war, coups and counter-coups, became a podcaster from a suburban living room and a maker of video documentaries. But a long line of files containing the myriad newspaper reports from his travels—some bound professionally into books by the prisoners at Changi jail—sit on a shelf in his study, testament to his amazing life in an era when print was king. And, while much of Garry's life now is based on the internet, he concedes that it has become a modern-day Tower of Babel. 'The thing that is lacking is true provenance. Can you believe what you read there? Bringing more sanity to this sort of thing is the best opportunity newspapers have got.'

A footnote: that man called Murphy, the former American soldier who fought for Fidel Castro and now claimed to be a frog farmer. Did Garry ever find him?

'Yes,' he says. 'It was at one of Castro's interminable harangues on TV. Murphy had accompanied Castro to the TV station but he took no part in the event. I found him near the studio door, behind the crowd of Castro supporters crammed into the studio. He had been with Castro in the Sierra Maestra mountains running the guerrilla war that eventually led to the overthrow of the Batista regime but would tell me nothing about it. Later on, Castro had him executed after charging him with being a CIA spy. Possibly correct.'

GERRY HARVEY

Brave new world

Gerry Harvey has the most cluttered desk in Homebush West—perhaps the most cluttered in the whole of Sydney. In his modest office at Harvey Norman headquarters, piles of documents stretch from one side of his desk to the other, then continue across the carpet to his office door. There's barely a square centimetre to spare on that desktop, which is probably why the morning newspapers are usually left draped over one of the visitor's chairs. On this particular day I notice that Gerry's name figures prominently on the front page of *The Sydney Morning Herald*. 'Racing sources' claim Gerry has just given $20 million to mining magnate Nathan Tinkler, who, despite his status as a mining billionaire, has reportedly hit a rough patch; the $20 million is an advance on the sale of 350 horses through Gerry's Magic Millions equine auctions.

I have to wait ten minutes or so to talk to Gerry, because he is on the phone to a TV reporter, explaining that, in all his dealings with Tinkler, he has never had a hard word, never had a problem.

'I don't know whether Nathan's paid the staff superannuation or not,' he tells the newshound on the other end of the phone. 'I've been talking to him two or three times a day and I didn't even ask. I just said, "Mate, you've got a lot of fucking bad publicity!"' And anyhow, this alleged $20 million lifeline is nothing to do with Harvey Norman; it's Gerry's own horseracing business, the one he now owns, after buying out his partners. So whether he has or he hasn't helped out Mr Tinkler, it's nobody else's business.

In the wonderful world of the mega-rich, $20 million is merely loose change, but, nevertheless, this reported largesse may puzzle the man in the street, given that the Harvey Norman empire has recently signalled a 40 per cent drop in profit and that Gerry has been sounding off for many months about GST-free online shopping and its withering impact on Aussie retailers.

Once he gets off the phone, Gerry is quick to explain that this setback to his vast furniture and electrical chain, the biggest in Australia, is nothing to do with the online competition he has been cursing for so long. After all, he says, fridges and lounge suites and bedding just don't sell online. No, a collapse in profit margins on electronic goods such as TVs, computers and communications gadgets is to blame. 'Computers are just dreadful,' he says. 'Our margins have been attacked, we've had this huge price deflation, people are buying tablets and smart phones all over the place and you make no money out of them. And then you've got flat-screen TVs that were $4000, then $3000, $2000, $1000, now $500: same TV. So that part of our business is being hit really hard.'

Gerry is sometimes called the 'grandfather of bricks-and-mortar retailing' in the financial press. He has been the wizard who has succeeded where other retailers have failed and, in 2012, was named as the thirteenth richest person in Australia. Despite the wealth, he keeps his feet on the ground, feet that are often shod frugally in resoled shoes. Yes, rather than buy new shoes, this $900 million man clings on to two 20-year-old pairs, and, according to his wife, Katie Page, he has been known to use cardboard to cover the occasional hole.

Katie, Gerry's second wife and the company's chief executive officer, is seventeen years younger than him and was born in Mareeba, far north Queensland. She is the daughter of a banker who kept the family on the move, a lifestyle Katie credits for producing 'strong and independent women who love life and go for it.' Nevertheless, the considerable age gap between the couple led her father, before the marriage, in 1988, to drive her past a local retirement village, cautioning that she might be living in one sooner than she had planned.

These days, she says, father and husband are good buddies—hell, they're almost the same generation. Katie and Gerry, who calls her Kate, met at a charity quest, a 'Miss Sydney sort of thing but based on intelligence.' Katie won, despite the fact that her future husband, who was on the panel of judges, didn't vote for her.

After two decades of marriage the two have eye-popping confrontations they call 'open-heart surgery,' in which frank and forthright opinions on business and other matters are aired in terms that could easily be mistaken for a matrimonial bust-up. But Gerry, who turned 74 in 2013, says it is all good creative friction. 'Sure they can be fiery exchanges. We've been doing it for years so after a while you live with it. When some bloke comes in here and I say something quite, er, robust to Kate, they'll say that if they said that to their wife they wouldn't talk for three days! But we can do it because we can be back to normal within minutes, change the subject and it's as if didn't happen.'

Mind you, the girl from Mareeba wields a fair bit of power, judging by the way Gerry lowers his voice when talking about the time Bob Hawke organised a meeting between Katie and Julia Gillard that went for three convivial hours. And you would have to say the girl from Mareeba has an acute ear, judging by the way she suddenly appears at the office door during this whispered confidence, instructing her hubby, 'Don't mention my stuff!'

A little later on she teases from her adjoining office, 'He'll be 106 this year. I have to check his office now and then to make sure he hasn't carked it.'

They have two children, and Gerry has another two from his first, seventeen-year, marriage. Now Gerry and Katie work together and live together and, says Gerry, it is a very rare relationship. 'I could never get a better woman, but she might get a better bloke! I like the fact that she's an individual. I've always had a fascination with women who are really intelligent and strong.'

It has proved a dynamic partnership, with the pair making regular tours of the company stores. When I visit they have just returned from a trip with Coalition leader Tony Abbott and several other business chiefs to an Aboriginal community at Arakoon, in New South Wales. 'Blokes from Rio Tinto, Fortescue—a few of them,' says Gerry. 'The idea was that we could all go up there and talk a bit of bullshit and do a bit of work: painting, laying carpets, landscaping, a new library for the community of 1200 Indigenous. Then we got back in the plane and flew to Cairns, and Kate and I drove from Cairns down to Gladstone doing all our shops. We do that every now and then.

'A few weeks before that we did the shops from St George, Moree, Dubbo and Orange, in western New South Wales. So we did about 25 of them, and I said to Kate that there's not one shop that we've walked out of and thought, *This is no bloody good, this is a waste of time*. We've thought, *These guys are trying hard, shop looks okay: it's not the end of the world*. Because some days I sit here in head office and get so depressed.'

Around Christmas 2011 Gerry launched a broadside over the way internet shopping, free of the GST, was hammering business in certain areas of bricks-and-mortar retailing. Now he says his forecasts came true. 'You've had shop after shop in trouble. Clothes shops, shoe shops, all those shops that are being affected by online purchases that are not paying all their duties and taxes. Sales for some retailers are all over the place, and businesses are putting off staff and closing doors.'

There was much publicity when Gerry seemed to decide that if you can't beat 'em, join 'em, and got into online shopping himself.

Now he is peed off that he fell for the hype. 'People said, "You've got to get this wonderful internet site up and running, and you'll see." Well, we spent all this money and nothing happened. Even JB Hi-Fi, who are way ahead of us, they came out and said only 1.6 per cent of their sales are on the internet. On that tour of the regional and country stores the internet sales were virtually zero. But the media goes mad about what is happening on the internet and how the sales are growing. This is a bit of a repeat of the dotcom boom. I'm going through the same exercise I did back then, saying to people, "Please look at the facts! You are being spun yarns, just get the facts. Go through the categories and find out what percentage are sold online." Fridges, for example. Most people think between 5 and 20 per cent; it's around 1 per cent: nothing! If you go through white goods, washers and all that—nothing! Go through lounges, go through bedding—nothing! And you go to all these country stores and ask, "What were your internet sales?" Ten grand is a good month, and half of those have already been in the store to check the product, like the old days when you got home then picked up the phone to buy. Virtually the only thing affected at Harvey Norman is cameras, but they represent only half a per cent of our turnover.'

But Gerry still rails against the injustice of GST-free online shopping because of the impact on other retailers. 'When I said in 2011 that there was a huge problem, I got all this publicity about how I was trying to protect Harvey Norman and all my rich mates, but I said, "Hang on, stop this bullshit. All the stuff I sell is *not* being brought in from overseas." I said I was talking about musical instruments, sporting goods, clothes, shoes, handbags, cosmetics, books: they were all going to get belted. But no, the media won't put that story in. It's just me protecting me and my mates. However, more retailers went out of business than ever before, and those that were left were crying louder than before because price deflation has hit not only audiovisual and computers but almost every other product you buy. A fridge and a washer is cheaper today than it was twenty years ago.

'Politicians won't attack the GST problem because they will lose votes. I get angry that we put people into positions of authority and they play the politics all the time instead of doing what's right. If a government today announced that everything that comes into this country is going to have GST on it, how many votes would they lose? Politicians think they would lose millions of votes; I think they would lose none. In fact, they might even gain some. Australians are basically fair-minded people: they know it's right.'

Nevertheless, there are still plenty who think Gerry's talking rot. Business executive Kieran Kelly wrote to *The Australian Financial Review* in January 2012, telling him to stop whingeing. 'He needs to be reminded of a few harsh facts about capitalism, the most pertinent of which is to innovate or die,' said Kelly, chief of Sirius Fund Management.

> *Harvey came to the public company sphere after a successful stint with Norman Ross. He quickly built a company that survived the 1987 crash and became a darling of growth stock investors of the past 20 years. He brought innovation to specialty retailing and prospered but now the business flounders. His wife Katie Page could have done worse than to put a copy of Walter Isaacson's biography of Steve Jobs under Gerry's Christmas tree. Jobs constantly tossed out old business models when they became redundant, staying one step ahead of consumer preference.*

Federal treasurer Wayne Swan took the opportunity to sink the boot in too. 'It's just not Christmas if retailer Gerry Harvey isn't whingeing about soft sales,' he told the media scrum. 'Back when we put the original stimulus package in place he spent a lot of time whingeing about that but ultimately it did lift consumption in Australia.'

Gerry once thought about a career as a politician himself but 'instantly dismissed' such a notion. 'It's not my game,' he says, 'because you've got to be a political animal to succeed, and I haven't got that urge. Politicians live it and they breathe it—in a way they're the right people and in a way they're the wrong people. You get all this debate going on a lot of the time, so they're all out there butting heads about something, whether it's gay marriage or asylum seekers, but they're not producing anything or running the country while they're doing it. I don't want to be involved in all that; I'd rather do something more constructive.'

Long years as a market leader have shown Gerry to possess a unique brand of business smarts. Against the advice of the 'experts' he has bought, rather than leased, most of the properties Harvey Norman uses for its stores. Thanks to the real estate boom it is a policy that has seen him acquire a massive property portfolio worth $2 billion or more, an asset that brings in a handy income stream in difficult times. And, ever canny about making a buck, Gerry speculates that he could probably borrow at 5 per cent right now and buy property with an 8 per cent yield. It's just that easy.

Born in Bathurst, as a kid Gerry wanted to be a farmer. His grandfather was on the land, and that is what he had in mind. 'But I didn't have any money for a farm,' he says, 'so I went to university in Sydney to learn how to make some. I had a part-time job earning 8 or 10 quid a week but I found I could make 30 quid a week selling vacuum cleaners door to door. I wasn't a good salesmen to start with, but I worked at it because I was seeing other blokes beating my sales all the time. They'd go out and sell fifteen vacuum cleaners a week and I'd sell two.

'When someone does that, when they beat you by a long way, you wonder, *Why? How can I turn that around?* Of course, if we were talking about running the 100 metres in 9.6 I could never turn that around, no matter what I do, but in something like this I had a chance. So I watched other people, used their lines, watched how they approached people and realised that it's all to do with how you connect with people. If you can connect with people they will buy things off you. All of a sudden I was a nineteen-year-old making

200 quid a week. So I dropped out of uni. I hated economics and accountancy, which is ironical because now I'm doing that all day at a desk.'

Yes, Gerry has 'connecting' down to a fine art. When he walks through his stores customers say 'G'day,' put their arm around him, want to be photographed with him. 'It's on all day,' says Gerry, whose laid-back manner puts the everyday Aussie at ease. 'They always call me Gerry, not Mr Harvey, and they don't feel out of place. Would that happen with Rupert Murdoch or Bob Hawke? That you feel you can say hello to them?'

By the same token, Gerry also enjoys the access to the rich and famous that comes with membership of that exclusive club. 'It's interesting with well-known people,' he says. 'I can ring some bloke I've never met who is very well known. I did it recently with orbital-engine inventor Ralph Sarich in Perth. I guarantee that if you had listened to the conversation for twenty minutes you'd swear I must have known that Ralph Sarich a long time, that he's a good mate. Never met him in my life!

'When you get two blokes who are well known they do talk as if they know each other. It's always happening. Like Peter Bartels—he used to run Myer—he rang me here one day, had a bloke who wanted to talk to me. He said "G'day," and I said, "Peter, how are you?"

'Bartels said, "Hey, Gerry, I've got this bloke here ..." Never met him, but if you are well known you can do that.'

But of course there are plenty of the rich and famous whom he already knows well, like the aforementioned Mr Tinkler and global media magnate Rupert Murdoch, a fellow business senior—now in his eighties—who has never shown any sign of slowing down.

The high profile that Gerry and his company enjoy—he spends around $100 million a year on advertising, and the 'Go, Harvey Norman, Go' jingle is one of the best-known in Australia—can also have a downside. In 2011 the GetUp! activist group targeted him in a campaign over native timber, claiming that 'instead of using existing plantation timber, which is plentiful and affordable, Harvey Norman furniture is made from ancient Australian trees that are logged then sent to China for processing'.

Gerry retorted that his firm was just being used for free publicity. 'GetUp! have decided they'll target Harvey Norman and they'll target Gerry Harvey because it's a name, it's a brand, and it will get them free media coverage,' he told the ABC's *Lateline*.

> *If they do it any other way, they're not going to get the coverage. So this is pretty disturbing as far as I'm concerned because we're operating entirely within the law ... We only use the timber that is certified by the industry ... Of all this timber that's harvested every year, 59 per cent goes into housing—that's framing—18 per cent into pallets and palings and 18 per cent into floorings and boards and only 5 per cent into the furniture industry. And of that 5 per cent, we take a tiny percentage. So, we're less than 1 per cent but if you believe what GetUp! are saying, we're big, bad guys out there using all this wood and destroying native forests.*

Despite being in his seventies, Gerry seems to have the energy of a man in his fifties. 'The trick is to live life as though you're 40 or 50,' he says, 'do the things a 40- or 50-year-old does and don't look in the mirror. Sometimes I see a really old bloke and think, *Shit you're old*, then I later find out he's ten years younger than me. You don't think you're that ugly until someone points it out and then you look in the mirror and think, *Shit, I can see what he's talking about!*' There is a reminder on his office wall: a photo of a fresher-faced Gerry Harvey in 2001 with John Singleton and Rob Ferguson, his two former partners in Magic Millions. 'We all looked okay,' he says ruefully. 'This is what happens to you over a few years.'

The partnership got a bit frayed around the edges too. 'There was a bust-up. It was never meant to blow up the way it did. We didn't make money for a couple of years. They were unhappy, we were all unhappy—it was a tumultuous time.' Now Gerry owns Magic Millions outright and sells half the horses in Australia.

Genial Gerry tries to treat everyone the same, but there is a hard-arsed flip side too. A few weeks after we meet, a finance journo named Nathan Bell wrote a column saying that Gerry should sack himself, and Gerry came out swinging. Against the advice of son Michael he gave a two-hour interview to the Fairfax press, saying a self-sacking would be fair enough if he were a spent force, but he wasn't. 'How come if we are doing such a shit job our shareholders' funds have grown over the past ten years?' he thundered. 'I will probably be here as long as I can stand … Between the Harvey and [Ian] Norman families we own 50 per cent of Harvey Norman, so if you decide to step down you would want to be pretty sure the person you put in was okay because it's your money. It's different at Myer, David Jones and most other retailers where managers come and go.'

Gerry cannot abide what he calls 'self-important people who get into positions of power and wield that power for their own benefit, pretending it's for the benefit of all the rest of the humans on this earth. The tragedy is that these sort of jobs are given to the wrong sort of people. They have this egotistical self-important persona. Those sort of people I just don't fucking like!' He names one on his small but selective hate list who 'pursued me and cost me a lot of money' and is mystified why governments appoint such people. 'I said to John Howard years ago, "Mate, where do you find them? How do you pick them out?"

'He replied, "I get a lot of complaints."'

Meanwhile, mega-retailer Gerry, whose family controls half the Harvey Norman shares, tries to steer his chain into the brave new world of 21st-century shopping. 'You do battle to understand what's going on,' he says. 'You talk to the best economists in the land, the best businessmen in the land, and we're all wondering, *What the fuck's happening here?* There's 5 per cent unemployment; with that sort of situation any other time in our lifetime, everything would be belting along. In five or ten years we'll look back and do a retrospective, the pluses and minuses of the internet. Perhaps we're actually going through another phase of the industrial revolution.'

JONATHON WELCH

You're the choir man!

It seems so sad, the reason Ken Welch took son Jonathon to the backyard that day to show him how to use the motor mower. 'There,' he said, having demonstrated the basics, 'now you'll be able to mow the lawn. I'm leaving tomorrow.'

The end of Ken's troubled marriage to Jonathon's mother, Olive, had been on the cards for years, but the actuality shocked their ten-year-old son. Soon after Ken departed, Jonathon fell ill. 'Flu-like symptoms,' he says. 'Aches, pain, fever. Mum took me to the doctor's but there was nothing wrong. I think I was just pining for my father. Mum's sister Ida—we called her Apple Cider—she came to our house, waited until my mother was out of the room and shook the bejesus out of me, saying, "Get up! There's nothing wrong with you!" Home was not a fun place at that time.'

Ken, an engineer with Errol Flynn–like good looks, had never related comfortably to his children. Jonathon suspects this had something to do with the fact that Ken and his brother had been left in the care of a nanny in the Melbourne suburb of St Kilda for seven years. Their English-born parents, Thomas and Ella, were in the diplomatic service and returned to the United Kingdom at the start of World War II. 'My father was aged from seven to fourteen over that time,' says Jonathon. 'They are formative years. It might have been part of the reason he was unable to communicate with us. On the other hand, he would get very emotional listening to opera at home. He would sit there weeping.'

Olive had been engaged to marry Geoff McComas, the late ABC newsreader, when Ken came along and stole her heart. It seems the newlyweds were happy at first, but, after children Andrea, Glenn and Jonathon came along, the cracks started to show. Unexpectedly, the couple adopted a daughter, Libby, when Jonathon was two, possibly an attempt to revive the marriage.

'My dad was a sweet gentle man,' says Jonathon, 'but he had trouble talking to me. When he became emotional he'd just cry—so at least I got something from him. He was always a ladies' man: he was married four times. His last wife was 30 years younger. My mother was very ladylike—although she liked to scream her lungs out at the football—and didn't talk much about the divorce. People didn't in those days. There was a social stigma. My parents had been married 28 years, but it was a very difficult relationship. My father and I became estranged. After he died I realised how little I knew about him. For example, I found out he had once swum the English Channel.'

The family home was in Ripponlea, south-east of Melbourne, where Jonathon attended the local state school. He was only seven when his inner showman appeared. Having spent hours memorising the words of his favourite book, *Winnie-the-Pooh*, Jonathon turned it into a musical. 'I put on a one-man show in the school library,' he says, 'and charged each kid sixpence to attend, so I suppose I had quite an entrepreneurial streak. I donated the money to the library to buy books.'

He soon recruited some of his friends into other shows—*Fiddler on the Roof, Paint Your Wagon* and *The Sound of Music*—all with original costumes and choreography. He was already singing at nearby St Margaret's Presbyterian Church, where Olive played the organ, and at age ten he began eagerly awaited piano lessons, like his siblings.

After moving to Caulfield North Central School, at that time headed by Rose Hanbury, wife of Australia's great quizmaster and later politician Barry Jones, Jonathon starred in his first Gilbert and Sullivan operetta, *Trial by Jury*, accompanied by Olive on piano. A bright student, Jonathon was accepted at Melbourne High School, where his exceptional singing voice was noted and encouraged by music teacher Peter Ross.

At the same time Jonathon joined the newly established Melbourne Youth Choir and blossomed to the extent that, after leaving school and being trained by a professional singing teacher, he was invited to join the chorus of the Victorian State Opera. Suddenly he found himself sharing the stage with the great June Bronhill at the Princess Theatre, the venue in which had watched musicals from the stalls at age five. His career blossomed.

A stint with Queensland's Lyric Opera followed and then, after a shaky audition (his big B-flat came out sounding like the horn on a semitrailer), in 1987 he was offered a place with the Australian Opera, with which he sang the title role in Benjamin Britten's opera *Albert Herring*. He could also boast of sharing the stage of the Sydney Opera House with Dame Joan Sutherland, in *The Merry Widow*. 'I remember walking along Circular Quay on opening night,' he says, 'thinking I was the luckiest 29-year-old in the world. Singing in one of the world's great opera houses with one of our greatest opera singers. I think it had been Dame Joan who got me hooked on opera in the first place. My mother had taken me to see her sing *La Traviata* when I was sixteen or seventeen. A truly extraordinary voice.'

However, on a personal level Jonathon's life had been rife with hurdles. He was twice seriously unwell: first came appendicitis that approached peritonitis and required drastic surgery that has caused lasting problems; second, he contracted glandular fever, which left him bedridden for months. 'I was really sick,' he says. 'Although for me it was the transformation of the ugly duckling into the swan, because I lost so much weight. I literally couldn't eat for three weeks. I remember my mother feeding me jelly through a straw. It also meant I repeated a year at Melbourne High, which wasn't necessarily a bad thing.' His mother died of cancer when he was only 23. His sister Libby developed a mental illness, and his other siblings, Glenn and Andrea, fell out over their mother's estate and did not speak for seventeen years. Also, his aunt Elsie fell ill and had to be placed in a nursing home.

Overlaying all this was Jonathon's growing realisation that he was gay, a subject he tackled head-on in his autobiography of 2009, *Choir Man*. 'It was such a huge relief that I wasn't the only gay in the village,' he wrote, having confided in a fellow gay student at high school. It was his 'first realisation that I would follow a path in life that was not seen as the norm … It was almost as if I was suddenly wearing clothes that fit me perfectly even though they might not be the fashion of the time'.

He says he made the decision to tell the story of his sexuality before someone else did. 'I've seen too many people suffer, not being comfortable about it. I was lucky to have an unconditionally loving family. Although I never had a chance to tell my mother, I don't think it would have been an issue—it wasn't with my father. It's through my words and actions I want to be judged.'

However, having had a religious upbringing he realised that his homosexuality was at odds with the Christian mores he had been taught. 'In the end I just had to shelve them,' he says. 'My mother's death sort of cut my ties with the church anyhow. But I am still challenged by religion. Who or what is God? I have no idea. I was recently in Uganda for three weeks with a choir of 50 from Australia. It's a very Christian country, and how they can have such faith alongside such abject poverty is inspiring to me.'

In 1993 Jonathon made a shock decision: he left the Australian Opera, one of the elite organisations on the Australian arts scene, telling friends and colleagues he felt he had 'other things to do.' He admits it was a 'scary' move and there were times he had doubts, but life moved on quickly. After a stint in event management he teamed up with two other opera singers to form a group called Tenor Australis, based on the famous Three Tenors. He also made his first foray into choirs, as musical director of the Sydney Gay & Lesbian Choir, and then decided to travel to America and Canada to visit some of their choirs. And that was where the real story began for Jonathon, when he became trapped indoors by a blizzard for three days with a friend in Canada.

'We read and watched movies,' he recalls. 'My friend had a copy of *Reader's Digest* and pointed out an article he thought would interest me. The headline was "With a Song in Their Hearts", and the story was about the Montreal Homeless Men's Choir.' It told of the 22 homeless men whom a conductor, Pierre Anthian, had formed into a 'ragtag collection' of choristers; the choir had made its debut singing Christmas carols at a Montreal subway station in December 1996. The choristers' ages ranged from 19 to 68, and they had become the toast of Montreal, Toronto, Paris and New York.

'A lightbulb went on,' says Jonathon. 'There was a picture of them and I could see the joy in their faces. I thought it was a great idea, and when I got home to Sydney, where I was living at the time, I went about forming a Sydney homeless men's choir.' Unsure how to start, he had some flyers printed and quickly learnt his first lesson: the word 'homeless' was a no-no. It might have worked in Montreal, but in Sydney the street people were offended. 'I realised I would have to think more carefully about labels,' he says. 'Many of the homeless don't identify themselves that way—they regard the street itself as their home.'

The Sydney Street Choir was officially launched on 16 October 2001 with the help of a variety of welfare agencies. There were ten potential choristers at the first session, ranging in age from late teens to early twenties. Jonathon's partner, Matt, provided morning and afternoon teas. They decided to put on a Christmas concert at

Paddington Uniting Church, joined by singer Marissa Denyer, and the audience was boosted by members of the Sydney Gay & Lesbian Choir. Jonathon quickly became a choir addict, forming such groups as the Australian Pop Choir, Pop Kidz and Pop Tots. After moving to Melbourne with Matt, he then became musical director of the Melbourne Gay & Lesbian Chorus.

His growing profile led to an approach from Jason Stephens, a film producer with a company named Crackerjack Productions, which was later taken over by FremantleMedia. Jason wanted to develop a TV program about a choir of street people with a professional musician as musical director. 'Jason wanted to set this up in Melbourne,' says Jonathon. 'He had heard about my choir in Sydney. His wife had come up with the proposed name, the Choir of Hard Knocks. I loved it. It reminded me of Jamie Oliver's TV program *Fifteen*, about young chefs from disadvantaged backgrounds.'

At Jonathon's suggestion, the production company approached the charity organisation Reclink for assistance then put the plan to the ABC. Deal done. *Choir of Hard Knocks* screened over five weeks in 2007 and was a ratings sensation. The choir went on to record two CDs, perform before prime minister Kevin Rudd at Parliament House, Canberra, at the Melbourne Town Hall and at the Sydney Opera House. The Sydney performance was telecast by the ABC and won a Helpmann Award, the annual gongs for Australian live arts named after Sir Robert Helpmann and founded in 2001.

Late in 2007 Jonathon appeared on ABC TV's *Talking Heads*, still riding high on the buzz of his choir's success. 'Choir of Hard Knocks has I think been one of the most extraordinary times in my life,' he told Peter Thompson.

> *It just feels like everything has come together the way it was meant to do. I'm absolutely at the right place where I need to be now in my life. The choir, since the program's gone to air, is obviously enjoying enormous notoriety and a great deal of interest ... I think the most wonderful things about*

*the time in Sydney with the choir was when they actually first
saw the Opera House from the outside. For many of them,
all they'd ever thought they would probably see would be a
picture of this amazing building. And so the performances …
were amazing, yeah.*

Yes, it was almost too good to be true, and, unexpectedly,
within two years it wasn't. In 2009 the Choir of Hard Knocks took
the hardest knock of all and, in fractious circumstances that never
seemed to be fully explained at the time, it fell from public view
because of a dispute over the income from the CDs, DVDs and
concerts from those glory years of 2007–08. As a result, Jonathon
and the choir split from Reclink, the charity organisation that had
partnered the concept: a bitter and regrettable end to what had been
an inspiring project. A few choristers, upset at what they saw as an
injustice, sought legal advice and even turned on Jonathon himself.
One claimed his life had been 'ruined' after his name and criminal
record were printed on a DVD.

Jonathon is still visibly pained to speak about it. For a long time
he avoided discussing the subject, hoping that his tribe of unlikely
choristers might eventually get what they saw as their just rewards,
but he was finally forced to accept the probability that they will
never resolve the dispute. Jonathon says he has learnt lessons from
the experience. 'The name "Choir of Hard Knocks" was problematic
from day one,' he says, 'because it was trademarked by the production company, which I didn't know. I never went into making the
TV series thinking it was going to be a huge success. Everybody kept
saying, "This is going to be enormous," but I just kept thinking, *I just
want to get on with running the choir.*'

He says it was like a 'bushfire behind the scenes' during the
break-up. 'There was a lot of money that came in from the concerts,
sponsorships, donations—I know that 150 000 copies of the first
CD were sold—and the choir members became increasingly upset,
wanting to know where the money was and what was happening to

it. My proposal was to set up the choir independently, with an independent audit of accounts, with Reclink remaining in partnership, but they said no.'

Reclink chief Adrian Panozzo is still adamant that all money raised—and that includes more than $1 million in 2008—went towards the Hard Knocks singing program. 'We are a registered charity with the Australian Tax Office so every year of our operations we are required to be publicly audited,' he says. 'I feel it was more a difference in philosophy. But it was definitely a separation and it was upsetting for our staff and volunteers at the time. Reclink continues to have personal relationships with some of the people. We see them in our daily lives moving round town and a lot of choir members still attend our programs.'

When the dust of conflict eventually settled, Jonathon and his choir regrouped as the Choir of Hope and Inspiration, and in 2012 the concept that had won the heart of TV viewers across the nation was reborn, bigger and more ambitious than before. From a small office in the arts district of Southbank, Jonathon and associate David Jones launched the School of Hard Knocks Institute, a broad-range educational facility aimed at teaching singing and many other facets of the arts. 'I thought, *Why just have a choir when you can have an entire school?*' says Jonathon, who registered the new name, cheekily borrowing from the 'Hard Knocks' brand. 'We wanted to create a whole range of arts and wellbeing programs, so, for a start, we have creative writing, drama, keyboard and drumming.'

There is even a course in playing ukulele, entitled 'Ukelear Power'. Within the first three months the new school gained the backing of 22 Australian arts, education and welfare organisations, including Mission Australia, Open Family, the Brotherhood of St Laurence and Box Hill Institute. For de facto classrooms, organisations such as Federation Square, Queen Victoria Market and even the Melbourne Cricket Ground have made space available.

'At the moment the programs are being piloted with many of the participants from our choir program,' says Jonathon, 'so we probably have about 100 and they range across what you might call the disadvantaged spectrum. So we have five blind members, three guys in wheelchairs who have either had accidents or strokes—we have people with acquired brain injury. Most ranges of mental health, going from bipolar, schizophrenia, eating disorders, you name it.'

Jonathon had been pondering the idea of a school since the TV series screened. 'Back then people kept coming to me and saying they would love to be involved, but I wasn't sure how to facilitate that. I realised I was only one person, there was only so much I could do, and I had an enormous weight of responsibility on my shoulders with the choir and the demands on me after the documentary. I've just turned 54 so for me the next ten years are really important in my working life. What I really want to do is build the capacity of many more people to run the programs.'

The Hard Knocks concept has spawned similar groups around the world. 'There has been a Choir of Warm Socks,' says Jonathon, 'and a Choir of One Knocker—a group of Brisbane women who have had breast surgery. There's even a Choir of Hard Knox at Knox Grammar School in Sydney. I got an email the other day from Mackay—there's a new one up there, Choir of Hidden Names or something. It is a great compliment, but I don't take credit for that and neither should Jason Stephens; that belongs to Pierre Anthian, who created Montreal Homeless Men's Choir.'

These days Jonathon is a well-known face around Australia. He says people often approach him with the enthusiastic greeting 'You're the choir man!' It confirms his belief that song and music are universal bonds, uplifting spiritual connections that bridge all cultures, languages and ages. He experienced this when he travelled to Uganda in 2012. 'English is spoken over there but it is not really developed. However, you can teach them a song. I taught them "Absolutely Everybody", that big hit from Vanessa Amorosi, and all of a sudden you had 400 little black faces and 50 white people singing along.'

He thinks the health ramifications of choirs are often overlooked. 'Two of the girls in our Australian group, Kim and Karen, have collectively lost 200 kilograms in weight. Unbelievable, I know. That's simply through singing once a week. The on-flowing benefit of that sort of thing to our health system and the saving in cost to the community in terms of things like diabetes are huge.'

The Choir of Hope and Inspiration practises weekly and performs regularly. Twenty of the original 47 members are still with the choir, which Jonathon says 'remains a really important stake in the fabric of their social life. Most members who have been able to move on have done so. No one yet has gone on to professional singing, but many have gone to part-time work or study. One of them is just finishing his masters in psychology. He has a brilliant mind.'

Thanks to his own experiences, Jonathon is ever aware of the influence he has on his fractured charges. Years ago at Melbourne High School, music teacher Peter Ross upbraided Jonathon publicly for messing up a piano intro to a song. 'Peter was horrified when my book came out and I told how that still affected me,' says Jonathon. 'How my palms still sweat when I sit down in front of people and begin to play. When Peter retired from Presbyterian Ladies College a couple of years ago he mentioned this in his farewell speech to the staff—that teachers had to be careful what they said because children will listen. I'm sure he'd forgotten all about it, but my book made him realise the important role that teachers play.'

IAN KIERNAN

Under full sail

Charles, Prince of Wales, has had a tough time of it on Australia's eastern seaboard. In an earlier chapter we learnt of the night that Amazing Bastard Peter Russell-Clarke, concerned about a possible royal dobbing-in, shut the door of his Melbourne restaurant in the startled face of poor Charlie, telling him to 'fuck off.' This chapter begins with the saga of Amazing Bastard Ian Kiernan, who put a flying tackle on a pistol-packing student who ran at Charlie at a Sydney function in 1994. (And as he and Ian lay sprawled on the Darling Harbour stage, none other than the New South Wales premier John Fahey wrapped his arms around the student's thighs.) As it turned out, the weapon carried by assailant David Kang was only a starting pistol, which meant that the worst he could have done was send Charlie off on a punishing 100-metre sprint—but that does not diminish Ian's heroics. 'I just jumped out of my seat and got him in a headlock,' recalls the founder of Clean Up Australia, who was being installed as Australian of the Year at the time.

'I've had blue heeler cattle dogs and, if you've had those, you know how to address an urgent situation.'

Kang (who copped 500 hours of community service before making the logical vocational leap to barrister) explained that he was attempting to draw national attention to the plight of Cambodian boat people, but he did a better job of drawing national attention to the new Aussie of the Year's ability to apply a headlock. The sharp crack from the pistol had provoked little reaction from Charlie, who stood bemused at the microphone, perhaps wondering what those damned colonials were up to.

'I went up to Charles later,' says Ian, 'and congratulated him on being so cool, just standing there while all that was going on.

'He said to me, "Well, you know, a couple of hundred years of breeding has got to produce some benefits," and I thought, *You poor bastard!*'

The years roll on, and in October 2012, Melbourne radio station 3AW latches on to a report about new Victorian laws that ban smoking on patrolled beaches. So who ya gonna call for comment? No contest there—it has to be Clean Up Australia! And now, on the phone from Sydney, is the legendary litter-buster Ian Kiernan. 'Responsible citizens who properly dispose of waste to recycling are subsidising the people who don't give a damn,' barks Ian with a well-practised grasp of the media sound bite. 'Because it comes at a cost if rubbish is dropped in public places. Why should responsible people have to pay for the irresponsible actions of litterers?'

Broadcaster Neil Mitchell asks him if it's time the government put some money into his organisation.

'We don't want to be funded by government,' scoffs Ian, 'because we want to be free to criticise when they deserve it, which is often. And to applaud them, as we are doing now.'

It's a brave stance because, with a flabby economy and amid company reshuffles, there's a problem: sponsorship for Clean Up Australia has fallen into a bit of a hole.

The Clean Up headquarters are in a cute but ancient cottage at Sydney's Millers Point, overlooking the traffic that flows ceaselessly onto and off the Harbour Bridge. On the day I drop by, most desks are empty.

'We've had to let staff go,' says Ian. 'It's been a tough year with an international takeover of one partner and the Global Financial Crisis hitting others with European parentage. It has all meant less cash to Clean Up and we've had to significantly scale back our operations to make up the shortfall. My CEO and I are determined to keep the doors open, even though it means we're volunteering our time.'

Ian says all this with the same cheerful confidence with which he seems to have met every other bump and pothole in life's winding highway. There was the dark recession year of 1974, for example, when, in his early life as a builder, he lost a $20 million property portfolio.

'That recession was shocking,' he says. 'People were in freefall. I had been renovating rows of terrace houses, buying them for $18 000 each, borrowing money at 7.25 per cent, renting them out and getting returns up to 37 per cent. It was a pretty good equation, and I thought I was a pretty smart young bloke, bloody oath I did. I'd seen something that others hadn't. In the end I had bought almost 500 houses.' He became so skilled at the game that sometimes estate agents needed to do no more than drive him past a potential purchase and he would decide yay or nay while looking at it through the car window.

It was an investment technique that had its pitfalls. On one occasion, while lunching in East Sydney after a week of heavy rain, he heard a god-awful crash, ran out onto the street and saw that three of his newly purchased terraces nearby had collapsed. 'Ruined my meal, I can tell you,' he says.

His property company was called Tierra del Fuego, perhaps an omen of things to come, for it is where Cape Horn, the sailors' graveyard of the early windjammer days, is situated. Back then, property whiz Ian had the fearless enthusiasm of youth, but he also had the flip side that comes along with it: blinkered naivety. A credit squeeze came along, interest rates shot skywards, and Ian's property empire went belly-up. He managed to sell two houses he owned privately, gave the money to a family friend with the instruction to 'make sure my family doesn't starve,' and signed over the family home to wife Judy.

'Then I did what any self-respecting young builder who sails boats would do,' he says. 'I got on my yacht, *Maris*, and visited 36 of the most beautiful islands I could find—Tahiti, Hawaii, the Marquesas—all in one year.'

And his wife? Did she go?

'No way!' says Ian, who took two crew instead.

The sojourn sowed the first seeds of his great awakening. 'When I was in Hawaii,' he says, 'I was living on the boat in the Ala Wai Canal. A lot of people did the same. It was illegal, and the authorities were always trying to get us out. It was war. But one night we decided to do something about the canal. What happens with the tropical downpours, all the ravines just gush rubbish into the Ala Wai. We picked up the rubbish and piled it outside the harbourmaster's office. He hated us: he was in charge, and here were all these illegal residents cleaning up. But what had happened was the same as what happened when I identified an opportunity with my houses: I had identified an opportunity to clean up the environment.'

Ian sailed back into Sydney Harbour on 16 September 1975, a year to the day that he had departed. He still owed a stack of money so cranked up a new building company using some of the members of his former construction crew. By December, Alfred Builders, named after his blue cattle dog Alfred, was in good shape.

Ian's marriage, however, had fallen apart. Unsurprisingly, the twelve-month sailing absence—and a brief but energetic polka with a Micronesian-American girl in Papeete—did the already-shaky Kiernan marriage no good at all. And sea-salt Ian admits it: he loves his boat and the sea above all else. 'I'm very comfortable on the ocean,' he says. 'I said to my sports psychologist once, "After three days at sea I go almost into a euphoric state. I have this wonderful feeling in my head and it's just fantastic."

'He said, "Oh yeah, that's connected with your biorhythms. You're doing what you are best designed to do."

'I never get bored. I've got this most beautiful boat, I'm floating around on this Huon pine grand piano, it's my own Boeing 747, and I always get seat 1A. It has my own gourmet galley, my wonderful reading and music collection, and if I get sick of the waterfront I can go and find a new one.' Even gales and storms seem to bring him pleasure. 'I'll often just sit in the hatch and watch, hour after hour. It's just so exciting, the power of nature.'

Now single, Ian was free to indulge his passion and sailed *Maris* whenever and wherever he could. He had bought his beloved 'grand piano' in 1958, when aged 30, from marine artist Jack Earl. Ian's year-long voyage had also sparked an interest in something new: sailing solo. 'When I was away,' he says, 'one of the crew members had a hernia and the other got a broken leg and had to be repatriated home, so I learnt to cross oceans on my own. I had a radio-telephone so had good communication if I needed it. It was a wonderful feeling of freedom, and, being a competitive person, I looked for an event where I could compete solo.

'I found a single-handed trans-Tasman race and entered that in my grand piano. It was fantastic. What happened was, a hurricane regenerated in the Coral Sea and came down into the Tasman and swept me home to victory. I was hooked!'

Ian wanted more. He entered another solo event, a trans-Pacific yacht race from California to Hawaii and finished 11th in a fleet of 25. This was actually better than it sounds: many of the competitors were in ultralight displacement boats that weighed in at 1 to 2 tonnes. *Maris* weighs 7 tonnes.

In 1981 a new race was announced for solo sailors sponsored by the British gas company BOC and covering 43 000 kilometres in four legs around the great capes of the Southern Ocean. Ian paid the entry fee and announced himself as an Australian challenger, but, despite his extensive credentials under sail and mates in the advertising game like John Singleton and Alan Morris of the Mojo agency he was unable to find sponsors for the $60 000 he needed to put out to sea. Glumly he had to watch another Australian, Nev Gosson—who had found sponsors—sail out of Sydney for the start, in Newport, Rhode Island.

The status of yachties in Australia took an almighty leap forwards in 1983, thanks to the America's Cup triumph, in which the brash Aussies took the America's Cup away from the Yanks for the first time in 132 years. In the same year Rod Muir, a Tasmanian-born radio tycoon and sailing nut, decided to get serious about the next BOC Challenge, in 1986–87. Ian just happened to be on board Muir's new 16-metre yacht *Dr Dan* when, in party mode, the affable millionaire pondered aloud about building a boat especially for the BOC task. 'It would be called the *Spirit of Sydney*,' said Rod. 'We'll get Benny Lexcen to design it and the best bloke in Australia to drive the bastard.'

Although Ian did not raise his hand that night, he ended up at the helm of *Spirit* two years later on that Mount Everest of a race; and indeed it was Lexcen, the man behind *Australia II*'s famous 'winged keel' in the 1983 America's Cup, who drew up the design. 'Benny was a character,' recalls Ian. 'I remember at the launch of a boat named *Ginko* he turned to the nervous owner and said, "Well, Gary, if she doesn't make it as an Admiral's Cupper she will make a bastard of a cruising boat!"'

Ian brought *Spirit of Sydney* home fourth in the BOC Challenge, setting an Australian record of 156 days. It was a daunting voyage, taking him from Newport in Rhode Island to Cape Town, Sydney, Rio de Janeiro and back to Newport, a route that involved sailing across the Sargasso Sea.

In his book *Coming Clean*, co-authored with Phil Jarratt and launched by prime minister Paul Keating in 1995, Ian recalls the moment his life calling became clear.

I can't overstate the depth of my disgust when I sailed in
to this pristine place of smoky blue water, dotted by semi-
submerged golden weed so vital to the marine food chain, this
sea of magic and myth—and found it littered with rubbish.
First a rubber thong, then a toothpaste tube, a comb, a
plastic bag ... the rubbish popped up on both sides of the bow.
I didn't know where it had come from—although the recre-
ational cruise industry must bear some responsibility in those
waters—but it took me back to Ala Wai Canal that Sunday
in 1975 when we cleaned up so much filth and thought for
the first time about what we, as sailors, were doing to our
playgrounds, our oceans.

Ian had been raised by the shores of Sydney Harbour. He had
seen the change over four decades: the broken glass on the tide line,
the plastic bags, the slime. 'At that time,' he recalls, 'we had raw
sewage on our beaches. Sydney Water was removing 30 per cent
of the solids from the sewage stream and dumping the rest in the
ocean, and it was washing up on our beaches. There was fury in
the community, but the government was doing bugger-all about it.

'So I had this idea—get people together like we had in Hawaii and
do a clean-up. I wrote off asking Laurie Brereton for help. Laurie was
minister for Ports and Public Works, and he's a mate, although I don't
reckon he thinks that any more. I've still got his reply in my file.

'"Dear Ian, as minister I'm thinking this is a good idea but I am
intending to commission a report ..."

'You know, that report would almost be finished now, 23 years
later! So the answer was "no" and we don't like "no". I said, "Well
bugger you, mate," and I got a bunch of mates together who were all
in the communications business—John Singleton, Alan Morris of
Mojo and Kim McKay, a project manager on the BOC Challenge.
They said, "You'd better get some money," so Singo picked up the
phone and rang Macca's.'

The Macdonald's chief Peter Ritchie had never heard of Ian Kiernan, but with the ringing endorsement of advertising tycoon Singo—'Kiernan's a good bloke, wants to clean up the bloody harbour'—Ian had the start of his Clean Up capital.

Morris was a canny choice too: the co-founder of Mojo had the earthy approach that was so close to Ian's heart. 'He and Allan Johnston, the other bloke from Mojo, once pitched to Coca-Cola in Atlanta, Georgia,' says Ian. 'Two little bearded blokes in leather jackets. The chairman of Coca-Cola was there, a very episcopalian sort of gentleman, and after the pitch the chairman, tugging on his cuffs, said, "Now, Mr Morris, this campaign—who will it be directed at?"

'And Alan Morris turned around and said, "Any c— with a mouth." If that isn't the most brilliant piece of marketing ... They didn't get the job, of course. They had been ushered in up the marble staircase; they left by the fire escape.'

Enthused, with the same brash spirit, but with a slightly more polished line of banter, Ian approached Mosman Council, which had earlier endorsed him as Mosman Bicentennial Citizen of the Year for his solo voyage. He told mayor Barry O'Keefe he wanted to clean up Mosman's seventeen harbourside beaches and got the official council nod. A committee was formed: Kim McKay, Mojo's Alan 'Mo' Morris and John Henderson, John Singleton and Mosman councillor Rod Jones.

It wasn't long before the target got larger. 'Mo phoned me one day and said, "Bugger Mosman, let's do the whole harbour."' And they did. On the remarkable day of 8 January 1989, an impressive 40 000 Sydneysiders came to lend a hand, and the next year it became national: Clean Up Australia attracted 300 000 people. In 1993, after Ian signed an agreement with the United Nations Environment Program, 30 million people in 80 countries took part in a Clean Up the World event held over three days.

'It's amazing how the importance of the environment has gathered momentum,' says Ian. 'I was made an honorary doctor of science at the University of New South Wales, which I was greatly thrilled by because I love science and technology. Fascinated by it. And it got me thinking, *What do doctors do?* They write formulae and equations, that's what they do. So I came up with Dr Ian's equation: $E = 1$. It's not $E = mc^2$; it's simpler than that. $E = 1$. Environment is number one. I use it all the time. I'm firmly of the belief that the environment is the primary issue that has to be factored in to every action we take. It's right at the base of everything. $E = 1$. The kids all get it. I get them to chant it out.'

Ian says social researcher Hugh Mackay has declared the Clean Up movement an outstanding piece of social engineering. 'And I agree,' says Ian. 'We have changed people's behaviour. When people get out there, make the decision to give up part of their Sunday to pick up someone else's shit, they see the scale of the problem and they start thinking, *What can I do about it?* And they start reviewing their purchasing policy and their waste-management policy. That's why I talk at schools whenever possible. I look at that wonderful multicultural face of Australia in these young kids and there I see the greatest investment we have in the future. They get it. They get $E = 1$.'

Now every day is clean-up day, Ian says. 'The tourism industry in the Kimberley doesn't do a great deal on Clean Up Australia Day because it is too hot at that time of the year, and it is the wet season, the monsoon season. But they have had a major problem: what they call "brown and white butterflies"—human waste by the roadside. Bloody horrible. And discarded beverage containers. So they did a clean-up in another part of the year, September. I went over for it. They cleaned 450 kilometres of the Gibb River Road, and they have done it every year since all the way to Hall's Creek. They've involved the Aboriginal people.

'I'm fascinated by our Aboriginal heritage. If only we could have paid more attention to them. There's a wonderful book called *Watkin Tench's 1788*, by Tim Flannery. Tench was a captain-lieutenant on the First Fleet and wrote about the white man arriving in Botany

Bay. Saw them slaughter 250 stingrays in one day, and 1200 snapper. You can imagine what the Aboriginals thought. Tench went with the Aboriginals and discovered the junction of the Hawkesbury and Nepean rivers. On the third night out they put on a corroboree where they mimicked every bumbling move by the bloody redcoats, these stupid people in heavy serge coats and stupid hats and they just got it like that. And Tench records it beautifully.'

While Ian's father, George, died at 75, too early to see his son's successes, Ian's Scottish-born mother, Leslie, witnessed it all. She turned 100 in 2012. 'Dad was more a horseman than a sailor,' says Ian. 'I still have his saddle and his boots. He fought in the war with the Argyll and Sutherland Highlanders and the Gurkhas. Got captured by the Japanese in Malaya, today's Malaysia, and put in Changi and on the Burma Road. They were given a life expectancy of 56.

'Dad met Mum when he was stationed in London. Mum's a Scot. They migrated here in 1936 because they could see the war coming. They bought a great big rambling unrenovated house in Vaucluse, in Sydney.'

Sightings of Japanese subs in Sydney Harbour spooked the Kiernans and they moved to a friend's farm at Raglan, east of Bathurst, for some time. Years later Ian went hunting for a property in the same area and mentioned the wartime saga to a local bloke. 'The farm was called Docairne,' said Ian. 'I suppose it's gone to subdivision now.'

The bloke shook his head. 'Docairne! We share a boundary with it!'

Ian was gobsmacked. That was the clincher: he had to buy the old spread, and he did. 'I'm a fatalist,' he says. 'Things have just happened in my life like that because they are meant to happen.'

Ian's trade as a carpenter and joiner began with a cadetship with Concrete Industries (Monier). 'I finished up as job captain on the State Office Block. Three towers. They've been demolished—that's my connection with mortality. Then I went to work for myself but discovered that you never get the last cheque, so I became my own most respected client.'

He is still building, recently restoring an old slab homestead in the Wolgan Valley, in New South Wales. 'Finest example of pioneer engineering construction I had ever seen,' he says. 'Limestone clinker walls, yellow-box and ironbark posts straight into the ground. White ants had got at it, but I had done this sort of work before.' So life gallops on for the amazing Mr Clean Up. 'I say to my wife, "I wish I could get bored,"' declares Ian, 'because my life is rushing past so quickly. We have a Portuguese ironing lady who comes every Thursday and every time she turns up I think, *She's bloody well here again! There's another Thursday I'm not going to have.*' The Kiernan credo in a nutshell: squeeze every last drop out of the mortal coil; don't waste a single hour. As Ian's old sailing mate the Bilge Rat used to say, 'Most people die at 40 and it takes another 30 years to bury the bastards.'

Angela Wylie, Fairfax Syndication

STEPHEN MAYNE

Crikey!

Okay, journalist Stephen Mayne admits it. 'I'm a shit-stirrer,' he says. An effective one, too. On a night of media infamy in 2006, Mayne was at the microphone, preparing to present a Walkley Award to Morgan Mellish of *The Australian Financial Review*, when News Limited scribe Glenn Milne charged at him like a bull in a monkey suit, shoving beanpole Mayne off the edge of the stage. 'You are an absolute disgrace,' said Milne, albeit with consonants somewhat furry around the edges, and pointed an accusing finger. 'You, you … you!' Led off by a stage hand, Milne then struggled in vain to return as Stephen reclaimed the mike.

'I have an announcement to make on behalf of Rupert Murdoch,' Stephen quipped. 'That was the former *Sunday Telegraph* political correspondent Glenn Milne—sponsored by Foster's.'

For a professional shit-stirrer this was gold, and Stephen, founder of the Crikey website, has made the most of it ever since. Advertising himself brazenly these days as a 'prolific media tart', he still flaunts a caricature of himself with a black and swollen right eye.

The prickly art of provocation is a hazardous one, and the internet, where Stephen pioneered his own brand of publishing, has a particularly cutting edge. Kerry Packer once asked him, 'Are you deliberately offensive or is it just natural?' Broadcaster Alan Jones declared, 'Stephen Mayne doesn't deserve a place in society!' The usually genial Eddie McGuire is said to have snarled, 'I wouldn't cross the road to give him a backhander or a writ.'

Yes, the writ is one of those hazards. Midway through 2012 Stephen had three threatened actions hanging over his head, all arising through his son-of-Crikey website, The Mayne Report. The trio of legal red flags all came via Melbourne's Manningham City Council, on which he was elected to office in 2008. To the horror of some, and the gratitude of others, Councillor Mayne evolved into a kind of embedded whistleblower, airing the council's dirty linen. The three potential litigants were a fellow councillor and two unsuccessful council candidates. The councillor had originally encouraged Stephen to run for office, but now, in a re-run of the night of infamy, was calling him a 'disgrace.' The Sunday Age outlined the municipal biffo at the time, quoting Stephen's accusation that some councillors had been pursuing personal vendettas and that he had been merely 'fulfilling his civic obligations by making council processes transparent'. In the end all three threats turned out to be hot air.

When I catch up with the provocateur himself at a city cafe, I take along a copy of the newspaper report. Stephen scoffs. 'This one's a nutter,' he says, pointing to one name. 'And this one had the voting preferences of people with criminal records.'

The law suit that really hurt came from broadcaster Steve Price in 2002, an action that cost Stephen his family house. 'It was one of three writs I got within the first year of launching Crikey,' he says. 'Three writs from three different states—against Crikey and against me personally. I was worried; it was enormous pressure. We were in strife with the Price one. There was a Supreme Court action, a contempt of court action, an aggravated damages claim: he was throwing the book at me and I knew I was in a world of trouble.'

It was not what Crikey had said about Price but what was contained in a media release from a political candidate that pulled the trigger. Stephen republished it without spotting the libellous slag-off. You may wonder how a bloke savvy enough to blaze a new trail in publishing, whom ex–Victorian premier John Cain says has a 'gift and a passion,' was not smart enough to safeguard his assets before sailing into these perilous seas—but the penny dropped too late.

After Price launched his action, Stephen tried to transfer the title of the family house into the name of his wife, barrister Paula Piccinini, but the Price team 'did a title search, got the bank records and knew we'd done it. So then we decided to sell the house. Sold it ourselves without an agent but, silly us again, we cooperated in a story in *The Age* about how to sell your own house. It alerted Price's team and they obtained an injunction over the sale. But Justice Bernard Bongiorno, God bless his soul, ruled that only $40 000 of the proceeds from the house sale should be set aside for a potential defamation judgment. On the advice of legal silk Julian Burnside, who acted pro bono, we offered Price $50 000, and he accepted.'

Happily, the arrows of litigation seemed to stay in their quiver for the next decade, until Stephen's blog accused the deputy mayor of Manningham Fred Chuah of trying to 'bypass regular council planning processes' to secure planning approval for a nursing-home development in the city's green wedge. Chuah sued and, after seven hours of court-ordered mediation, The Mayne Report eventually announced a settlement. The deal included a public statement in which Stephen tugged the appropriate forelock, but Chuah, who was chairman of the nursing-home board and whose wife was the home's chief executive, got into hot water too. A Councillor Conduct Panel later found that Chuah had 'engaged in conduct intended to mislead and deceive other councillors' and told him to apologise. Instead, Chuah resigned. The Mayne Report rolled on.

There is one organisation that has been notably immune from Stephen's barbs for the past seven years—the RACV, which was a favourite Mayne whipping boy until 2006, when Stephen's wife was elected to the RACV board. 'That's quite an amusing element,' he says, 'in that I used to be the RACV's biggest shit-stirrer, but since she was elected I haven't said "boo."'

Paula's appointment as youngest ever RACV director contrasted starkly at the time with Stephen's own quixotic jousts at the ballot box. Back then he declared, almost proudly, 'I failed to get elected in 30 consecutive contested ballots from 2000, including 24 public company boards.'

Try, try again. He ran as an independent candidate in Higgins, in southeast Melbourne, against treasurer Peter Costello in the 2007 federal election but garnered only 1615 votes, and he ran again in the Northern Metropolitan Region in the 2010 Victorian state election; no-go there either. He tried again in a state by-election in 2012, finishing fourth out of sixteen starters for the seat of Melbourne. However, later that year, having cut his teeth at municipal Manningham, he cracked it for Melbourne City Council.

Persistence, not to mention longevity, seem to run in the genes. Stephen's English grandfather, engineer Phillip Mayne, was the last surviving British officer of World War I; he died in 2007. Among his heirlooms were four letters from the Queen, sent on his 100th, 105th, 106th and 107th birthdays. The old fella died in his sleep before making 108.

'He was a great guy,' says Stephen. 'Came to Australia several times. Very strong on education. Grandpa was the first of his family to go to university; he gained a scholarship to Cambridge. Every one of his successors in the family has completed a university degree— three children, eight grandchildren, twenty great-grandchildren. I mentioned this at a Melbourne University commerce alumni dinner one time and they specifically created a scholarship for someone whose family had never been to uni before.'

Stephen had invited his grandfather to write for Crikey, and he produced half-a-dozen columns on life lived through three centuries. Stephen was able to describe him in an obituary as the 'world's oldest columnist'. He didn't pay his grandfather for his contributions, but that was the nature of the beast. 'Sweat shop, free content,' quips Stephen, evoking the original concept he used when founding Crikey, soon after the fall of Jeff Kennett's Victorian government. It seemed a lunatic plan—virtually no income, 80 hours' work a week, give the content away free—and there were many at the time who wondered if he had lost his marbles. But eleven years later John Cain, introducing Stephen as a guest speaker at the State Library, declared that the Crikey founder had become Australia's 'best-known shareholder activist,' who poked and probed and asked the uncomfortable questions. Cain did not say 'shit-stirrer' once, but he did remark that there were 'many people who wished Mayne would just go away.'

Stephen's road to Crikey began in 1989 when, as a twenty-year-old, he landed a job with the *Herald Sun*, today the nation's biggest-selling daily paper, and thrived, reporting the world of stock markets, profits and losses. He eventually moved to *The Age*, then noticed a job ad for a press secretary for Kennett's dynamic new state government. 'I worked for eighteen months in Kennett's office,' he says. 'Did a good job, got on well with everyone, and I think I helped sell the government case for massive austerity. But I had to leave because I had bought an apartment off the plan in the old Jolimont railway yards and they settled early and I didn't have the cash. So I asked for a pay rise. Alan Stockdale, the treasurer, put me up from $50 000 to $55 000, but the business editor job at the *Herald Sun* came up and they offered me $65 000. So I left to get enough to finance my apartment.'

The Kennett team bade him a fond farewell. 'I got all these lovely cards, messages from Kennett and Stockdale. They even called a press conference to say what a great job I'd done, and it was all very positive. But they assumed I would stay loyal to them, so they didn't even lock down my computer or take my pass away. For two weeks I was printing out every press release, talking to bureaucrats, looking at files, planning my stories. They had no concept I would be an independent journalist.'

The Kennett welcome mat was soon withdrawn, as Stephen broke successive stories that rocked the government boat. By 1997, Stephen had grown so disillusioned with the Liberal regime that, fuelled by the knowledge he had gained while on staff and spurred by events afterwards, he appeared on the ABC's *Four Corners* as a whistleblower. 'It was part of my plan to unseat Kennett,' he says, 'and I threw everything at him; but he survived. I said, "Too good, I'm leaving the state," and went to Sydney as business editor of *The Daily Telegraph*. Then I joined the *Financial Review*, but all the while I was thinking of running against Kennett. When the *Herald Sun* splashed a story under the headline "The Order Is Silence", reporting that Premier Kennett had prohibited all his party's candidates from debating their Labor counterparts, it went off in my head. I resigned my job so I could run against him.'

The move was a disaster. Four days after moving to Melbourne and throwing his hat into the ring, Stephen was ruled ineligible because he was still on the electoral roll in Sydney. Suddenly, he was out of work without prospects, and his furious father banished him from the family home until he found employment.

In tears, Stephen took to his computer and wrote an 11 000-word essay on why he had tried to run for office. He posted it on a new website he called Jeffed.com, which parodied a pro-government site set up for the Liberal campaign, Jeff.com. Stephen's father read the essay, understood, and lowered the drawbridge. The Jeffed.com website bored into the government that Stephen had once served, countering the good messages from the official Jeff.com.

Says Stephen, 'It was actually Kennett, in launching Jeff.com, who was saying that the internet was a legitimate, groovy new political campaigning tool. So my Jeffed.com had a lot more credibility than it would have otherwise.' From a standing start, Jeffed.com drew 115 000 page views in thirteen days, more than the Labor Party website, and was credited by some for cementing Kennett's shock defeat.

'There was a level of liberation in publishing Jeffed.com,' says Stephen. 'It was the first time I could really say what I thought without editors, publishers, lawyers, advertisers, colleagues, politicians influencing it. I had genuine control, and the liberation ... particularly publishing that 11 000-word stream of consciousness, and having people like Jon Faine and Paul Lyneham ringing up and saying, "This is great, amazing, extraordinary," and plugging it and reading it.' By the time of the election Stephen had bulked out his essay to 18 000 words. 'I think the mistake Kennett made,' he says, 'is that he should have sued the moment it went live and scared Faine off it, said, "This is just so defamatory and I'm taking out an injunction," but he just let it go.'

With Kennett gone, Jeffed.com went into mothballs, but, despite a Walkley Award under his belt, Stephen found he had burnt all bridges back to the mainstream media. He took on a column called 'The Bitch' for publisher Eric Beecher's magazine *The Eye*. 'I wrote a series on AGMs and Beecher didn't run any of it, so I thought, *No, even Beecher is too straitlaced for me*. I decided to do my own thing. For six weeks over Christmas and New Year I plotted the new site, then, bang, we launched.'

Crikey was born on 14 February 2000, Valentine's Day, but there were no hearts or flowers. One of the four original shareholders, Sydney journo Andrew Inwood, had come up with the name. 'It had to fit into a headline,' says Stephen, 'had to be easy to spell and convey a message of "holy shit!", and "Crikey" did all of that. We took thirty $30 subscriptions at the launch. The website was free, with a password-protected archive which was bollocks—who was going to pay to read an archive? But after a few months I added a sealed section, which had the defamatory stuff, and that's where the model of premium content arose. The website became less important as the daily email took over, and we built up the best email list in the country.'

But the first two years were a struggle. He and Paula went from a bankroll of $300 000 to a credit card debt of $65 000. 'And we got married eight months after we launched Crikey,' he says, 'then went off on a ten-week honeymoon. It was ridiculously decadent for someone who had just launched a new business. Crikey really took off in 2002.'

It's hard to believe that this burr under the Kennett government's saddle was once a staunch Liberal. While delivering the 2011 Stephen Murray-Smith Lecture, at age 42, Mayne said that he had 'been signed up by Sophie Mirabella for the Young Liberals' in 1988, the year Murray-Smith died. He continued,

> *Still, as Murray-Smith's own journey demonstrates, we all take interesting pathways through life. I went from being a Jeff Kennett spin doctor in 1994, criticising John Cain, to running against the Liberals in Kennett's seat of Burwood in 1999. I also went from staying with Andrew Bolt in Hong Kong in his apartment for five nights during the 1997 handover to China, and having him at our wedding cocktails in 2000, to having him storm the ABC studios in 2005 when I was filling for Jon Faine to declare that 'the ABC is disgraced by your presence.'*

But then, shit-stirrers can take offence too. In 2008 Stephen fell out briefly with Di Gribble, one of the co-purchasers of his Crikey website, over a statement she made about him in an interview with the RACV magazine *RoyalAuto*. In fact, it was an article I wrote as part of a long interview series, and it quoted Gribble as saying Mayne had 'run Crikey out of his front room with a couple of badly paid young people. It was poorly resourced and was regarded as being unreliable.'

Says Stephen, 'We had our biggest blue. I felt she was not fairly representing me.'

Gribble, an Australian publishing legend who died in 2011, had teamed with Eric Beecher to buy Crikey from Mayne in 2005 for $1 million.

Beecher said Crikey was

> *something incredibly innovative, as there's nothing quite
> like it anywhere in the world. It was a momentous thing for
> Stephen Mayne and his team to invent and run. We intend to
> retain Crikey's essential ingredients: disclosure, ferreting out
> important information that people don't want you to know,
> being an active and lively part of the fourth estate that acts
> as one of the crucial checks and balances in the Australian
> democracy.*

Stephen credits a lot of his crusading zeal to his mother, a
fiercely ethical woman, but he seems to have had a natural flair for
stirring the possum from a young age as well. As he told the ABC's
Peter Thompson in 2008, when he was in Year 9 at school, he was
the locker room monitor, meaning he had the key to the room.

> *And I will admit that I used to dispense a little bit of justice
> there, because I hated violence. Still do. And I hated confron-
> tation. And at an all-boys school, of course you're going to
> get bullies. And so my way of meting out justice to the bullies
> was I would wait till everyone had gone to class and I would,
> say, steal their shorts on the day they had physical education
> classes and, therefore, they couldn't go and, therefore, they
> would get a detention. And, for me, that was, 'Well, you
> just beat up this poor kid. I'm going to get you in trouble.
> I'm not going to front you, cos you'll just beat me up, but
> I'm going to make you pay in another way ... Occasionally
> I would put paper up the locks of someone so they couldn't
> open their padlock. They'd have to get a new padlock if they
> were particularly bad.*

The busy Mayne mobile phone can chirrup at any time, and,
indeed, on this particular November afternoon, it lights up repeatedly. One text message, he advises, comes from an Australian

Shareholders' Association informant with a 'big story on slush fund contributions,' asking, 'Are you around?'

Stephen puts down the phone. 'Not an ASA issue,' he says, highlighting another facet of his hyperactive life. After being elected to the ASA board, Stephen resigned late in 2012 to take a paid position as the association's policy and engagement coordinator. It is a gig that sees him gallop around the country throwing the fear of Hades into company AGMs.

Every year he heads off to the United States to harass Rupert Murdoch at News Limited, Rupert-baiting having become something of a hobby. 'There is no more powerful family in the world than the Murdochs,' he explains. 'It was Rupert, more than any other media mogul in history, who pioneered the business strategy of parlaying political power into commercial gain. And that's why you happily run loss-making newspapers: because you can bully governments into concessions and other favours that make it a good investment. He's done this by ruthlessly and pragmatically backing different political leaders and governments in exchange for a relatively unfettered ability to expand and dominate the media market place in a most unhealthy way.'

It has taken me more than a month to pin down the peripatetic Mayne, but I have quickly understood why. His @MayneReport Twitter feed chatters on without end, like a social media GPS, detailing the activities demanded by his multitudinous roles. 'ASA is holding 38 822 proxies from 16 REA Group shareholders,' says a tweet 35 minutes old. 'Am going to ask about excessive $182m in cash and $93m in franking credits.'

Twenty-nine minutes later: 'Read paper speech from REA chair Hamish McLennan and now CEO Greg Ellis talking to a few slides. About 40 in the room.'

On Twitter Stephen describes himself as 'ASA policy guy, Crikey founder, Melbourne City Councillor, professional speaker, ABC regular and publisher of www.maynereport.com'. Even private downtime in the silly season seems to carry a business overlay. On Boxing Day 2012 he told his 13 600 disciples on Twitter, 'Looking forward to playing golf at The Heritage Yarra Valley in next few days. Westpac dropped $10.4m in receiver sale'.

Stephen has just been newly elected to the Melbourne City Council when we meet, and he announces on arrival that he has just been appointed the previous evening as head of the council finance committee. A very busy Amazing Bastard—but his crusading lance is never far away. 'Nothing gives me more pleasure than taking on the rich and powerful,' he says. 'But in the game of radical publishing, the goal is not profit. It's maximising the diversity of opinion and voices. And the goal is simply surviving.'

WOLF BLASS

The full bottle

When Wolf Blass went into hospital a few years back for a hernia operation, he went five-star, booking a suite at a private Adelaide hospital near a leading restaurant so he could have meals delivered. And, given the worrying proximity of the Blass family jewels to the surgical slicing zone, precautions were taken against any mishap. Wife Shirley, with a strong matrimonial interest in the matter, left a note attached: 'Don't slip with the knife, look after little Peter'. When Wolf awoke after the operation he found an answering note from the surgeon in the same location, saying Peter was safe—mainly because his unusually diminutive size made the little fella too difficult to find.

The surname Blass translates from the German as 'pale, colour-less', which seems quite inappropriate for this German-born thrice-married wine-industry empire-builder. This is a bloke who quite possibly holds the world record for shortest ownership of a Rolls-Royce. That's the canary-yellow job he bought in 1987, sent away immediately to have a sunroof fitted then promptly wrapped it around a Stobie pole while fuelled up on booze. Sadly, it was 3 a.m., so he never got much value from the sunroof and, when the coppers tracked him down, he blew 0.138 on their party whistle. They needed police dogs to find him.

'I walked away from the accident,' he admits now. 'Walked away for some reason. And for the next two or three weeks, wherever I went, people would go, "Woof! Woof! Woof!" It became a little bit of a joke.'

He was president of the Carbine Club in Adelaide at the time and the day after the prang was due to host a Formula One function for 600 people. 'Everybody said, "Wolfie, you wouldn't be on stage, would you, after what happened?"

'And I said, "I'm the fucking president and I've got to be up there."'

He used the occasion to gush remorse, delivering a first-person lesson on the dangers of drink-driving, and his spin doctors then persuaded him to give his TV ads for Classic Dry White a rest for a while. Instead (nudge-nudge, wink-wink), he did some ads for that other dry white—milk.

'I was lucky,' he says. 'Only lost my licence for four months.'

Nothing 'colourless' here. Shirley, his third wife, once belted him in public for groping another woman at a bar. They were in their dating days back then and, as Wolf explains, 'I had been a bachelor for a long time.' Even so, cupping the rear end of a flirtatious femme was not the wisest manoeuvre, particularly when the lady's boyfriend was standing nearby. Shirley was at one stage the owner of a retail store called 'I Am Woman', and, that night, Wolf certainly heard her roar. She slapped him and told him to smarten up and go home.

She says it was one of the few occasions she has seen Wolf weep. 'He told me I was the only woman who cared enough to do that.'

Wolf still knows how to sell himself. We are sitting in the luxury high-rise Melbourne apartment he bought for the lady who smartened him up. He sports an expensive gold watch, shiny gold rings and elasticised gold bands holding back his shirt-sleeves. On the table he has modestly laid out three books about himself (well, he *has* called himself the cockiest winemaker in Australia), and you do suspect that many of the Blass quotes have been diplomatically massaged, because—surprisingly, after his precocious success in Australia—Wolf still struggles with fluency in the English language.

He has also laid out a copy of *Winestate* magazine carrying a four-page article on his Wolf Blass Foundation, which was established in 1994. The article reveals that, unexpectedly, the great promoter has been having trouble letting people know about this $4 million gift to the industry that made him famous. The idea of the foundation was to help fund wine projects, but in the twelve years to 2012 applicants had taken only $800 000. Australia's cockiest grape-crusher was disappointed but had decided to fire up his publicity machine. In the name of good wine, he wanted to give money away.

Born in 1934, Wolf is comfortably well-off. In 1996, five years after Wolf Blass Wines combined with Mildara, the Mildara Blass group was acquired by Foster's for $560 million, a figure that contrasts starkly with Wolf's raggedy-arsed wartime origins. Born in 1934 in Stadtilm, in central Germany, he was reduced to stealing food and fuel from the Nazis as Adolf's war machine fell apart through 1945. 'It was a time where, as a youth, you became a bit of a street fighter. I definitely did not have any discipline. I was moved from one school to another because of my behaviour but I always managed to pass the examinations—through sheer luck, I would think.'

His maternal grandfather, Otto Sohn, owner of the Sohn bottling complex, had managed to keep business going through the war years, pacifying government and military officials with generous supplies of schnapps and vino. 'My father, Friedrich, was rarely home,' says Wolf. 'Ninety-five per cent of men in the age group to 45 were in the army or administration. Grandfather was very successful. He was a practical man, an entrepreneur—building a very good business. His two sons were also at war, so my mother was an executive of the company during wartime. He was disappointed none of us boys became scholars.'

For Wolf and his schoolmates it was a disastrous time to get an education. Increasing bombardment by the Allies forced schools to relocate repeatedly. There was also the dreadful spectre of the German concentration camps. Buchenwald was close to Stadtilm, and as defeat loomed for the Third Reich the evacuation of prisoners began. Eleven-year-old Wolf and his cousins one day saw a 'big, big column' of people being marched from the camp. 'We were told they were criminals,' says Wolf. 'There were thousands of them. They wore striped outfits and the weak ones were shot and the bodies were just left lying by the road. The occupation forces later made the Germans pick them up.' It took some years before the horrific truth dawned. In his childhood innocence, he had witnessed a death march. It has haunted him for decades.

In late 1945 he was sent to boarding school, the former Adolf Hitler Sports School, in Wickersdorf, not far from his home. 'Germany was occupied by the Americans, then the British, then the French, then the Russians. They were quite civilised, the occupation troops, but for us it was turmoil. There was no system of civilisation. You had to get ID cards; older people had to go through a political system of clearing references. There was a shortage of food, and that was the determining factor of our lifestyle.'

Wolf and a mate decided to leave school and, with suitcases in hands, they walked to the railway station through the forest to avoid detection. Having no money, they jumped aboard a coal wagon and travelled close to the border of the Russian sector.

'There was a huge uproar,' says Wolf. 'My grandfather had the police investigate; nobody knew where we were. At that stage my mother, Irmgard, was with her parents in the western French-controlled zone. I knew the name of the village and that was my destination. At one stage I caught a train and fell asleep and went in totally the wrong direction.'

A French officer spotted the thirteen-year-old in the village of Alzey and drove him the 3 kilometres to his grandparents' home in Dautenheim, where his mother was staying with his two younger brothers, Peter and Fritz. According to Fritz, Wolf was so dirty and unkempt that their granny failed to recognise him at the doorstep, mistaking him for a beggar and shutting the door. 'Our mother said, "Hang on, I'll have a look." She went to the door and we could hear her cry, "Hey, it's Wolfie!"'

Wolf made several trips back to his grandfather's vineyard, in East Germany. 'Same thing,' he says, 'no passport, through the forest, very handicapped conditions, not realising how dangerous it was. Almost like it was part of a game. It became a big issue in the family: what the hell were they going to do with the boy? I had never really been part of any family life so my father thought it best to get the boy into a wine farm. They were mixed farms with livestock and everything else. This Edmund Diehl, a friend of my father, had a very big wine farm. Father thought that it would be good for me to get some work and it would relieve the family of the responsibility.

'But Diehl had been a high-standing party member of the Third Reich and his attitude carried over into his personal life: a dominant, dictatorial person without any respect for anybody in his workforce. He treated us like POWs. There was a 2-metre wall around the farm buildings; we worked eleven hours a day, seven days a week. It was one of the cruellest memories I have; unbelievably it is still in my mind. I thought, *This can't be life*. I stayed one year and knew I had to get out, but I never mentioned to my father one word about the brutality of this man. I did not want to hurt him.'

Wolf put an ad in a wine magazine looking for an apprenticeship in viticulture and found a position 20 kilometres away at a farm on the River Nahe. There were two other apprentices there of similar age, and, though they were all worked hard in the vineyard the first year with pick and shovel, there was camaraderie and freedom. 'We had a lot of fun,' says Wolf. 'And we were taught something about the trade—wine-bottling, wine treatment, vintage operations. But because it was a mixed farm we also had to get up early in the mornings and clean the stables, carry the milk to distribution centres.

'The owner was mean. He drove an old Citroen and if he was driving behind the coal trucks, when coal fell down he stopped the car and picked it up. He didn't pass good food over to us apprentices, but we were smart enough to know where all the food was. We spent a lot of time with the workforce in the village and shared our good luck with them.'

By age eighteen Wolf had finished his apprenticeship and gained his certificate in viticulture. He travelled to Frankfurt, where his parents were living, and got a job with the Hans Schneider company, where he learnt more about the winemaker's craft from the foreman, a man named Knoll. At nineteen Wolf also enjoyed extracurricular tuition from the boss's 24-year-old daughter, a divorcee. 'I learnt lots of tricks' is the way Wolf sums it up.

'Life became meaningful. I knew that whatever directions I'd go, my mind was set to perform. I became very hungry for education. I went to a sparkling wine company on the Rhine to learn that part of it and in 1956 became *Kellermeister*, which is a sommelier, for Carl Finkenauer.' At this old family firm, founded in 1828 at Bad Kreuznach, Wolf honed his skills in white wines, and when the company expanded to produce sparkling wine Wolf went to work briefly at a large bottling company named Seitz to master the machinery involved. 'I also learnt fruit-juice operations—apple juice, blackcurrant—that was all new to me. I was a very ambitious fellow.'

The lifestyle was good: Wolf spent a fair amount of time driving around Germany in an old Volkswagen, visiting wine festivals. It was a rust-bucket with a white arrow down the side, and, as he was destined to do with his Roller in Adelaide years later, Wolf wrapped it around various objects in his travels, miraculously without injury.

However, when he landed his next job in London, with Copenhagen Wines, Wolf had to grow up fast. The firm was a disaster. Pilfering was rampant, and staff seemed to have no idea about the product, importing sweet German wine in barrels that contaminated the contents. Before Wolf arrived, one delivery of barrelled wine had exploded.

He soon moved on to a more respected outfit, Avery's of Bristol in south-west England, where his accent was mistaken for southern African. He did nothing to contradict this notion: after the blitz, Germans were not winning popularity polls among the Brits. Wolf settled in, worked on his English language (watching *Hancock's Half Hour* on TV also provided a tutorial in the British sense of humour) and enjoyed the bachelor's life. However, it was this very status that eventually redirected him Down Under.

'I had the offer of a very good job in Venezuela,' says Wolf, 'and the negotiation was very successful, but in the final decision-making they said they should have a married, settled person. They probably checked up on my private life! But I had another offer of a job in Australia with Kaiser Stuhl. The offer came from Ian Hickinbotham of the Barossa Valley's Grape Growers' Co-operative, a brilliant technological person ahead of his time. I visited Australia House in London and tasted the Australian wines they imported there. I thought, *Shit, I can't go wrong here.* They were very ordinary. Then I went to the Australian Migration Centre to find out about the Barossa Valley. Not one person there knew anything about it. At school we had been told Australia was sheep country, hot, might not survive the next century because there is no water—that type of stuff. But that's all we knew.'

Hickinbotham insisted that before heading to Australia Wolf complete a three-month refresher course, researching the latest techniques in winemaking and bottling. 'Three-quarters of the questions about bottle pasteurisation I did not understand,' Wolf admits, 'so I had apprehension about what this job would be. The flight to Australia was a nightmare with all the stops for refuelling. Frankfurt, Rome, Cairo, Istanbul, New Delhi, Singapore, then Darwin. Thirty-six hours on a propeller plane. When the stewardess opened the door of the plane I walked down onto the tarmac and said, "Gee, you must have had huge rainfalls," but she said they had not had rain for months. I didn't know anything about the tropical climate, you see? The humidity! Everything was moisture. And I asked, "Is this Australia?" It was definitely a shock to the system.'

There were more shocks to come. The Barossa Valley seemed to Wolf like another planet. 'We drove through Gawler, a little township, and I thought it was like a cowboy town. I almost asked, "Where are the horses?" It looked like the Ponderosa.'

He arrived at Nuriootpa and was invited to the Angaston Country Ball at the local town hall. 'When we entered, all the girls were sitting on the left-hand side and all the bloody blokes were on the other side,' he recalls, still astonished at the sight. 'I thought it was hillbilly country. There was no alcohol. You had to be 200 metres from the hall to have a drink.'

At weekends he discovered that women would sit indoors to drink while men would congregate around a beer keg out in the garage. Wine? Barely any at all was drunk by Aussies in the 1950s. It was indeed another planet.

The co-op proved to be a hillbilly outfit too. 'It was on its last legs,' says Wolf. 'But this is where the genius Ian Hickinbotham motivated people to get the sinking ship floating again.' The growers, unable to sell their grapes to the valley's winemakers during the Depression, had formed the Kaiser Stuhl company as their own winery. It was named after a flat-topped hill in the valley—it means 'king's seat'—but the Australian appetite for wine was still in its infancy and business prospects were bleak.

The Kaiser Stuhl team launched a sparkling wine called Pine-apple Pearl and within three years were making 80 per cent of the sparkling wine in Australia. By the time Wolf's contract was up, in 1964, the company was producing a dazzling array of brands that still linger fondly in the memory of baby boomers today: Yalumba Pearlette, Kaiser Pearl, Mardis Gras Pink Pearl, Sparkling Cold Duck, Cheo Frizzante, Gala Spumante, Pineapple Pearl and Cherry Pearl. These were the forerunners of the wine coolers of the 1980s.

Despite the success, however, Wolf had problems with some of the workforce at Kaiser Stuhl—'The work ethic for some was about four out of ten'—and struck out on his own, encouraged by the fact that Kaiser Stuhl offered to pay his airfare to California to accept a job offer there. 'I realised I must be good!' says Wolf.

He worked briefly at Woodleys as a blender, and then as a freelancer for several years, travelling about in a Volkswagen as he had done in Germany. His clients won medals and trophies, and it did not escape Wolf's notice that most of the winning wines had been made with produce from the Langhorne Creek region on the Fleurieu Peninsula, south of Adelaide. Wolf credited the unique combination of annual flooding from the Bremer River, the silt, the soil structure and the eucalyptus trees. It produced a flavour unlike other wine regions.

In 1966 Wolf registered the name Bilyara, Aboriginal for eagle-hawk, which evoked his German background. Three years later he was asked to run the Tolley Winery at Nuriootpa. The owners were happy with the results but not so happy that Wolf had simultaneously launched his own Bilyara brand from a small plot he bought outside Nuriootpa. By 1973 both Wolf's Tollana wines and his Bilyara wines were established names, but the Tolleys did not like the arrangement. Confronting him with an ultimatum one day, they gave Wolf an hour to decide: would he give up his own wines?

'I told them to stick it,' says Wolf, who cranked up his own business with a $2000 loan. Thus started the Blass juggernaut that eventually saw the $560 million sale to Foster's.

But it has not just been the product. Wolf has been the Dick Smith of the wine trade, a one-man trademark who had a natural flair for publicity. When he launched Pineapple Pearl for Kaiser Stuhl it was in a bottle shaped like pineapple, and the gathering had their glasses filled from a mock petrol pump. He made his bow-tie part of the brand, an accessory that had a practical origin. 'When I was working as a freelance consultant—rubber boots and overalls, changing the wine styles of six or seven different companies on $21.50 an hour—I had the tie on and that was interfering with my practical work, and I thought, *No, I'm not going to lower my dignity. I'll wear a bow-tie!*' His exuberant European personality has not wowed everyone. 'I've had a lot of detractors, but the more I got knocked, the harder we worked to achieve our goals.'

And he managed to have three marriages along the way. Raelene, seven years younger, was first. That union lasted nine years and produced daughters Susan and Sharyn. Wolf blotted his paternal copybook by going to Melbourne to see the Aussie Football League grand final the weekend Sharyn was born. Next came Martine, twenty years younger, whom he met at the Melbourne Cup. That marriage produced son Anton, but when the child was four Martine left for another man. That left a wounded Wolf free to court the elusive Shirley Nyberg, the lady who 'smartened up' the Wolf man. Shirley had three sons from an earlier marriage and was so cautious about marrying again that, when she eventually agreed in 1996 to Wolf's repeated proposals, she bought a racehorse called Brave Decision to mark the occasion. For Wolf, it was third time lucky. 'Shirley's beautiful, sexy and she keeps me bloody straight and honest,' he says. 'And we love each other.'

DERRYN HINCH

A pawn and a king

On perhaps the most spine-tingling day of Derryn Hinch's spotlit innings thus far, a hire car delivered him and wife Chanel to the wrong destination. It was the day when the transplant team was waiting at Melbourne's Austin Hospital with his new liver, but the driver, looking for a low-publicity side entrance, got it wrong. When the car pulled up, the Hinches peered out the window at the Melbourne Brain Centre.

'Well,' says Derryn, 'some people do say I need a new one.'

Like the Sinatra track 'That's Life', which Derryn used as his theme throughout a marathon radio career, the bearded opinionator has been up and down, over and out, a pawn and a king. He has been jailed, divorced, sacked, divorced, hired, divorced and remarried. He has been both indestructible and mortally ill, both extravagantly wealthy and parlously poor, but, like Ol' Blue Eyes, whenever he has been down, he has always managed to pick himself up and get back in the race.

Even the good times seemed to come with the odd kick in the tail. In 1981, as a brash 3AW newcomer, he beat for the first time the 'unbeatable' Bert Newton on Melbourne radio in the ratings, but was off-air with vocal cord polyps. And in his millionaire days, he made a point of principle about drink-driving by using a Roller chauffeured by a pert blonde, only to discover later that she did not have a driving licence.

It's hard to believe there was a weekend many years later, at Woodend, near his former Macedon vineyard, when his pockets were empty: he was down to his last $6.49 in the bank, but he could not even access that because the Commonwealth Bank ATM minimum was $20. He still doesn't quite know how that happened. 'It just did,' he told Andrew Denton on *Enough Rope* in 2003.

> *I mean, I spent a lot. Then a couple of things went bad and*
> *I got sacked a couple more times, and it just, you know …*
> *but I sold everything and paid it off. I sold the Hawaiian*
> *places. I sold the vineyard. I sold everything. The lowest time,*
> *I suppose, all I had left—and that was hocked too—was the*
> *farm. It was what I call my 'Grizzly Adams' period. I lived*
> *for a year in, you know, the flannelette shirt and gumboots.*

Even a memorable day like his first wedding was laced with those characteristic Hinch dramatics, when his bride, Lana Wells, a Herald & Weekly Times journo, was given away by an uncle—just before he dropped dead at the altar. 'Gave a whole new meaning to "death us do part",' quips Derryn, who has married another four times, twice to actress Jacki Weaver.

He has confessed guiltily to bedding other women during his first two wedlocks—what he called that 'awful male attitude' in which a one-night stand didn't count—but today he doesn't regard any of his previous hitchings as a failure. 'They just ran their course,' he says. 'You end up going in different directions.' And, oddly for a bloke who has twice been convicted in court for, in essence, protecting children, he has never wanted any of his own. 'Too career-oriented,' he says. 'But Jacki's son, Dylan, is like a son to me. He has two little kids who are really my grandchildren. I was there for Dylan's form-ative years, 11 to 21. You know, when he was fourteen I asked Jacki how I was doing with him, saying, "I've never had a fourteen-year-old son before."

'She said, "Neither have I."

'It's like men think women have this inherent knowledge that comes from the womb.'

It has long been a joke among his mates how Hinch gravitates inexorably to pregnant women. Missing at a party? You'll find him chatting with an expectant mother somewhere. 'I love that glow,' he says. 'Still can't get over it.'

But it takes a special sort of Amazing Bastard to get sacked from radio, hired for TV, have a liver transplant, go through a court trial and serve five months' house arrest all within a couple of years. The house arrest, ordered by a magistrate for naming two paedophiles, came only weeks after his transplant operation and was unprecedented: he was totally shut off from any form of communication with the outside world. No broadcast, no Twitter, no blogs, no comment. The Hinch-free zone ended in December 2011, when he sent a midnight tweet to the Twitterverse: 'He's back. New Liver. New Life. Same old #Hinch. Fresh attack on bad law. And the magistrate was wrong. Life in this old bastard yet'.

But, true to his theme song, he was shot down again the following August. 'I was blindsided,' he says. 'Never saw it coming. I'd just done an interview with astronaut Buzz Aldrin. I was pleased with that—it was the only one he did in Australia, and he didn't charge money, which he has been known to do. I'd got to him because I covered the moon shot; I'd watched him go to the moon in 1969. I came off air and the program manager Clark Forbes was waiting for me, saying station manager Shane Healy wanted a word.'

Derryn thought it was 'the Vizard thing': he and morning host Neil Mitchell had attacked their station for hiring former TV host and comedian Steve Vizard, a bloke who had been in corporate hot water over shares. But it wasn't the Vizard thing; it was the sacking thing, something Derryn had copped fourteen times before.

'I'd been at the station ten years,' he says, 'and *Drive* was rating number one. They told me they were taking a new direction. I said, "The only new direction from the top is down."' He now suspects his five-month absence (without pay) on home detention did him harm. 'And I was asked by the 3AW program manager how long I was going to keep going with this "paedophile thing,"' he says in astonishment, noting that the royal commission announced later that same year had vindicated his long and emotionally draining campaign against child molesters.

True to his reputation as a Human Headline, Derryn was all over the front page of Melbourne's tabloid *Herald Sun* the next day, with a strapline at the top pointing inside to a report apparently deemed less important: the deaths of two workers on an oil rig.

Over at the Seven Network, a senior executive reportedly slapped the paper down on a desk and declared, 'Why the fuck isn't this bloke working for us?' A few days later, he was. Once again, he was back in the race.

'They decided there was still some tread left in these tyres,' says Derryn, who, a Human Headline to the last, almost ran over a woman in his giant Cadillac on the way to the studio for his farewell radio show, on 30 November 2012. 'She dropped her mobile phone on the road and jumped after it. She had disappeared from sight in front of the bonnet: that's how close it was. Nitwit!'

Though it has lasted more than half a century, the Hinch career in the headline industry was not his first choice. His mother, Betty, used to claim that the young Derryn's early desire, when growing up in New Plymouth, New Zealand, was to be a wharfie so he could 'sit on the end of the jetty and watch the ships go by.' In fact, his first job application—possibly propelled by a yearning to escape the confines of Kiwi land—was for the New Zealand navy, but he was put off by regulatory red tape that controlled everything down to the number and colour of underpants ('two pairs, white', which seems wholly inadequate). Nor was he impressed by his Uncle Ken's recommendation of a career in banking.

However, Clem Cave, one of the Hinch family's neighbours in New Plymouth, happened to be news editor of the local bugle, the now-defunct *Taranaki Herald*. Cave suggested to the fifteen-year-old Derryn that he might try his hand in the newspaper trade, and, after barely scraping through Year 11, Derryn signed on as one of the *Herald*'s two new cadets in January 1960. Full of teenage swagger, he had his ego kept under some sort of control by his mother. 'Must be a very quiet news day,' she told her son when a story about him appeared on the front page. 'You don't want this, do you?' she asked, using the same page to line the bottom of a bird cage.

The Hinch career has always been in overdrive. At 18, he pretended to be 21 to land a job as police reporter for the Sydney *Sun*. At 22, pretending to be 25, he was United Press International bureau chief in Toronto, and at 28 he was New York bureau chief for John Fairfax newspapers—they thought he was 32.

Hinch is an unusual surname, but it has made its mark on the media before. 'I was going through some papers of my late grandfather, Alf Hinch', Derryn wrote in his book *Human Headlines*. 'I found a single sheet of brown paper called the *Daily Herald*. Written on it in pencil were hardship stories of life in a logging camp. During the Great Depression, in the 1930s, my grandfather was one of the huge army of unemployed New Zealand men who, craving any job, left their wives and families and went off to live in tent cities in the bush on the north island, earning a meagre living clearing and cutting timber … The editor of the paper: Alf Hinch.'

In New York, Derryn was introduced to the boss of the Macquarie Radio Network Stan Clark and, with some extra beer money in mind, suggested he might file the odd broadcast back home. In a rare admission of the jitters, he records in his book that he was so nervous before he filed his first effort—a piece about Australia's prime minister John Gorton meeting President Nixon—that he asked his wife, Lana Wells, to leave the room and go for a walk.

'But I suddenly discovered that I like the spoken word', he wrote. 'Loved the honesty and the urgency and raw emotion of it.' And so in 1978 he rolled into Melbourne to join 3XY. Hinch Radio was up and away. He switched to 3AW in 1979, overhauled local radio king Bert Newton within two years and stayed on top until 1987, when tycoon Christopher Skase, having bought the Seven Network, lured him to TV. 'He called me from his private jet one Sunday afternoon,' says Derryn, 'and offered $400 000 a year. I told him he would have to at least double it and hung up. Then I walked into the kitchen and told Jacki I had probably made one of the biggest mistakes of my life.' But Skase rang back. He upped the offer: $1 million a year. In 1987, that was a king's ransom.

Derryn could be a hard man on talkback radio. You could hear the atmospheric pressure rising when he let fly at some caller he thought was talking crap, often ending with 'You're an idiot, goodbye.' He knows that, for all the Hinch fans out there, a caval-cade of detractors are out there too. Addressing the Melbourne Press Club in late 2012 he said, 'I've lived a year longer than I expected—and a year longer than some people hoped.'

One detractor was Melbourne tough guy Mick Gatto, who phoned the station when Derryn's health was failing to say 'I hope you go to your grave soon, you maggot.' Another post-operative unwell-wisher was Steve Price, who had been program manager and broadcaster on the same station. Working in opposition as a colum-nist for the *Herald Sun*, Price wrote, 'The waiting list for healthy organs in Australia is up around 1700 with more than a hundred waiting for a liver. So what qualified Hinch for the new one other than time spent waiting? Was his high profile an advantage? Were donor advocates desperate for the sort of wall-to-wall publicity giving Hinch a new liver would bring?'

Price was right about the wall-to-wall publicity, but Derryn found out later that his celebrity status actually counted against him.

'My surgeon Bob Jones had told his team that even if a new liver had been available in the first three months, they could not give it to me,' says Derryn, 'because it would appear to be giving an advantage. In the end Bob says they probably waited too long: that, by the time they operated, I probably had about two weeks to live.'

His liver problems had first been diagnosed in 2006 with cirrhosis and a subsequent bout of septicaemia, but a 'pesky spot' turned into something more sinister in 2010. Tests revealed it to be cancer, but Hinch, with an 'unwavering conviction' that he would prevail, fired up a new blog called *My Liver, My Life*. 'I turned it into a project,' he says, 'as a journo would, writing about someone else. That's how I dealt with it.' The blog, still on the web, shows Derryn continuing to throw punches two weeks after the transplant, in July 2011:

> *Nobody has been able to use that headline that has been doing the rounds on Twitter: Liver rejects Hinch.*
>
> *And speaking of the Internet. The craziest hoax transplant story appeared on the weekend:*
>
> *'Scientists have found they can create chimeric animals that have organs belonging to another species by injecting stem cells into the embryo of another species.*
>
> *'Derryn Hinch is rumoured to have received a pigs liver in his recent transplant operation.*
>
> *'The researchers injected stem cells from rats into the embryos of mice that had been genetically altered so they could not produce their own organs, creating mice that had rat organs.'*
>
> *Not only rubbish, but a cruel hoax on the donor and family whose decisions made my second life possible.*

The donor is usually anonymous, but in this case the donor family, noting the timing of the Human Headline's well-publicised operation, put two and two together and contacted him. Turned out that Derryn's new liver had come from a young man named Heath

Gardner, who had died of a gunshot wound and whose 27 years of life had been more than colourful. Wild and rebellious, Heath had used drugs, had been 'known to police', and had hung around motorcycle gangs.

When Derryn was shown a photo of Heath covered in tatts and with arms wrapped around a topless girlfriend like a gangster from *Underbelly*, his thoughts turned uncomfortably to the spectre of AIDS. 'I thought, *Holy shit!*' Derryn recalls. 'He looked like that slain criminal Andrew 'Benji' Veniamin.'

When he rang his sister Barbara in New Zealand, she said it all: 'Typical of you, Derryn. Why couldn't it have been a 50-year-old accountant who played lawn bowls?'

There was more: the topless girlfriend turned up two months later as a contestant on the reality TV show *Please Marry My Boy* in a low-cut hot-pink top with micro-miniskirt, wanting a 'real man who can look after me.'

Says Derryn, 'Talk about six degrees of separation. After the TV show she reportedly hooked up with a guy I knew: a tattooed bikie who made news when his mother disappeared and her body was later found in a drum in the river.'

Steve Price wasn't the only person to ask whether Derryn deserved a second chance after mistreating his body for so long. A *Good Weekend* magazine spread written by a freelancer who had been given 'unbridled access' to the Hinch life for a fortnight was published soon after the transplant—an article Derryn describes as a 'hatchet job' that painted him as a 'self-centred callous hypocrite' undeserving of his new chance at life.

Undeserving? Well, Derryn admits to his self-destructive ways in earlier years, when he would quaff at least four bottles of vino a day. He and his Rat Pack mates would lunch over 'bankers' hours—one to two.' That's 1 p.m. to 2 *a.m.*

'It didn't seem that bad,' he says. 'I'd get up at 5.17 a.m., at the office by 6, finished by 1 p.m. and you're free again till the next morning. So you have a bottle at lunch, another bottle later in the afternoon; at dinner you'd have a bottle; then reading or writing or watching TV you'd sip away on a fourth.' He admitted to 60 *Minutes*, which taped the whole transplant procedure, 'I was a fucking idiot, absolute fucking idiot. Just to sit down and stare at your own stupidity … it's as confronting as anything I think you can face.'

But did he not deserve a second chance? Derryn says he underwent 30 hours of tests before even getting onto the waiting list and, like any other hopeful recipient, would have been struck from the roll if the cancer had spread. His liver cancer was a primary cancer, not secondary, from somewhere else. Only 5 per cent of cases fall in that category. 'I was very lucky,' he says.

So Derryn has had his fair share of critics. He has also had at least one professional lampooner: a TV comic character named Hunch, played by Steve Vizard, the very bloke Derryn had told listeners in 2012 should not be on radio. While conceding that the former TV host was 'intelligent, clever and entertaining,' Derryn had argued that the insider-trading case seven years earlier meant Vizard had lost the right to broadcast his opinions. 'Steve Vizard is still in disgrace in this town,' he said. 'You can say he has been punished and has paid for his sins. Not true. He is still paying for them.'

But Derryn can also forgive and forget. Mark Day and John Blackman, both broadcasters who had worked with Derryn on 3AW, are two on the list of those with whom he has both fallen out and later puffed the peace pipe. They all had, at one time or another, been on 3AW together, but that seemed only to fuel the flames, and, to management's delight, ratings soared. Derryn accused Day of being a pimp because he earnt money from escort ads in *Truth*, the scandal rag he co-owned with Owen Thomson. 'Day virtually accused me of arson,' says Derryn, 'of so-called Jewish lightning, because there was a fire at Sardi's, a restaurant I owned.'

Blackman had his Hinch moment after he was headhunted by a new station and remarked upon departure that '3AW has lost its soul.'

Derryn disagreed: 'It has just lost its arsehole.'

However, some years later the boys buried the hatchet. 'We've buried so many hatchets,' says Blackman, 'my backyard is rusty.'

During the 1990s, when your author was writing the tail-twisting 'Spy' column in *The Sunday Age*, I was on the Hinch hit list too. One day he sent a steaming letter to editor Steve Harris, the sort of missive you might expect from a bloke who wrote two books on Scrabble, declaring, 'Lawrence Money is a scabrous, tawdry, reckless, irresponsible, inaccurate, bitterly envious camp-follower'. Indeed, one of Derryn's senior staff, Mike Frazer, leapt up at a function saying the only reason he had attended was 'to punch Lawrence Money in the nose'. Yet there I was twenty years later, schnozzle intact, lunching with the Headline at his favourite local eatery—Dish at the Royce Hotel in central Melbourne, not far from his apartment—with a copy of *A Human Deadline* (inscribed 'We've shared a few bumps along the voyage. Regards, Derryn') in my briefcase.

Derryn's usual table, which is actually two small tables pushed together, is in a corner far enough from the front door to discourage too many passing cries of 'Look, Ma, there's Darryl Hinch!' Yes, it amuses him that after he has spent so many years in the public eye so many of his glued-on fans still screw up his name. Darryl, Derrick, Darren. Even Endora in TV's *Bewitched* got hapless son-in-law Darrin's name right occasionally.

So Derryn it is—Derryn Nigel Hinch, who turned 69 in 2013, a man eternally on a mission. In the oft-quirky way he views the world, Derryn sees his post-transplant life almost as a life for one and a bit. Facing a possible jail sentence in 2012, he saw an injustice that might have escaped many: it meant that part of someone else would have to go to jail too. And, lunching with Derryn, I did have the thought that, in a nice kind of way, it is a déjeuner à trois. Certainly, Heath's mother, Lynda, and his two sisters, who had attended Derryn's book launch the previous month, were comforted by the notion that through losing their boy new life had been given to another.

Dining with Derryn these days is a far cry from the decadent banquets of yore. His potion of choice is a non-alcoholic Edenvale 'shiraz'—a rich red drop from a bottle with an impressive label— which teams nicely with his favourite plate, a vegetarian salad with eggplant, falafel, parsley and mint. That day at Dish, Derryn sipped his red and made one of his Hinch/Hunch prognostications: that Twitter would be alive within hours with word that 'Hinch is on the piss again'. But it ain't going to happen. The Headline has dried out for good. 'During my house arrest—it's not all fun, y'know— they would sometimes knock on the door at around nine-fifteen at night for a random breath test. One evening I'd probably had three-quarters of a bottle of Edenvale around dinner, but I blew 0.00.'

The liver he murdered with the hard stuff, a pock-marked, desiccated anatomical fossil, is pictured in his book. He and wife Chanel held it in their hands, fascinated by the death sentence it had imposed on its owner.

'Do you often see livers this bad?' Chanel asked the medicos.

'Only at autopsies,' was the reply.

Derryn describes it as a 'Dorian Gray liver,' and as it had sucked the life out of him many a wellwisher had thrown him a hopeful lifebuoy: an embroidered handkerchief blessed at Lourdes, details of a 'wonderful faith healer in Manila', a guaranteed cure made from the pureed contents of a can of asparagus. He took it all with good grace despite his utter scepticism about 'miracle' anything.

However, he gave Chanel much credit for her support during his travails and, at our lunch on 22 November 2012, spoke of her with great affection. Their marriage had weathered his jailing, his illness and his surgical salvation. Chanel, a naturally shy person, had blossomed in the Hinch-driven limelight. He said they were still living as they had from the start—in separate apartments in the same buildings and in fact Chanel's parents had subsequently moved in to an apartment in a floor between them. But the arrangement suited them well. 'It's funny,' said Derryn, 'people still ask Chanel: "When are you two moving in together?" And she says: "Probably never." One of her colleagues said: "How can you do that?" and she asked how long he'd been married. "Twenty years," he said. So Chanel asked: "Aren't there times you would like to be alone in your own little place" and he said "Every day!" So I think there may be an element of jealousy there at times about the way we run things.'

And that was the last time I saw Derryn before he contacted *Age* columnist Suzanne Carbone three months later to drop the bombshell—his marriage was over. Although he and Chanel would continue living separately in the same building, Derryn declared that 'with my new-found health I have decided to spend my remaining years focusing on my career.' I emailed the Human Headline in astonishment but did not get a reply. I saw him at a Melbourne Press Club function shortly afterwards—he did not mention it. February 2013, when he made his announcement, was the month of their seventh wedding anniversary. Another 'bump along the voyage'. That's life.

A.W. BURTON

The final salute

Amazing Bastards are all amazing in their own way, so there is no particular priority in this collection; the extraordinary life of late-listed Derryn Hinch, for example, is just as gobsmacking as those of the blokes further up front. However, to a man, they all fit that W. Somerset Maugham template: they have grabbed hold of life and forged new trails that others have followed. There is an additional level of Amazing Bastard: blokes of whom you may have never heard but who number in their millions; gallant and good-hearted men—grandfathers, fathers, sons, grandsons—who may not shake the world, but who are the foundation stones for a better one.

I will finish this book with a tribute to my own personal champion, the amazing Arthur William 'Buddy' Burton, a brilliant, witty, generous, truly humble man, who never sought acclaim and in fact actively eschewed it. He had no children and knew no father—his dad, William Thomas Burton, was killed in action in World War I and never saw his only child—so Buddy was raised by his grand-mother in a humble Footscray home, in Melbourne. He was dux of Auburn Central School in Hawthorn in 1929, gained a scholarship to Wesley College, starred scholastically there and later at Queen's College, became a skilled and compassionate GP, a medical secretary for the Victorian branch of the Australian Medical Association and a Knight of Saint John. He was a very private man who never spoke of his many good deeds and cut short anyone who tried to broadcast them. It was only at his funeral, in 1996, that at last I was able publicly to tell this, his story.

Among the many pieces of verse and prose that Buddy Burton could call to mind to suit any occasion there was one particular snippet from Arthur Guiterman's sardonic pen that he would recite when events conspired to demonstrate the fragility of human life. The verse reminds us that even the sword of the great Frankish king Charlemagne eventually was reduced to ferric oxide, or rust, and Buddy would deliver those rhyming couplets with his trademark expression: a twinkle in his acutely intelligent blue eyes, a wry smile, perhaps a crooked finger rubbing the end of his nose.

It's a poem that reflects quite a few of the facets of this remark-able man. His extensive memory for literature, most of which harked back more than 50 years, to his college days. His subtle, droll and lightning-quick sense of humour. His formidable knowledge of history and the classics. His meticulous attention to detail—and as an example I refer to the chemical formula for rust. I once made the mistake of quoting the Charlemagne verse back to him, saying, 'ferrous oxide.'

Said Buddy curtly, 'Ferric!'

He had what you might call 'Buddyisms', which were so much a part of his character. Those dry, slightly cynical throwaway lines he'd use to put things in perspective. When you wished him a happy birthday, for example. 'One step closer to the pavilion,' he'd respond. Or you might be moaning to him about some paltry inconvenience.

'Me heart bleeds,' he'd say, and you would quickly stop complaining. Or you might mention a small setback at work. 'You can be stiff,' would be the retort. Or a group of women might have gathered at home to talk to his wife, Betty, interrupting his morning's work. 'Bloody chooks yackety-yacking,' he'd mutter.

But he was a paradox, this man. When he emerged from his study he would treat the very same chooks as he would any member of the opposite gender: with great chivalry and courtesy, forever opening doors for them and fussing over their comfort.

And, of course, if you came to him with a real problem, something that genuinely weighed heavily on your shoulders, you knew you had a veritable Rock of Gibraltar to lean on. This utter reliability was a quality that gave great comfort to my late mother, Doris, when her marriage to my father ended, leaving her to support three young children alone. For Mum in the early years, and for us children later, Buddy was a sort of personal Superman. It was enormously comforting to know that whatever the problem might be, there was this authoritative, all-knowing, seemingly infallible bloke who could take control.

In 1972, as a young father in Canberra, I was concerned about infant daughter Samantha, who was born with a minor eye problem. Beset with anxiety, I wrote to Buddy, who sent a letter that I still retain:

I am replying in haste to your latest letter as directed. A dermolipoma is defined as a congenital growth beneath the bulbar conjunctiva. It is not a cancer and never will be. Removing it should be a breeze. Your eye bloke appears to have the necessary qualifications and I can see little point in carting your offspring around to others in the trade. In fact, now you have acquired skills in carpentry, I can't think why you don't do it yourself!

Both parents were put immediately at ease, the operation was carried out—although not by me—and, as predicted, it was a breeze.

Buddy was simultaneously one of the most generous and the most modest of men. So modest that he would become genuinely annoyed should you tell anyone how he had helped. Particularly so if you were foolish enough to try to thank him personally. 'Quite unnecessary,' he would say, and change the subject.

When my beloved mother died suddenly, in 1981, so young at 60, I managed to circumvent Buddy's defences and wrote him a letter thanking him for all he did for her—and us—during her lifetime.

He wrote back, 'Any small thing I managed to do was a pleasure'.

Small thing? I am still gobsmacked, stunned, at his benevolence after mum's divorce. 'If you allow me to choose the schools,' he told her, 'I shall take care of the children's education.' And so he did. A man who was not greatly wealthy, and not even a blood relative— he just happened to marry my mother's sister—put me and sister Rosemary through two of the finest, and most expensive, schools in Melbourne. I went to his old school, Wesley, and Rosemary to Korowa Girls' School, where Betty had been a teacher. He was saddling up to put younger brother John through Wesley too when another extraordinary uncle, a dentist with three kids of his own, chipped in to help.

A few weeks before I started at Wesley, Buddy took me along to Buckley & Nunn's department store and fitted me out with the entire summer and winter uniforms, and presented me with a new Gladstone leather bag with my initials on it and a fountain pen embossed with my name. Everything brand new. For a boy from a struggling home, where Mum had to count every penny, it was an unforgettable thrill, and I strode off to school that first day 10 feet tall.

Many years passed before I fully appreciated the priceless gift I had been given, a gift he never mentioned or would allow to be mentioned. Many years passed before I recalled, with newly opened eyes, the way he had made do with his old radio, his old TV set; many years before it dawned on me how he and Betty had curbed their travel plans until we children were through school.

Betty, a brilliant woman who could more than match it intellectually with her husband, was a national president of the Young Women's Christian Association and headed the Good Neighbour Council. She never begrudged the household economies necessitated through Buddy's good works; besides, they both regarded chattels and material goods as minor matters.

Buddy's quiet generosity continued: he put my sister through college; he helped me buy my first house. 'There was no need,' he said when I wrote yet another letter of thanks, but I suspect he was chuffed that the property was close to his own, allowing me to stroll round to visit once or twice a week for many years afterwards.

In retirement, Buddy decided to do a law course, which, predictably, he galloped through with honours, and then, seeing the need, wrote the landmark book on Australian medical ethics and the law. Coincidentally, he studied his law course with the son of his great friend Michael Salvaris, with whom he had studied for his medical degree years earlier. The son, Mike Salvaris, became a social-rights advocate and academic.

Buddy was chuffed when I took over the 'In Black and White' column in Melbourne's afternoon newspaper, *The Herald*—he had been good friends with the column's founder, Bill Tipping—and he feigned outrage at, but I am sure secretly enjoyed, the occasional mention in my daily column of the old unnamed medico who kept issuing pieces of wisdom from his red wing-back armchair. It's a piece of furniture that now stands in my study, a treasured pulpit from which he amused me, educated me and advised me, and where, sometimes, after slopping too much brandy on the pudding at Christmas dinner, he nodded off briefly.

Buddy was the most fastidious and meticulous of men. His garden shed looked like an operating theatre, the tools all laid out on white towels and always replaced in their position after use. His car boot, after ten years' use, was in the same condition as it had been on the day of purchase. He was organised, resolute, unswerving. Of course, this could sometimes be a bit hard to deal with, because in his view there was only one proper way to do everything. Three Buddy edicts come to mind: You were never, repeat, *never* to phone him after 9 p.m. on a weekday; if you visited anybody in hospital you never stayed longer than ten minutes; and in his later years you never tried to contact him between 2 and 4 p.m. because that was when he had what he called his 'afternoon zizz.' (After he arose, he would have his evening whisky, which he would always precede with the Gaelic toast to the health of those who might be present: '*Sláinte mhath.*'

How much can you owe one man? Buddy is the one who taught me to fish, supplying rod, reel and book on fishing knots. He is the one who ignited my interest in an outside world, offering to give me a quid in Melbourne's Olympic year of 1956 if I could memorise all the flags of the competing nations. I couldn't, and he didn't. No free rides. Buddy is the one who—prescient as ever—summoned me to his study at age twelve and promised to give me 100 quid if I did not smoke until age eighteen. I didn't, and he did; and the sum ($200 by then) went towards the purchase of my first car, an EJ Holden, which I drove for six years and 320 000 kilometres. And I still have never smoked a cigarette. Buddy is the one who put my name down for the prized membership of the Melbourne Cricket Club, and in my late twenties we teamed up to go to the footy together, a wonderful mateship that extended for the next quarter-century (albeit with little supporter joy, both of us being Melbourne Demons men).

It was easy for strangers to misinterpret Buddy's sometime abrupt manner and believe he was uncaring. Yes, he scoffed at sentiment and cut down any overt gestures of affection with his scything wit, but I was not surprised to find touching evidence of his soft underbelly after he went into aged care. Carefully stored away at his home were a tender love letter to him from Betty during the war; the scholastic medal he won as a child at primary school—still in the original box; and, to my delight, the giant cartoon cards I had drawn for him on his pivotal birthdays, cards that gently lampooned some of his quirks and triumphs. He had kept them all. 'That's quite something,' he had said on each occasion, smiling at his nephew's efforts. 'Quite something!'

Buddy was a natural leader and manager. He was punctual to the last second, never forgot an appointment, and was immaculately groomed, with hair that never thinned or went grey. His world was very cut and dried. Pop singers were 'hairy unwashed creeps,' advertising was 'a total waste of money,' newspapers were (tongue-in-cheek, I hope) 'journals of misinformation.'

Right up to the end he was still pulling the levers. On a visit to Melbourne's Peter James Centre, to which he was admitted with dementia associated with his Parkinson's Disease, we asked a nurse how he had been.

'A bit grumpy,' she replied. 'He sacked me today, but he gave me one month's pay.' There it was. Our family champion would never change: still running the show but always with a good dose of compassion.

I visited him on the day he died, in 1996. Nearing 80 years of age, he was looking tired and thin. It was a Saturday afternoon and he was sitting quietly, dappled in the feeble winter sunlight that slanted in through the dining-room window. He reached out and shook my hand, and I held it a while, gave him a hug and felt the boniness of those old shoulders that had carried so much, for so many, for so long. The hug had been a long time coming, for it was a bold intimacy of which you would never dream in his younger days.

How curious is the cycle of life. It had been Buddy who had taken me aside in the family home at age ten to break the news of my grandmother Mary Adamson's death in England, just before she was due to return home, and Buddy who appeared at my home late on that terrible October night in 1981 to tell me of the sudden death of my mother. Now Buddy had reached the same door, which he had been preparing to open since his Betty died.

'Once your ever-lovin' goes,' he had said, many times, 'the sooner you follow, the better.' A few hours after I left him that afternoon, he slipped away. That kind and generous heart was finally still. He had reached the pavilion he had long talked about, and I imagined him arriving bang on time, impeccably groomed, with the usual knife-edge creases in his trousers and impossibly shiny shoes. His was a life of noble service, of self-sacrifice, of 1001 unsung acts of kindness. The father he never knew, William Thomas Burton, cut down on the battlefields of Europe, would have been so proud of the son he left behind, for Arthur William 'Buddy' Burton was an extraordinary man. And an amazing one.

ACKNOWLEDGEMENTS

Grateful thanks to all the blokes in this book who welcomed me in to their homes or offices and were so generous with their time—despite my larrikin urge to classify them all as 'bastards'. I salute Allen & Unwin's Sue Hines for her enthusiasm for the concept, Foong Ling Kong for nursing it along—and Ann Lennox for seeing the book through to publication. Special thanks to copyeditor Penny Mansley for her formidable researching and checking skills.

HH
Baker 8¼
Marth 9¼
Cambdon 11¼
Breen 14½
LD